Contesting Justice

Contesting Justice

Women, Islam, Law, and Society

Ahmed E. Souaiaia

STATE UNIVERSITY OF NEW YORK PRESS

Cover images courtesy of the author.

Published by
State University of New York Press, Albany

Printed in the United States of America

For information, contact State University of New York Press
www.sunypress.com

Production by Eileen Meehan
Marketing by Anne M. Valentine

Library of Congress of Cataloging-in-Publication Data

Souaiaia, Ahmed E.
Contesting justice : women, Islam, law, and society / Ahmed E. Souaiaia.
p. cm.
Includes bibliographical references and index.
ISBN 978-0-7914-7397-9 (hardcover : alk. paper) 1. Islamic law—Philosophy. 2 Islamic law—Methodology. 3. Koran—Hermeneutics. 4. Polygamy (Islamic law) 5. Women—Legal status, laws, etc. (Islamic law) 6. Islamic law—Social aspects. I. Title

KBP50.S68 2008
340.5 ' 9—dc22

2007017444

10 9 8 7 6 5 4 3 2 1

To my mother

Contents

Illustrations

Figures

Tables

Preface

It is difficult to write a book dealing with a controversial topic such as women in society, religion, and law. It is even more difficult to discuss the topic of social justice in the context of a historical time frame that spans more than one thousand years. A study with these parameters would involve concepts and assumptions that may or may not be clear to the reader for it is necessarily interdisciplinary. For these reasons, I will use this prelude to define some of the concepts and key words. Given the space constraints, I will use such terms without providing elaborate supporting evidence, and I hope that readers will keep in mind these brief explanations and focus on the specific substance that is the heart of this work. It must be mentioned nonetheless, that I have addressed most of the issues associated with these terms, especially the concepts and principles associated with Islamic law and jurisprudence, in other works (*On the Sources of Islamic Law and Practices* (article), and *Verbalizing Meaning* (book).

I use the word *"Arab"* to refer to a person or a group of people who claim a kinship to a branch of the Semitic people and whose founding father is Ishmael. As such, and in terms of religion, an Arab could be Muslim, Christian, Copt, or even a Jew. A *Jew* is similarly defined; hence, she or he is a person who is linked to Abraham through Isaac and for the purposes of this work, I exclude "Jewishness" as an ethnicity. A *Semitic person* therefore could be Arab, Hebrew, Assyrian, or Ethiopic. The *Semitic religions* consist primarily of Judaism, Christianity, and Islam, for they were founded by Semites, although not all the adherents to these religions today are so.

Throughout the text, I sometimes make generalizations about Muslims and Muslims' beliefs and practices. To me, a *Muslim person* is one who adheres to (or one born to Muslim parents and who does not deny) the common beliefs and practices of Islam generally anchored by the two categories known as the "articles of faith" and "pillars of Islam." A *Muslim community* consists of individuals who collectively adhere to and share these common beliefs and practices. Today, a typical Muslim is a person who adheres to the teachings of Islam as understood, explained, and canonized by the scholarship of the major Islamic schools of thought. I understand *Islamic schools of thought* (*madhāhib*) to be the major theological, jurisprudential, and legal tendencies that were founded by renowned religious authorities such as Ja`farī al-Ṣādiq, Abū Ḥanīfah, Mālik, Ibn Ḥanbal, and al-Shāfi`ī (hence, the *Ja`farī, Ḥanafī, Mālikī, Ḥanbalī,* and *Shāfi`ī* schools). *Sufism* (or Sufiism) however, refers to a plethora of mystical tendencies all of which share the belief that knowing God is possible through spiritual experiences that are guided by a knower (*`ārif*). Sufism is not a distinct school of jurisprudence and theology; rather, a Sufi adheres to one of the established schools of thought that is prevalent in his or her community.

Islam is the name of the religion preached and implemented by the Prophet Muhammad and preserved by his followers in consistent, albeit varying systems of beliefs and practices. The word itself is a derivative (*maṣdar*; verbal noun) of the Arabic root that means, among other things, to submit, to resign, or to surrender oneself.

Since this work relies primarily on Islamic literature, I use some key religious words as defined by Muslim scholars with the understanding that the same words may mean different things in other Semitic traditions. For instance, the word "*Prophet*" refers to a person selected by the deity to lead a tribe or a clan to which he belongs. A *Messenger* on the other hand, is a person the deity selects to lead the larger human community. Generally, Messengers are backed by a divine scripture. As such, Muslim scholars see all Messengers to be Prophets, but the reverse is not true. Some Muslim scholars contend that God has sent as many as 125,000 Prophets but as few as five (some say twenty-five) Messengers.

The adjective "*Islamic*" is used to refer to inanimate objects, concepts, or behaviors that are inspired by Islam. For instance, we say Islamic art, Islamic cities, Islamic thought, and Islamic civilization. But we say a *Muslim* (person) and a Muslim community, which consists of individuals who are Muslim. The *Islamic world* is thus used to refer to the community influenced by Islam even if there is in its midst non-Muslim individuals or minorities (hence the Islamic civilization). The Muslim world on the other hand, refers only to the communities of Muslims. In other words, even if a group of Muslims is found in a non-Muslim country, they could be considered part of the Muslim world. Similarly, a Christian group of people living within a predominantly Muslim country is part of the Islamic world.

Islamic law is the corpus of legal rulings and determinations that are inspired by or based on Islamic teachings. I use Islamic law as the quality of positive law that a modern state can directly enforce. Although it may be used by some Western scholars, I do not use the phrase "Muslim law" because it may imply that such a law was never influenced by outside traditions. I use "*Qur'ānic law*" to refer to the legal rulings that are explicitly stated in the Qur'ān and that did not require extensive interpretive efforts to formulate them.

The phrase "legal rulings" (*aḥkām*) refers to the pronouncements of the law regarding specific cases. The *legal rules* (*qawā`id*) on the other hand, are the five judgments; as such, they are finite and they are the domain of the jurist not the *faqīh*. The *legal proofs* (*adillah*) are the explicit and implicit traditions found in the sources of law (Qur'ān and the Sunnah) that are used by Muslim jurists to link the legal rulings to the revelations. The *legal justification* or *legal purpose* (*`illah*) refers to the reason behind any given proscription or obligation. Since the Qur'ān did not always identify the justifying reason behind prohibiting or requiring (obligation) something, it was left to jurists (*mujtahid*; pl. *mujtahidūn*) to identify the legal justification and once discovered, it was used to extend the legal rule, by way of analogy (*qiyās*), to cover cases not addressed in the earlier sources. For example, and given the topic of this work, establishing justice is seen as the legal purpose of inheritance and polygyny laws. During the formative period of Islamic law, analogy was the primary tool of *ijtihād* which is the exertion of maximum efforts in determining legal rules, legal rulings, legal proofs, and/or legal justifications.

The *sharī`ah* is the *abstract* concept that includes the legal rules and legal rulings as derived from the legal proofs. Each Islamic school of thought envisions a specific *sharī`ah* that reflects its own theological, religious, and jurisprudential principles and teachings. Islamic law is the codified rendering of the *sharī`ah* for the *sharī`ah*, as I understand it, is the law and principle at the same time and it serves as a guide to producing a particular positive Islamic law. A good example that underscores the difference between *sharī`ah* and Islamic law is the legal code that governed the Ottoman Empire (*majalla*); it is based on the *sharī`ah* but it is not *the sharī`ah*. Since the mechanisms of enacting Islamic law are dependent on social and political forces at any given time period, Islamic law—unlike *sharī`ah*—shares some features with other legal traditions such as Common Law and other modern legal systems.

Muslims believe that the *Qur'ān* is the revealed Word of God, which scholars and ordinary Muslims memorize and recite verbatim (recite it in its entirety or selected parts of it). The *Ḥadīth* on the other hand, is God's nonverbatim revelation to the Prophet (meaning is revealed but the verbalization of any one tradition is the Prophet's). Although there is a technical and semantic difference between the two, I nonetheless use Ḥadīth and the Sunnah interchangeably. The *revelations* are "truths" that did not originate from human rational, logical, philosophical, scientific or any human intellectual (or otherwise) activities. For Muslims, revelations are the information and the knowledge communicated by the deity to a person (inspirations and visions; as was the case with most prophets), indirectly (mediated by angels; the way the Qur'ān is said to have been revealed to the Prophet Muhammad), and/or extraordinarily (direct talk; the Qur'ān speaks of only one instance of this kind of communication: Moses who is known for Muslim as *Kalīmu Allāh*).

An *Islamicist* is a professional and qualified scholar of Islamic studies who may or may not be Muslim; such a term should not be confused with an *Islamist* who is generally a Muslim who sees Islam as a comprehensive way of life that governs the individual as well as the collective life of the community. *Islamism* is essentially a political and social project rooted in a religious discourse (*marja`iyyah dīniyyah*). It is a movement that seeks to establish *sharī`ah* as the basis of politics and governance in Muslim countries. In Arabic countries, followers of this movement are referred to as the "*islāmiyyūn*" to distinguish them from "*muslimūn*" who may or may not support the "Islamization" of society projects promoted by the "*islāmiyyūn*." In the West, some refer to the Islamist movement as the fundamentalist movement. Given the specific historical context of "fundamentalism" in Christianity and in the West, using the connotation "Islamic fundamentalism" might be an oversimplification and mischaracterization of Islamist movements.

Throughout this work, I sometimes use the phrase "status of women," which may seem vague. Where it is not made specific, the reader should understand it to mean the economic, legal, and political status of women.

In the conclusion of this work, I recommend that building and protecting *civil society institutions* is a more effective way of improving the status of women than relying on legal reform or on increasing the representation of women in judicial, legislative, and executive bodies. I understand the civil society institutions (and processes) to manifest themselves in three layers listed below in order of importance:

1. Separation of governing powers (executive, legislative, and judicial). This foundational process is fundamental and each branch of government should be elected (selected) through a separate process and performs its duties in full and uncontrolled independence.
2. The initiation and safeguarding of critical public service institutions whose responsibility involves dissemination of information and the education of the public. For instance, the media and press outlets, schools and universities, and professional and labor associations should form the bulk of civil institutions of this layer.
3. Legal protection of civic and civil entities that represent the ethnic, cultural, religious, professional, occupational, and private interests in the larger society. The concept of civil society is essentially a Western idea but I argue that, in the Muslim world, a new understanding of civil society is necessary in order to accommodate the cultural, religious, and societal elements that are unique to Muslims. I suggest that those interested in these topics consult my other works where I discuss these topics in great details.

This study is not about defining these words or defending the above understanding; rather, I introduced them axiomatically so that the reader is aware of my assumptions and is able to follow the rationale of my arguments.

Acknowledgments

The author is grateful for the help and support from a number of colleagues who read drafts of some of the chapters of this work (and some have read the entire manuscript), each from his or her academic discipline point of view, and commented on it. Among them I would like to mention David Powers who reviewed the sections dealing with Islamic legal philosophy more than once and was very generous with his time and suggestions. I am also indebted to my colleague and friend Fekhereddine Berrada for his support, encouragement, and editorial insight. Lastly, I would like to thank the anonymous reviewers for their constructive comments. I am confident that these colleagues' suggestions improved this work, and I remain the sole responsible party for any and all shortcomings.

I am sincerely grateful to my students who have contributed in one way or another to the development of this research project throughout the years. I especially thank students and members of the larger community in the West and in the Muslim world who spent many hours reading and filling out numerous surveys. Their patience, time, and support are greatly appreciated.

Introduction

In Islam, the concept of justice is at the core of a number of theological, jurisprudential, legal, and philosophical doctrines. For instance, one of God's attributes is being just. The doctrine of reward and punishment is founded on divine justice: it is written that each and every human being will be treated fairly based on his or her personal acts and achievements.[1] The school of Mu`tazilites considers justice to be one of two doctrines: *`adl* or *`adālah* [justice] and *tawḥīd* [singularity of God]. Muslim theologians and jurists contend that the laws governing civil and criminal offenses uphold divine justice and remedy unjust acts by the aggressors. The concept of justice is very common in Islamic thought. To be sure, the majority of Muslim scholars (past and present) see justice as the raison d'être of legislating and governance: Islamic law and jurisprudence is to realize God's justice on earth. The importance of justice and fairness in the Islamic discourse justifies making such concepts central themes of this work.

This study explores the limits and range of social justice in the Qur'ānic, interpretive, and legal traditions. Initially, my working hypothesis (as well as the thesis of many scholars: Leila Ahmed, Barazangi, A. Wadud, and Asma Barlas, among others) contends that since the Qur'ānic passages dealing with the two primary cases of this study (polygamy and inheritance) emphasize justice and fairness, it must be the male-dominated interpretive processes that have disfranchised women and produced laws and social practices that are disadvantageous to them. This hypothesis is premised on the assumption that justice is a social construct, which would mean that by manipulating its definition or opening it up to new perspectives (in this case Muslim women's perspectives questioning the traditional paradigm), a new understanding and applications of the concept of justice would emerge. Upon the examination of the historical documents, the role of men and some women (`Ā'ishah in particular; given her role in transmitting many traditions that are part of Sunni compilations) in developing legal and religious traditions, and in the light of the analysis of the survey data (interpretive opinions), I now argue that, especially in the Islamic religious discourse, the concepts of justice and fairness are necessarily informed and shaped by the cultural and political environment wherein they *were* conceived. In other words, justice and fairness are not absolute values in the eyes of members of a religious community; rather, justice and fairness are *time-specific* social constructs *manufactured* by the prevailing understanding, local customs, and practices. In the Islamic discourse, justice is time specific in that it was defined during, and did not evolve beyond, the formative period of Islamic law and practices (first two Islamic centuries). Justice is also manufactured in that the formulation of the concept was not necessarily normatively derived from the primary sources of religious and legal teachings as religious Muslim scholars claim. The time specificity and artificiality make the Islamic concept of justice fundamentally different from the modern Western one, which is characterized as an evolving social construct.[2] One of the key differences is that in the Western view, justice is susceptible to change depending on the societal environment. The Islamic religious concept of justice is locked and therefore societal changes alone will not necessarily result in the emergence of a new understanding and new application of justice. The analysis of the concept of justice as it relates to the legal and economic status of women in Islam has far reaching implications regarding the origins and development of Islamic law and practices in general.

To support the above claims, I rely on the evidence found in religious texts as well as that in the ethical and jurisprudential literature that informs human behavior. For instance, the Qur'ān contains passages that suggest an impenetrable and hidden wisdom even in destructive acts such as murder. As a conceptual basis, I argue that the Qur'ānic story of the "Knower" has the role of communicating values and shaping behavior through paradigmatic speech and idiomatic stories (chapter 1). Similarly, I present the power of persuasion of Qur'ānic legal philosophy in shaping social behavior through the concept of *communicative justice* that employs binaries (such as fear and enticement) in order to achieve compliance and even self-denial. I show that Islamic legal theory operates on the emotional level in order to elicit desired social behavior and acceptance of legal rulings even if they apply differently to men and women (chapter 2). From the Islamic legal tradition (corpus of law), I examine the laws of polygamy and inheritance in order to explore the full range of interpretations and discuss whether there exist other legal determinations and legal rulings that are more propitious to women (chapters 3 and 4).

In order to further assess the explicitness of the Qur'ānic verses dealing with inheritance and in order to verify whether women's participation in the interpretive process could provide a counterweight against men's assumed bias, I have compiled and analyzed data consisting of interpretation of legal texts by 908 participants. The aggregate data (as well as the comparison of the interpretations by numerous groups of equal numbers of males and females) *did not show any male or female bias*. In other words, women's participation did not produce interpretations that are favorable to women. In the light of this study, I argue that civil institutions that promote education, independent thinking, diversity, and advocacy will enable competitive processes of reading and implementing legal and religious traditions in a way that is just and fair.

The analysis of the data, however, is conclusive in showing that the Qur'ānic enunciations are explicit and specific about female relatives' inheritance and abundantly vague or silent about male relatives' inheritance. Despite this explicitness, in most cases (numerous examples are provided in chapter 4), Muslim scholars augment or diminish female heirs' shares as if they were dependent on male heirs' shares. It stands to reason that an unknown value is measured against or derived from the known one and not the opposite. Classical Islamic law scholars (both Shi'ite and Sunni) do not follow this logic and they treat the shares of males as given and irreducible values. The data analysis underscores this conflict between theory and practice.

Parenthetically, the data also show a small (1% to 6%), yet consistently higher percentage of female interpreters (participants) being more specific in their understanding of the letter of the law. This factor (along with evidence collected from historical documents) further supports my argument that women's participation in the interpretive process alone would not necessarily rectify existing unjust and unfair practices and rulings. Furthermore, women's close adherence to instructions and letter of the law could signal their propensity to uphold established rules and customs even if such rules are to their detriment. Admittedly, the statistical figures are too small to allow for broad generalization, but it signals a trend. Research in the social and behavioral sciences has shown that women tend to be more law-abiding citizens than men.[3] It is therefore troubling to realize that women, more than men, are prepared to obey laws that disadvantage them. I must emphasize that this point is peripheral. It was suggested by the data but it is not central to my main argument, and I hope that future research will deal with the extent and implications of this finding on the status of women and minority groups.

I conclude by presenting discussions of and solutions for some of the unjust practices from various points of view. Muslims, Islamists, and Islamicists' recommendations range from preserving and maintaining the status quo to calling for radical interpretations or rejection of the existing systems. I argue that building civil society institutions is *the* practical and effective approach for bringing about positive change and ameliorating the economic, social, and political status of women and other disadvantaged social groups.

Although this work is intended to be a critical appraisal of the literature and disciplines that informed and shaped the legal status of women in the Islamic civilization,[4] it should not take away from the historical significance of that which some women had achieved during the early years of Islam. Scholars are cognizant of some progress made by Muslims in the area of gender equality and women's rights and this study does not dispute those findings. However, throughout the history of the Islamic civilization, it is also undisputed that women have fewer opportunities to achieve economic and political power thus far almost monopolized by men. Therefore, it is essential that the bases of discrimination against women and the premise of gender-based civil and economic inequality are addressed. The background information and proposed methodology of this work should further delineate the importance and pervasiveness of the themes that are selected for discussion.

The evidence from the time of the Prophet Muhammad suggests that women were treated differently not just because of their gender, but because of their economic and social status.[5] The fact that there were very wealthy women even prior to the rise of Islam suggests that women who came from a "noble" Arabic background were able to own property and run their affairs. What is true also is that those who lacked the elevated social and economic standing suffered abuse, exploitation, and marginalization. Wealth was, as it is now, a source of power and influence.[6] As a result, those who were wealthy were influential and powerful, and those who lacked wealth were weak and exploited. With the rigid and biased rules of transfer of wealth from one person to another and from one generation to the next, the tight control over the means of production, and the unfair usurious financial rules and practices all have widened the gap between the rich and the poor.

Predictably, in this kind of environment, women, laborers, and slaves remained disadvantaged by the unfair rules of wealth transfer and excessive accumulation of capital in the hands of the few. It was very difficult for this social group to break through the economic and cultural barriers placed in front of them. Children born to poor parents were more likely to be a burden, and therefore they were not desired. As a result the practice of "infanticide" (*wa'd*) was widespread during the pre-Islamic era. If this practice was common, it undoubtedly must have had an impact on the attitudes toward women in general.[7] Not only would men have a negative attitude toward women, but women themselves must have felt the shame that was described in the Qur'ān and that shame must have shaped their sense of worth and being. I would contend that it is necessarily the case that the ill treatment (and negative categorization) of a group of people has a greater and lasting negative impact on the psychology of the persons (individually) than physical abuse. Regrettably, that might have been the case during the pre-Islamic times in Arabia;[8] but some of these attitudes might have survived and continued to play a role in shaping the behavior and views of members of the emerging Muslim community.

What we know about the status of women from that time period with some degree of certainty is that such a status was decided by social standing and family name. A good example of the importance of these factors in determining the status of women is the background and role of the first woman in the life of the Prophet Muhammad, Khadījah.

Not only was Khadījah a wealthy woman, but also one who did not seem to live by the code of "ethics" and traditions known to have governed the society during that time. Then, widowed or divorced women, even if they were young, were undesired by most men, let alone a man of nobility. Because of this cultural limitation, men tended to enter into special contracts with each other that would oblige one not only to take care of the other's family but also to marry his widow if he were to be killed or to die.[9] As a result of these practices, we know of many men who married the wives of their deceased brothers, and uncles and nephews marrying the wives of one another upon one's death. Khadījah on the other hand, not only kept control of her wealth but also hired a manager instead of entrusting it to a male relative as was the general practice. Furthermore, she, a woman in her forties, proposed to and ended up marrying a man nearly half her age. When taken in that context, or even in the context of modern times where age difference is still a factor, for a woman to marry a much younger man is indeed ground breaking and out of the ordinary. For the duration of their lives together, Muhammad and Khadījah exemplified the warm and respectful relationship between spouses of any time. It is possible that his respect and admiration of Khadījah had left a lasting impression on him. His attitude toward other women, widowed or otherwise and young or old, shows an impressive maturity and a commendable sensitivity.[10]

Prophet Muhammad's example in treating women influenced even the most conservative of the Arabs. For instance, `Umar, who is known for chastising women for arguing with the Messenger and for appearing in public, moved to the "center" during his caliphate years and appointed al-Shifā' Bint Abd Allāh al-Makhzūmiyyah as the Head Controller (office of *muḥtasib*) in charge of the markets in Madīnah.[11] He offered the same job controlling the markets of Mecca to Samrā' Bint Nahīk al-Asdiyyah who went around whipping merchants, buyers, and sellers who violated the law.[12]

There are numerous reports that show that women, during the time of the Prophet Muhammad, were not only entitled to own property and managing it themselves, but also to work so that they are charitable and contributing members of the society. When Jābir Ibn `Abd Allāh prevented his maternal aunt from working on her farm and tending to her trees, she consulted the Messenger who encouraged her to work so that she would have the means to give to charity and help the needy.[13] In other words, even if it were not necessary for a woman to work to support herself, she was still encouraged, based on this report, to work so that she would be able to offer charity and contribute to the betterment of the community.

Not only did early Muslim women participate in civil and political matters,[14] but also they served in the front lines during wars, which is a step forward considering that even today the armies of modern Western nations restrict women's participation in combat. For example, there are numerous reports that recorded the role of Nusaybah Bint Ka`b al-Anṣīriyyah al-Māziniyyah in the battles of Uḥud, al-Ḥudaybiyyah, Khaybar, and Ḥunayn. In all of these and other battles, it seems that she served in the front lines to the point that she was wounded in twelve places in a single battle and nursed her injuries for a year.[15] Her service earned her admiration from the Prophet who commented at one point: "The day of Uḥud, every time I turned left or right, I saw Nusaybah fighting." Even after the death of the Prophet Muhammad, Muslim women continued to enlist and fight in the all-volunteer armies that traveled afar from the Islamic capitals. Historical records show that women enlisted for fighting in places as far away as Cyprus, and some died there. Umm Ḥarām for instance, whose grave is still preserved in the city of Larnaca in Cyprus, enlisted and fought during the rule of the third Caliph `Uthmān.[16]

The role of some Muslim women in politics and military affairs is a historical reality and one need not work hard to unearth evidence for this matter. The widely documented and reported rebellion led by `Ā'ishah against the fourth Caliph `Alī shows a highly sophisticated degree of political maturity not only among some women but also among men of that time period. Not only did men support her ideas and basis for challenging the Caliph, the highest political and religious authority in the Islamic civilization, but also men marched under her command to fight and die. In other words, it seems that there was an acceptance of women's leadership for her to be able to take such a leading role in a highly controversial event.

In a similar fashion, the daughter of the Prophet Muhammad, Fāṭimah, did not ask her husband, the well-respected and influential `Alī, to speak for her and ask for her inheritance; rather, on numerous occasions, she argued her cases and challenged the logic and authority of the first Caliph Abū Bakr.[17] She became a central figure that shaped Shi'ite thought and practices. Women's activism and political dissent was not restricted to famous or privileged women but even ordinary citizens participated in shaping the daily life of Muslims throughout Islamic civilization. After the death of the Caliph `Alī, women like Sawdah Bint `Umārah Ibn al-Ashtar, Bikārah al-Hilāliyyah, al-Zarqā' Bint `Uday Ibn Ghalib Ibn Qays al-Hamadhāniyyah, `Ikrishah Bint al-Aṭrash Ibn Rawāḥah, and `Urwā Bint al-Ḥārith challenged the Umayyad Caliph Mu`āwiyah, and the records show that these and other women participated in the political and military activities of that time.[18] Historical accounts show that women were indeed effective leaders and respected speakers. It is reported that when Umm Kulthūm Bint `Alī Ibn Abī Ṭālib spoke, "one could hardly hear any noise, as if people stopped breathing."[19]

Similarly, many Muslim women contributed to the arts, literature, and the sciences throughout the Islamic civilization.[20] Religious sciences were influenced by women, and many of the architects of Islamic jurisprudence and theology were impacted by the contribution of Muslim women scholars.[21] Their role in transmitting Ḥadīth hardly needs evidence and their scholarly integrity was never questioned. In fact, it is reported that no woman transmitter was ever accused of falsifying Ḥadīth reports, a feat that cannot be claimed by all men involved in the transmission of traditions.[22] Among the Muslim women who taught Ḥadīth was Maymūnah Bint Sa`d from whom the Caliph `Alī learned some Prophetic traditions.[23] The renowned scholar Ibn `Asākir learned Ḥadīth from some eighty women.[24] Fāṭimah Bint `Abbās[25] was a leading scholar in Egypt and Syria, and Nafīsah Bint al-Ḥasan Ibn Zayd Ibn al-Ḥasan Ibn `Alī had led al-Shāfi`ī's funeral prayer when he died to honor him for leading her in Ramadan prayers.[26] In Baghdad, Shuhdah (aka Fakhr al-Nisā' = the Pride of Women) taught courses in literature and history, and many influential scholars attended her classes.[27] The Hanbalite school of thought (the most conservative of the four Sunni schools of jurisprudence) was at one point dominated by a female scholar, Fāṭimah Bint Ḥamd al-Zubayriyyah (aka al-Shaykhah al-Fuḍayliyyah), who taught and wrote in the arts and sciences in Mecca.[28] Prominent Muslim women like the mystic (Rābi`ah al-`Adawiyyah), poets, and leaders had contributed to the rise of the Islamic civilization that lasted over a millennium.[29]

Notwithstanding all these individual achievements, it is evident that when one examines the legal and economic status of Muslim women in modern times, one realizes that it did not improve. Furthermore, when considering that the Muslim community was a leading force in the world civilization at the time (eighth to fourteenth-century time period), it is reasonable to assume that it provided opportunities to a large segment of its people. When taken in the context of and expectations from a civilizational powerhouse however, the improved status of women becomes anecdotal, for it is possible that for every woman who held a high status, there were many who were among the disadvantaged political, economic, and social classes. In other words, drawing conclusions based on anecdotal evidence amounts to unsupported generalization. To illustrate, imagine one looking back at America (as the seat of the modern civilization) hundreds of years from now; one could argue that women, African Americans, or members of other historically disfranchised minorities during the twentieth and twenty-first centuries were justly and fairly treated and enjoyed the same opportunities as people of European descent. One could support these claims by historical records that show the existence of powerful women Senators (women like Hillary Clinton), Black Supreme Court Justices (such as Clarence Thomas), several women holding cabinet positions in a number of administrations, and influential minorities represented in the arts and sciences. But as members of this community here and now, we know that African Americans are in fact still disadvantaged and are subjected to unjust and unfair conditions. Women, despite the fact that they constitute more than 50 percent of the population, are still underrepresented in leadership and executive positions that come with power and prestige (governors, presidents, CEOs, etc.). Native Americans are still living in appalling conditions. Understanding claims of women's achievement in the West (and factoring in the significant time and cultural differences separating the Western and Islamic civilizations) should give us valuable insight into the extent of claims of equal status awarded Muslim women. In the final analysis, most women in general and most Muslim women in particular, have a difficult journey ahead of them on the road to achieving social, economic, and political justice and equality.

The Islamic civilization, like any civilization of its caliber, undoubtedly had its achievements, its heroes, and its icons. But with that progress and achievement, it also had its second-class citizens, its victims, its slaves, its cheap labor, its consumers, and its privileged elite. When the errors and abuse caught up with the aging civilization, it was the weak and underprivileged that suffered first and most; and women were, as they are in most civilizations, the bulk of that underprivileged class of citizens. Today, many Muslim women are caught between the application of the misunderstood past and the synthesis of traditional law that has been filtered through the eyes of the elite, resulting in their abuse in the family and in society at large. Family laws are stacked against them, cultural practices target them, and political expediency subjugates them. In most cases, religion and the law play a major role in their continued exploitation and marginalization inside and outside the Muslim world.

Among the primary areas that continue to impede the integration of women into the larger society are some legal rules and social practices that traditional Muslim scholars generally portray as settled precedents that cannot be challenged. The claim of settled precedent will be tested in this study by way of adopting the same methodology and doctrines that were used by scholars of classical Islamic law and jurisprudence.

It is true that in some countries (Saudi Arabia and Iran for example) women are coerced into wearing specific attire and inheriting according to a predetermined system of shares that may or may not address the specific individual's needs. However, there are millions of other women living in the so-called modern (or moderate as some may choose to call them) Muslim countries and in the West choosing to abide by classical Islamic law and practices.[30] In fact, there are many staunch promoters of life according to the *sharī`ah* who are women and who are living in the West. In light of this reality, legislation and political decisions that are implemented in some countries to promote and uphold the rights of some women have the opposite effect on other women. Since Western countries do not allow the existence of separate legal systems such as religious courts,[31] we cannot determine whether some or all Muslim women would "choose" such courts. For this reason, I sometimes discuss the issue of attire instead of cases of personal statutes in order to contextualize the pressure exerted on Muslim women and the nature of the choices they make. For example, Turkey, in the name of secularism and for the purpose of providing a neutral environment for all women, bans the wearing of headscarves in some public and work places. The effect of that same initiative is that Turkish women who wish to wear what they see as a religiously mandated attire see their rights (civil and/or religious) being encroached upon by the state.

Subsequently, in liberal societies as well as in the conservative societies, women are caught in a power struggle that victimizes them and places them in the midst of an ideological war that they did not initiate. In conservative societies, some women lose the right to wear what they choose to wear. On the other hand, in some liberal societies, some Muslim women lose the right to wear what they want to wear. In both cases, the liberal discourse and the conservative religious discourse have in common more than each of them would care to admit:

Both are about control and values. The difference is that one is mandated and enforced in the name of humanism, secularism, and modernity (and even security and integration as the recently proposed law in Holland suggests); the other is maintained and enforced in the name of God, society, and morality.

A balancing act between these competing claims requires a strong grasp of the values and beliefs that inform the identity and the choices of individuals and communities. Moreover, the power of religion to move and motivate adherents ought to be soundly understood as a force whose purpose is to establish a controlled political, economic, and social environment. In the final analysis, humanist liberal thought works toward relieving the members of the society of their fears and anxieties by suggesting to them that they are masters and controllers of their own destiny. The religious conservative discourse, on the other hand, accomplishes the same goal of alleviating anxiety by teaching the individual that her acts are part of a grand plan and by comforting the collective by the sense of predictability that is the result of the adherents' adherence to religious and moral absolutes to some degree or another.

In order to understand how these goals are achieved and how these processes are brought to bear on the life of individuals and communities, it is essential that the elements of the religious, cultural, philosophical, and legal systems that shape and inform the acts and beliefs of peoples are adequately explored. In other words, questions concerning the existence of moral absolutes, legal mechanisms, and ethical guidelines that bring about human volition and action should be examined and answered in the light of medieval and modern discourses.

Arguments for the inclusion or exclusion of an individual or a group of individuals from the larger society are generally founded in law and ethics. Law consists of rules that meet the requirements of reason or necessity that sustains the cohesion of society. In contrast, ethics covers the set of rules and conventions that are shared by smaller groups but that may or may not be accepted by the collective as inviolable laws. In the West, it has been accepted that ethical guidelines are more or less personal and that when a conflict arises between a moral imperative and a legal ruling, the legal ruling should prevail. Predictably, the economic, political, and social forces within any given community may contribute to elevating a moral guideline to a legal ruling; hence, making it binding upon the larger society. However, ethical and moral guidelines are ever present when individuals and organizations provide direct services to their charges. Citizens select their political leaders based on their moral and ethical preferences; and politicians and executives carry their duties fully mindful of those preferences.

Arguably, ethical and moral guidelines are shaped by the family and by the religious establishments. Therefore, religion plays a continuous role as a social control mechanism in every society. In the case of the Islamic civilization, the role of religion is prominent. First, the fusion of religion and politics in the Islamic community is more evident. Second, and from its beginning, Islam played a fundamental role in the formation of the law. As a result of these elements, it is hard to separate ethical guidelines from the legal rulings in Islam. It may be argued that offenses that are punishable in the Hereafter are moral or religious matters; whereas, offenses punishable in this world are purely legal. But even this distinction is challenged when some modern Muslim states enact laws that punish and enforce regulations that were not historically a function of the state (or government).[32] The emergence of the so-called moral police in places like Saudi Arabia and Iran to punish those who violate dress codes or individuals who skip prayers are innovations that further blur the boundaries between law and ethics.

Women are the segment of society affected most by the new state jurisdiction. In religious as well as in secular societies, women are used by conservatives and liberals to score political points.[33] As a result, we find women being subjected to specific legislation that puts them at a disadvantage simply because of their gender. For example, in conservative societies, women are forced to wear specific attire under the pretext of preserving cultural authenticity and national identity. In liberal societies, women are also forced to *not* wear specific attire so that the secular heritage (more precisely *laïcité*) and the character of the society are not challenged. In the name of preserving the workplace as a neutral space, women in Turkey and France are banned from wearing headscarves in certain government buildings.

The status of Muslim women can be appraised by examining a number of issues such as the ones mentioned above. In this work, a modest attempt will be made to recount the historical, philosophical, and legal contexts that contribute to the negative and positive impact on women.

This study is normative, analytical, and quantitative. Legal studies in general and Islamic jurisprudence in particular emphasize the role of explicit statements in determining the intent of the legislator and the purpose of the law. In other words, the more explicit the legal proofs (legal basis), the less elaborate interpretation is adopted to consider the validity of law and its conformity to the statutes (or constitution). For example, and for purpose of clarity, freedom of speech is a constitutional right in the United States of America because the First Amendment explicitly protected it. Abortion rights on the other hand, are not an explicitly stated constitutional right, although the U.S. Supreme Court has ruled that such a right is implicit in some cases related to the issue of abortion and reproductive rights. The difference in opinion about the basis for abortion rights does not necessarily stem from personal beliefs, but rather from the nonexplicitness of the constitution on abortion. In other words, while some jurists argue that abortion rights are rooted in a right to privacy, it remains true that interpretation was needed in order to find a basis for the claim. Furthermore, protection of privacy is not conclusively derived from the explicit text of the constitution. Since privacy was not clearly mentioned in the text of the Constitution, in 1890 then-to-be Justice Louis Brandeis inscribed "a right to be left alone" which was then used as a basis for such a claim. This right has developed into a liberty of personal autonomy protected by the Fourteenth amendment. The First, Fourth, and Fifth Amendments also provide some protection of privacy, although in all cases the right is narrowly defined. Over time, the constitutional right of privacy has developed alongside a statutory right of privacy that limits access to personal information. These two examples from Western legal traditions clearly underscore the importance and function of interpretation. It could be argued that it is interpretation that gives power to otherwise ambiguous and dormant declarations and makes them relevant to the issues and values of the specific community. Similarly, the debates about certain claims of social justice and civil rights and the centrality of the ambiguous constitutions and by-laws presents the issue of explicitness in the forefront of the legal and moral discourse. In other words, is ambiguity a jurisprudential necessity in order to accommodate changing circumstances and changing values of societies or is it simply a shortcoming or an oversight on the part of the framers and authors of constitutions and laws?

Theoretically speaking, communities that accept the rule-of-law principle still dispute certain claims when the language of the law is not specific enough. In a similar fashion, Muslim scholars asserted the same theory when it was declared that no laws that violate the explicit Qur'ānic enunciations should be accepted as part of the *sharī`ah* laws. That is to say, if there is an explicit text that supports a particular claim, then such a claim ought to be enforced.[34]

Since this study is not about discussing the validity of the above theories, I will assume for now that this theory is valid and that the Qur'ān contains explicit and implicit statements that distinguish between the inviolable and disputable rights. Nonetheless, determining the degree of explicitness is another challenge facing legal scholars and philosophers of law from all legal traditions. In the case of Islamic jurisprudence, expertise in the Arabic language, familiarity with historical context, proper disciplinary training, and mental capacity are prerequisites for deriving legal opinions from the primary legal proofs. The more ambiguous the text of the legal texts, the more rigorous the prerequisites are in qualifying the interpreter. However, it is reasonable to assume that explicitness can be measured by the accessibility of the text of the legal proofs by the largest number of people in a way that produces identical interpretation. In other words, if a large number of individuals (randomly selected) who are fluent in the language in which the legal proofs are expressed reach the same determination of the law, it is reasonable to conclude then that the legal proofs were explicit. On the other hand, if the same process leads to radically divergent interpretations of the legal proofs, it could be concluded that the legal proofs were not explicit but rather implicit. The decree of implicitness can be established by the degree of divergence in opinion of the interpreters and visa versa.

On the basis of the rationale described above, this study firstly relies on normative analysis of the legal proofs as well as the established legal opinions relating to polygamy[35] and inheritance laws and practices. Secondly, the legal proofs (three verses of Qur'ān dealing with the two general cases) were made available to randomly selected individuals who are fluent in Arabic or English (or both) and were asked to determine the shares and rights of specific individuals based only on the text given to them. The results (collected data) were then categorized and analyzed (categories such as: males-females, practicing Muslims-non-Muslims, Arabic speakers-non-Arabic speakers, language experts-non-language experts, age groups, etc.).

One may ask whether Islamic law allows for this kind of data gathering and analysis as a basis for interpretation and derivation of formal legal opinion. To that end, it is essential to note that the foundational principles of Islamic jurisprudence in Sunni and Shi'ite schools of thought embrace this methodology. The doctrine of *informed assumptions*, discussed in detail in the chapter on inheritance, is exactly the kind of method that is employed here. In other words, none of the methods adopted in this study are foreign to Islamic jurisprudence. Rather, such methods are further refined so that the structure of the surveys identifies as many variables as possible in order to account for every element that may have an impact on the end results.

In summary, in addition to textual and normative analysis of the primary and secondary literature available on the subject matter, this study relies on data analysis (quantitative study) in order to support the overall thesis. Traditional Muslim scholars contend that the strictest of *sharī`ah* laws are based on the most explicit Qur'ānic texts. That assumption is tested by interpreting the original texts and four translations: if the interpretation of the legal proofs converges on a specific determination of meaning and effects, it is then reasonable to conclude that the verses dealing with the cases at hand are explicit. Of course it is possible that the convergence might be due to settled understandings influenced by exegeses or widespread practice. However, the presence of a large number of interpreters who are not Muslim (and given that everyone was instructed to ignore any and all outside information) would mitigate any bias or traditional exegetical interference.

If there is a substantial difference of opinion from one interpreter to another, it is reasonable to assume that the legal proofs were not explicit and that the legal rulings are the result of extensive interpretive processes that may or may not be reflective of the intent of the legislator. Furthermore, the data that were generated allow further verification. For instance, the large data of interpretations serve to (1) test the validity of the assumptions by Muslim scholars regarding the basis of their opinions and rulings and (2) provide a basis for any divergence from the traditional views. The results were not only valuable in determining whether or not (or to what degree) the given verses were actually explicit, but also in supporting other possible determinations of the meanings and shares. Of course, this method itself rests on the assumption that the degree of explicitness of a text is directly proportional to the degree of wide consensus (among independent [blind-survey] readers/interpreters) on a specific interpretation, which is discussed further in chapter four.

The data generated from the examination and analysis of the original Arabic text and the translations allow for considering the translations as a first generation of interpretation while the interpretation of the translation by other randomly selected readers serves as the second generation of interpretation. By establishing this layered paradigm, I was able to develop a formula that accounts for the margin of error in interpretation in the original language and in the second language, hence the validity of the claim of an organic link between the legal rulings and the legal proofs. If it is shown that interpretation is just as powerful as the legal proofs, it follows then that in order to have a balanced and more accurate interpretation of the legal proofs, all interested parties ought to contribute to such a body of interpretive laws.

Although the title of this work suggests that the author will be dealing with issues of women, understandably, no single publication could cover all the things that matter to Muslim women, let alone women from around the world. This study is not a conclusive appraisal of the status of Muslim women nor is it one that deals with all of the most important issues. It is in the final analysis an academic endeavor addressing very sensitive and controversial topics. As an academic endeavor, it selects themes that can be analyzed methodically. The Qur'ānic verses dealing with the distribution of inheritance are accessible and they assign specific numbers (fractions) to each of the heirs therein mentioned; hence, it was easy to subject these verses to empirical analysis in order to understand the way Muslim scholars interpret and interact with religious texts. As controversial topics, polygamy and inheritance rights generate heated debates, especially in the context of religious and cultural studies. For that reason, I will find it necessary to introduce argumentative narratives and counterclaims by conservatives, reformers, and liberals of the Islamic world. Given the importance of the issues and the need to listen to various voices, the "normal objective" and "sober" academic discourse ought to tolerate the controlled divergence from that which are ordinarily and customarily its characteristic traits. For these reasons, the methodology of this work will be a combination of analytical, descriptive, normative, and argumentative approaches and it is hoped that the readers will tolerate the variations.

1

Legal Absolutism and Ethical Relativism

A civilization is a manifest expression of collective, sophisticated, and adaptive values in critical areas of public life. The said expression must be propagated and preserved by effective iconic and monumental means. Although a civilization is not necessarily a moral good, the positive achievements must outweigh the negative aspects. To be elevated from a major power to the center of gravity of a world civilization, a community must establish peaceful cities with inclusive citizenship, achieve complementary organization of labor, acquire refined sciences, literature, and culture, elect/select attuned government, institutionalize complex and inclusive religious system, and exhibit the flexibility and capacity to dominate other cultures in a non-coercive manner. With this understanding of civilization, it becomes clear that no community can achieve such a status by excelling in one or few of the critical areas. To the contrary, there must be a comprehensive and all encompassing agenda that contribute to the well-being of the economic, social, and political life. In other words, it is not only the laws nor is it the political system that guarantees success; rather, it is through the collective input in all areas that legendary status of a civilization is realized. To be sure, one should not look for the secrets of success only in the centers of power, but also in the subtle discourses that shape public life, ethics, and social dynamics. Communities establish social order and declare collective expectations by relying on iconic, paradigmatic, and idiomatic tales that communicate public morality, which in turn dictate the place and function of women, ethnic groups, and individuals. In this context, the Qur'ān is full of "stories" that are not necessarily legal but just as effective in creating the "ideal" *ummah*. In order to understand the moral basis for the Islamic social order, I will begin by introducing and analyzing one of the most fascinating and intriguing stories of the Qur'ān: Moses' encounter with the "knower." This background information should lay the foundation to my argument against legal reform as the singular solution to widespread discrimination against women. Because this story shows that cultural and societal expectations are sometimes more oppressive than laws, I contend that encouraging a culture of diversity and pluralism that stretches the ethical and moral boundaries is, in the long run, more effective than short-sighted legal actions and solutions.

Throughout history, acts of murder, imprisonment, and war made human life and liberty a contested value. In religious and secular discourses, the context of any of the above acts made it possible to relativize the rights to life and freedom. They can be forfeited: The saving of some life might be cited to legitimize the destruction of another. In Islamic ethics, such acts are possible but they cannot be done under the umbrella of aggression:

> My people! I have prohibited upon Myself aggression (*ẓulm*), and I have proscribed it for you too; so do not act aggressively towards one another.[1]

Although it is difficult to define aggression in the modern political context especially,[2] it is fairly easy to characterize acts of aggression as violent undertakings by the powerful against the weak for no reason but to maximize one's dominion and hegemony.[3] Aggression, as an act of violence, can only be justified when it is committed to redress a prior act of violence. Violence is any direct or indirect restriction of the movement and liberties of another person. Such restrictions may take the form of killing, injury, imprisonment, or depriving one of one's mental or material capacity and ability to pursue a normal life. In my view, to deprive women of equal opportunity to pursue a dignified and fulsome life constitutes an act of aggression. In the Islamic traditions, it is said that, before God, there is no other act more egregious than aggression and for that reason the deity promised to treat aggressors as his "personal" enemies in the Hereafter.[4] In Islamic thought, the antonym of aggression is justice; and therefore, only acts in the name of justice and fairness may justify the taking of life or liberties of a person. Despite the existence of guiding principles such as the above, more often than not, we learn of acts that seem to be unjustified. That is when ethical and moral arguments emerge as a means to justify or criticize social and religious practices.

What should (or ought) one do if one knows for a fact that a person will cause some harm (in the future) to another person or to many people? Should a parent or both parents be allowed to kill (abort?) a child if they were to know with absolute certainty that such a child, were he to reach adulthood, will be an unrepentant criminal and a lethal menace to them and to others? Should a person or the government be allowed to restrict the travels and movement of adults and discerning people upon knowing that an eminent danger is awaiting them? Should the rights of the few be sacrificed for the rights of the many? If so, should women's rights be curtailed for simply being women because the community leaders see them as a disturbance to social order? And finally, how do we acquire the special knowledge (if it exists) that allows one to make these judgments; and which knowledge is supreme: acquired, revealed, or gifted knowledge?

At first glance, these inquiries may appear to be a series of hypothetical questions similar to the ones asked in modern-day university level courses on ethics, moral philosophy, and jurisprudence. In reality, these are the kind of questions faced by executive leaders, judicial authorities, and law enforcement agencies. Curiously, however, some of these are also the kind of situation presented in the story of Moses when he had an encounter with a person identified in the Qur'ān as a "knower" and a servant of God (or al-Khaḍir in the exegetical collections). It provides a backdrop to the philosophical and jurisprudential discourse that informed Islamic law and practices throughout the history of the Islamic civilization. If we were to understand the arguments of this particular story, it would be easier to grasp the reach and scope of Islamic law and especially laws dealing with matters of social justice and individual entitlements.

For Muslims, the story of Moses' encounter with the "knower," like the rest of the Qur'ān, has moral and possibly legal implications. It teaches and justifies, it instructs and implies, it commands and inspires. It provides adherents with the comfort of knowing that there is a higher purpose and a nobler goal for acts even if they are not understood. In Islamic practices and traditions, one does what one can in keeping with the guidelines of legality and morality but doing so does not guarantee attaining the ultimate truth or the desired ends. For Muslims, the end and the beginning are in the hands of God. "It is fate (or *maktūb*)" Muslims declare every time an event (such as loss, death, or injury) strikes. In short, it is not up to the individual Muslim to negotiate the outcome of the passing of time or to explain the unexplainable. Moses' encounter with the "knower" is a powerful reminder of the limitations of human reason and need for broader perspective. More importantly, the passages of this story outline the moral and ethical foundation of acts when they are juxtaposed to legal judgments. For the author of this story to choose Moses—the man of the Tablets, the preacher of the Commandments, the legal genius—and contrast him to the "knower" of ethical judgments—a man of penetrating insight and mysterious wisdom—this setting is indeed compelling.

In understanding the balance between law and morality in Islamic tradition, I hope to achieve a sound understanding of the Islamic worldview in the broadest sense possible. In this chapter, firstly, I will introduce the story as told in the Qur'ān and in the exegetical works. Secondly, I will analyze the story in order to highlight the arguments that support the main thesis as posited in the introduction to this work. Finally, and in the light of the analysis and discussion, I will draw some conclusions and propose some answers to the above and other questions.

To Know or Not to Know: The Basis of Acts

> And tell of Moses when he said to his assistant: "I will not rest until I reach the junction of the two seas or die trying." When the two reached midpoint, they forgot their fish which then quietly made its way into the sea. When the two passed beyond the location, Moses said to his assistant: "Bring us our lunch, indeed we have achieved an acceptable leg of our journey." He said: "Remember when we

retreated to the rock, there I forgot about the fish—and indeed it was Satan who caused me to forget about it—and it amazingly made its way into the sea." He said: "That is what we were after." And the two backtracked retracing their footsteps. There they found one of Our subjects to whom we gave some mercy from Us and We taught him a great knowledge from Us. Moses asked him: "It is great maturity that I desire, can I tag along so that you may teach me from that which you have been taught?" He replied: "You will not be patient with me; how could you be patient about that which you have no foreknowledge?" He said: "God willing, you will find me patient and I will not disobey any of your commands." He said: "When you follow me, do not ask me about anything until I explain to you its purpose." The two began their journey together and when they boarded the boat, he punctured it. He said: "You punctured it to drown its people; indeed you have done a wicked act." He said: "Didn't I tell you that you will not have patience with me?" He said: "Do not judge me by my forgetfulness and do not make it harder on me." The two continued until they encountered a boy; he killed him. He (Moses) said: "Did you just kill a pure soul that did not cause the loss of soul? Indeed you have undertaken a sinful act." He said: "Didn't I tell you that you will not have patience with me?" He said: "If I ask you about one thing after this, then do not accompany me; indeed you will be excused from doing so." They continued until they reached a village. They asked for food and they were refused and denied any hospitality. Therein, they found a wall that was about to collapse. So he rebuilt it. Moses then said: "Maybe you should ask the people of the town to pay you for rebuilding it!" He said: "This is the time of parting company. However, I will inform you of the interpretation of that for which you had no patience. As for the boat, it belonged to poor individuals who make a living by fishing in the seas. I wanted to disable it because there was a usurping king after it. As for the boy, his two parents were two faithful individuals but he would have driven them to arrogance and ingratitude. We wanted their Lord to offer them instead a child who is charitable and merciful. Finally, the wall belongs to two orphan boys from the town and there under was a treasure left for them by their righteous father. Your Lord willed that they reach adulthood and retrieve it. That is your Lord's mercy; I did not do it on my own. That is the interpretation of that for which you had no patience." [Q18:60–82][5]

The above passage is the full story as told in less than three pages of the Qur'ān. The only person mentioned by name is Moses. The location and the names of the other figures were described in specific terms by exegetes.[6] Muslim scholars are not sure why certain information is left out in the Qur'ān although that is not unusual. Some argue that information is purposefully left out because it is not critical to the legal or moral purpose of telling the story. Others contend that the Qur'ānic style intentionally leaves critical information out in order to empower prophets and religious authorities to interpret it within the specific context and circumstances. Whatever the case may be, clearly the style of telling this story has focused attention on the three acts by the knowledgeable subject of

God (the knower) and contrasted them to the judgments issued by Moses who was given the divine commandments that prohibited these same acts. Even if the story is deemed nonhistorical, its philosophical implications are extraordinary. In other words, the selection of the acts (the three events) and the observer (Moses) do suggest a rationale behind the "telling" of this narrative, which does not appear to be that original in its totality.[7] In the Qur'ānic contexts however, it brings to light the relationship between legal and moral imperatives on the one hand, and the value of life and human dignity on the other hand. This objective was achieved by making Moses, a personality that is universally associated with law and commandments, a central figure who is on a journey to learn beyond what he was taught.

Before I analyze the story and theorize about its ethical and legal implications, it is necessary to start with the interpretations of the traditional Muslim exegetes. Not only will the presentation of the views of Muslim commentators shed some light on the role of interpretations in the religious discourse, but it also helps in comparing and understanding the function and place of morality and ethics in the scripture and in the commentaries respectively.

Ostensibly, the usual cryptic style of the Qur'ān rarely tells a full story. However, in addition to this story, only the story of Joseph may come close to biblical style narratives that recount a story in a suspenseful and conclusive manner. Moses' encounter with the curious figure, identified in exegetical works as al-Khaḍir, is narrated with dialogues. The commentaries that will be analyzed in this chapter relate to the passages of the Qur'ān, all of which are taken from the chapter entitled *al-kahf* (the cave). The names (except Moses') and some other details are found only in the *tafsīr* collections.

According to al-Ṭabarī and Ibn Kathīr, after a passionate and empowering speech to the Israelites, Moses was approached by a member of the audience and asked if there is any other human being more knowledgeable than him. Moses replied negatively arguing that with the revelation and the Commandments that God has bestowed on him, he had become the most knowledgeable person to ever live. Not long thereafter, Gabriel came with a message from God to rebuke him and inform him that there was in fact another person whom the deity had blessed with extraordinary knowledge. Disappointed and curious at the same time, Moses and his helper Joshua undertook a long journey to find this man.[8] The only clue they were given was that a dead fish would come alive and disappear once they reached the place where lived this "knower."[9]

After some time had passed along the coastal lines of some unspecified seas,[10] the pair decided to rest. Joshua laid the jar containing the fish on the ground and they both fell asleep. During that time, the fish made its way into the water. Upon waking up, they resumed the journey, although Joshua noticed that the fish was missing. After some time, they decided to rest and Moses asked Joshua to check on the fish and serve him some food. At this point, Joshua blames his forgetfulness on Satan and reveals to Moses that the fish swam away when they were asleep. Upon hearing the news, Moses realized that he had missed the location of al-Khaḍir so they backtracked all the way to the location where they lost the fish.

It did not take them long to find the mysterious person who seemed to have known about them and was expecting their arrival. He nonetheless entertains himself by asking Moses for the reason of traveling to see him despite the fact that he has a challenging task of leading his people. Moses answered by expressing his desire to learn from him some of what he had been given. To this, al-Khaḍir replied by predicting that Moses does not have the patience to observe and learn. When Moses insisted that he is patient, al-Khaḍir exclaimed: "How could you be patient in the face of that to which you have no exposure? You are given the knowledge that allows you to judge the apparent justness of acts but not the knowledge of the unseen." The predictions and warning did not discourage Moses. He promised that he will be patient and he will not antagonize him. To this al-Khaḍir agreed on the condition that he is not challenged about the validity of what he does.

They started by walking along the coast soliciting rides from boat masters. Not only did the crew of a new, reliable, clean, and decorated boat offer them a ride, but they did not even charge them for it. Despite that, al-Khaḍir sabotaged the boat by cutting a hole in it and concealing it and thereby rendering the craft unfit for sailing. Irritated by the seeming ingratitude and criminal behavior of his companion, Moses complained judgingly: "Did you puncture it to drown its crew? Indeed that is an abhorring act." Upon hearing the criticism, al-Khaḍir reminded Moses that he was warned against such behavior. Moses apologized and begged him to forgive his forgetfulness.

They left the boat and started to walk in the town where they encountered a number of children playing. One of these children was a clean, polite, and well-behaved boy. Without warning, al-Khaḍir kills the boy by intentionally striking his head with a rock. Appalled by the cold-blooded murder of an innocent child, again Moses objected to this undertaking and expressed his disapproval. Once reminded of his impatience, Moses declares that he agrees to end the arrangement if and when he violates it one more time.

They left that town and went to another one. The people of this town were neither hospitable nor accommodating to these traveling strangers: They denied them water, refused them food, and declined them rest. Despite the townspeople's attitude, al-Khaḍir decided to waste his energy and time rebuilding a wall of a house that is falling apart. Possibly amused and probably irritated by the irony, Moses commented: "Maybe you should ask to get paid for doing that!" Upon hearing that, al-Khaḍir asserted: "That is it. We are done: You go your way and I am going mine. But before you do that, I will inform you of the interpretation of that which tested your patience. As for the boat, it belonged to some poor individuals who rely on it for a living. However, were they allowed to continue their voyage to the next city, its ruler would have usurped it from them and deprived them of their means of support. The boy on the other hand, is a child of two believing and righteous people whom he would have tortured and coerced to disbelieve. I did what I did so that they are given another merciful and kind child. Lastly, the wall stood as a protection of and marker for a treasure that was left by two righteous parents for their two orphan children. Rebuilding and maintaining the wall until they are old enough to extract it was the purpose of my undertaking."

Some early Muslim scholars saw this story as a metaphor for the vastness of divine knowledge and a lesson in humility. The context they provided suggests that even those given special knowledge such as revelations are still limited in their wisdom. Some Sufi masters and Shi`ite theologians rely on this story to instill in the mind of their followers the need for a teacher (*`ārif*) or an *imām* respectively.[11]

For Shi`ites, the existence of the Qur'ān or the books of interpretations and laws is not enough to guide the adherent to the right path. There must be a living knower or infallible living person who leads, teaches, and initiates. For Sufis, life is a journey into learning, and knowing that requires a seasoned master and guide. For Shi`ites, reason and intellect are fallible and because of that there must be an infallible person who can interpret and apply the divine knowledge at any given time. The presence of a *`ārif* or an *imām* is therefore seen as the manifestation of God's grace, wisdom, and mercy upon his creations.[12]

For Sunni Muslims, the story teaches humility and speaks for God's vast and absolute knowledge. This view is underscored by an anecdote that is embedded in the exegesis dealing with these verses. It is reported that, while the "knower" and Moses were riding on the ship, a bird landed near the sea and took a sip of water. The "knower" then pointed to the bird and told Moses that his knowledge compared to God's is similar to the amount of water taken by the bird from the sea: it is so minuscule that it hardly adds to or subtracts from the divine knowledge.

Sufi scholars argue for a literal meaning (*ẓahir*) and a hidden meaning (*bāṭin*). The literal meaning is that accepted by the majority of Muslim scholars and they do not contest those interpretations. However, Ibn al-`Arabī contends that there is another meaning for the story:

> When Moses spoke to his young companion (*fatāh*), it was analogous to Moses the heart (*qalb*) speaking to the young soul (*nafs*) when it first attaches itself to the body (*badan*); telling it that he will not stop journeying until he reaches the intersection of the two worlds: the world of spirit (*rūḥ*) and the world of form (*jism*). They are the pure and clear in the human form and locus of the heart.

As one can see from these interpretations, the same story could be used as a building block for the creation of a comprehensive worldview that is informed by the beliefs and ideas of the adherents of any given religious entity. The same story can be "modeled" in a way that will reenforce the teachings and practices of the community.

Muslims, regardless of their theological tendencies, do not see this story as an imperative or a command that asks them to imitate the knower. For legal and ethical scholars, the style in which the story was composed, *khabar* (neutral narrative), relieves Muslims of any obligation or prohibition. Nonetheless, it teaches them to accept the unexplainable: things that are seen as acts of God.

For the purposes of this study, the story of the knower and Moses is significant in that it is indirectly used to argue for a "natural" order of things: Women, disabled, underprivileged, the poor, the exploited, and anyone not sharing the bounties of this world are consoled by the promised bigger plan that may explain their worldly distress. For that reason, I consider this and other metaphors in the Qur'ān and Islamic traditions significant. The status of women in Islam cannot be understood in the context of isolated legal rulings and limited practices. Rather, it is dependent on a broader worldview that is anchored on philosophical, theological, legal, and practical considerations. As the popular cliché states, knowledge is power. In the case of the Islamic discourse on ethical questions, knowledge is context. Those who know ask those who do not know to trust them in creating categories, assigning entitlements, and awarding rights. For the majority of Muslims, not even religious scholars claim access to divine knowledge. Religious authorities, in their view, possess methods and processes of ascertaining that near absolute knowledge is acquired. The absolute knowledge is especially required in matters of law and religious practices.

Cognition through Models and Paradigms

The above story (and many other similar stories that I will introduce in the following chapters) suggest that there is an extraordinary function played by models, anecdotes, paradigms, allegories, and parables. They are stories stripped of most of the specifics and particulars and told in an imaginative way in order to provide clarity and assign meaning to abstract concepts. A model allows the author to place the listener into the story and make her a character, an actor, an agent, a participant not only in the story, but also in imposing the meaning of the model on the events of today. The use of paradigms and models is a powerful tool that explains, and most importantly, makes the past relevant to today if not a replay of it anew. It is a powerful tool when the consumer of these images sees herself as part of the story. When that happens, status is established, privileges are preserved, and acceptance is guaranteed.

The utility of models and metaphors in society is underscored by the frequency of their appearances in the Qur'ān and Ḥadīth . The story of Moses and "the knower" is thus one good example of how stripped-down parables are employed in assigning meaning and establishing social order. In this particular case, the three events of the story justify acts that appear to ordinary (or not so ordinary as is the case with Moses) people to be unfair and unjust. The impact and effect of this approach is to encourage acceptance of things the way they are, tolerate conditions regardless of their immediate impact, and resign oneself to the course of events. In terms of our case study, it can be argued that parables give meaning and purpose to one's status as being a significant part in a bigger and extraordinary world that may not be well understood in its totality. In other words, such tools (parables and models) suggest to women that their status and their rights are not measured by comparing them to members of the other sex or members of other species for that matter; rather, by the function they provide and the place they hold in the "bigger picture." That is being on the belief and thought level. On the practical level, jurists will establish more mundane rules and guidelines that will ensure that everyone performs her or his function in the desired manner and time; and that is the role of legal philosophical discourses.

The majority of legal rulings governing the status and rights of women are not decided only by anecdotes and hypothetical arguments. Admittedly, their status is informed by metaphors like the one about the knower and Moses but the practical steps are decided by explicit and implicit directives that adherents are asked to follow in their personal and communal lives. The next chapter focuses on the parts of the Qur'ān and Islamic jurisprudence that concretize the boundaries and govern the social order in the Muslim community. The overview and explanations of Islamic jurisprudence will provide the reader with another layer of Islamic tradition analysis that will help establish a solid background. I argued in other publications that some of the laws of inheritance in Islamic law do not conform to the explicit legal proofs found in the Qur'ān.[13] It is essential, therefore, that I examine the legal theory that constituted the basis of the legal rulings on Inheritance. The next chapter will accomplish that task.

2

The Domain of Ethics and the Law

I contend that in order to understand the status of women in the Islamic discourse, one must have a good grasp of Islamic legal theory, which is the foundation of Islamic law. Not only is Islamic law eminent in governing the individual and collective life of Muslims, but it was Islamic legal scholars and ethicists who categorized "God's speech" and gave it meaning. Stated differently, given that Islam governs all aspects of the adherents' life, it is fair to conclude that such control of the social and personal life of the individual and the collective is accomplished by canonizing the religious traditions. The process and results of creating the canon and categorizing the so-called legal proofs offer an opportunity to analyze and understand the legal and philosophical reasoning which is entrusted with giving power and authority to Qur'ānic and Prophetic enunciations. It is through interpretation that the Qur'ānic words are given clear meaning and it is through the clear meaning that men and women are awarded rights, entitlements, responsibilities, privileges, status, and an identity in the eyes of each other and in the eyes of God. So what are the characteristics of Islamic jurisprudence and Islamic ethics? Furthermore, if Islamic law is expressive of God's will and God's will is to codify and implement divine justice, then what is "just" and "fair"? Finally, if one is treated unfairly and unjustly, what remedies are there to redress the injustice?

In Islam, not only what is said in the Qur'ān is of paramount importance, but also how it is said has legal and ethical implications. With Muslims seeing the Qur'ān and the Sunnah as the primary sources of Islamic law and practices, the interpretation and the context of their content becomes central to understanding Islamic thought in general. Although Islamic legal and philosophical thought is bound by the specificities of the Qur'ān and informed by historical events, the role of reason and tradition was as important, as it has been essential in the development of Western philosophy of law and jurisprudence. For this reason, I have opted to present Islamic legal and ethical tradition in comparison with Western moral and jurisprudential philosophy.

Paraphrasing a thesis that is widely held by scholars and practitioners of law in modern times, one could argue that "one cannot legislate morality."[1] This seemingly innocent conclusion is actually a code phrase for a scholarly position on the nature, origins, and jurisdiction of existing laws and law-making institutions. The fields of legal philosophy, political theory, and jurisprudence are rich with thought-provoking essays. A variety of schools of thought like consequentialism, hedonism, deontologism, and positivism all have attempted to explain the interplay between society, the individual, and the state.[2] During the medieval times in Europe natural law theory also gained significant following.[3] In Islamic civilization, from the time of the Mu'tazilites until the rise of mystic philosophers like al-Ghazālī, the same themes were the topic of much heated debates; the outcome was very different. While modern Western legal traditions invariably have separated themselves, theoretically and institutionally, from religious agencies, Muslim communities still consider classical Islamic law as a foundational platform for at least some branches of law.[4] It can be argued that some specific characteristics of Islamic jurisprudence are the reason for the persistence and longevity of Islamic law.

In this chapter, I will argue that ethics and legalism in Islamic thought were, and still are, inseparable. Ethics and morality imbue Islamic law with its power to motivate and to move the person to act in accordance with whatever code of conduct and system of commands and obligations he or she happens to honor. In order to make a person act in a particular way or behave in a certain fashion, it is sufficient to manipulate his or her belief system in a way that is inducing to the desired result. This is how Islamic law—like other ancient and modern communities' legal traditions—operates as evidenced by the various Qur'ānic and traditional references linking faith, motive, and behavior.

In ancient Greece, thinkers like Plato and Aristotle argued that a virtuous man is ultimately a happy man. In other words, morality and happiness impact the agent inasmuch as virtue leads to happiness. The debate on human nature therefore focused on determining the nature and form of virtue. Finding a definition of virtue became the first step in identifying that which makes a happy person. In Platonic thought, virtue is that settled disposition that enabled man to act consistently and reliably in a virtuous manner. For instance, courage, moderation, and justice were all seen as moral virtues that settle in the agent to make him act most of the time courageously, moderately, and justly. Such a man is a happy man.[5]

Early modern Western thought focuses only secondarily on the agent, but primarily on his acts. The questions of motivation, volition, and actions that engaged the thinkers of the Enlightenment were formulated in a way that asks about the power that motivates a person to act courageously, moderately, wisely, and justly.[6] The most appealing and influential theories associated with these questions argued for the attainment of happiness as the ultimate motivator. People act in order to maximize happiness for the greatest number of people. On the agent level, some opined that a person will act if and only if that act will result in relieving or avoiding pain and maximizing pleasure.[7] Some deontologists argue for morality being the byproduct of a system of threats and obligations.[8] In other words, they contend that morality presupposes the system of commands and norms.

The tendencies that shaped ancient and modern ethical theories are too numerous for us to list here. However, the presence of the themes of happiness, pain, and pleasure in ancient, modern, and in the Islamic traditions makes the comparative approach to the study of such themes most appealing and beneficial.

The methodology of this chapter, and in the entire book for that matter, is complex due to the complexity of the topic. In part, a purely analytical (typical of the field of moral philosophy) approach will be applied to certain themes in order to maintain disciplinary standards inasmuch as treating ethical subjects is concerned. In addition, a combination of descriptive and normative approaches will be adopted in order to formulate and define what may be seen as purely legal themes. The reader must be warned that, since there is no clear break between what is purely legal and what is purely ethical in Islamic thought, the methodologies of this study do not reflect clear boundaries. Rather, I will shift back and forth between the philosophical and analytical approaches depending on the subject being discussed at any moment. We begin by asking how much of a role do concepts such as happiness, pleasure, and pain play in formulating and sustaining Islamic law and jurisprudence? Secondly, to what extent is Islamic law and jurisprudence dependent on morality? How does Islamic legal philosophy see men and women?

Chronology of Islamic Thought

For more than twenty years, the Prophet Muhammad exerted unparalleled religious and political authority. Islamic thought and practice during the Prophet's lifetime was tacitly or explicitly shaped by his personal example.[9] In fact the Qur'ān declared him to be the living example of the ideal person.[10] Even in areas for which divine guidance was not ascertained, any dissent by his followers was subjected to his personal accommodation; but he could never be overruled.

Upon his passing away, the Qur'ān served as the theoretical springboard for guidance, while the Prophet's trodden path (Sunnah) was adopted as the supreme interpretive authority. His Companions, or disciples, acted as the bearers and authenticators of his manners, thoughts, and practices.[11] Despite the Prophet's extensive teachings, diligent care, and deliberate decisions, the Muslim community faced the biggest test immediately after his death.

Even before the conclusion of the rites of burial, many of the top community leaders met at the yard of some clan leaders (*saqīfat banī sā`idah*) in order to appoint a political successor.[12] Before the end of the day, and as a result of the decisions that were taken, four principles were established: (a) the religious and logical necessity of having a sous-sovereign leader,[13] (b) the dominance of Quraysh in governance over all other tribes (hence, ethnicities),

(c) the requirement of public endorsement of the leader, and (d) the obligation of obedience to the leader.[14] The consequences of these four doctrines had lasting effects on the development and the nature of the Islamic civilization. Despite the early solidifying of a particular system of governance and law making, most of these principles were nonetheless challenged throughout the history of the Muslim communities. The ruling class and its policies survived and prevailed not on account of lack of social movements that contested their logic and foundation; rather, by reason of the force and power of precedent and social norms.[15]

In terms of social movements that challenged the status quo, one could mention the Kharajites who cast doubt over the form and place of the Caliphate.[16] They argued, and acted upon that argument during the reign of `Uthmān, that the Caliphate was neither a religious nor a logical necessity. Moreover, since they held the view that faith and practice (*īmān* and *`amal*) are the only unbreakable and inseparable qualifying conditions in the leader, anyone—not just a man from Quraysh—be he a former black slave or *woman*, can hold that post.[17]

The Shi`ites on the other hand, appealed to the nature and attributes of God to argue that His grace and care (*luṭf*) assured humanity the gift of continuous divine guidance in the form of revelation of the scriptures and the presence of an infallible leader (*al-imām al-ma`ṣūm*). In this scheme, both lawmaking and governance become a form of divine providence.[18] God provides absolute laws and the rulers enforce them. These laws, however, are interpreted by infallible persons so that the certitude of the laws is not jeopardized by fallible human interpreters. Not only should the laws be divine, but also the interpretation and derivation of the laws from their primary sources and evidentiary proofs (*adillah*) should be carried out also by a person who is guarded from erring.

Not long after the first major civil war and after the end of the righteously guided Caliphate era, reason-based schools of thought started to gain wide following. Early rational thinkers adopted reason in order to balance contextual and universal understanding of the Qur'ānic teachings. This intellectual trend, later known as the Mu'tazilite school of thought, lasted for nearly two centuries. Expectedly, their zealous trust in reason to explain mundane as well as metaphysical matters triggered an angry reaction from traditionalists. Subsequently, Mu'tazilism collapsed and Ash'arism (founded by a former Mu'tazilite thinker) emerged. Despite many attempts to systematize Islamic theology, no coherent orthodoxy was realized. Instead, the dominant trend that distinguished the post-Mu'tazilite era from the past is the resignation to accepting explicit Qur'ānic and Sunnaic enunciations about theological, ethical, and legal matters without asking why or how (*bilā kayfa* and *bilā limādhā*). Despite the significant contribution of Greek philosophy and Persian and Indian literature to Islamic thought during the last tier of the Abbasid rule, it was the school of legalism[19] that gained the widest attention and following.[20]

Ethics, Morality, and the Law

Undistracted by the glare and the glory of logical debates that raised the profile of theologians and philosophers to universal fame, a handful of legal scholars focused on studying practical sciences (*al-`ulūm al-`amaliyyah*).[21] This endeavor consisted primarily of sharing, preserving, and transmitting religious traditions and practices in order to guide the adherents' life according to the path set forth by God and His Messenger (*sharī`ah*).[22] Besides the fact that legal scholars, as well as theologians and philosophers, have considered the Qur'ān and the Sunnah to be the primary sources and anchors of their inquiries, it is Muslim ethicists and jurists who categorized the speech of the Qur'ān and the Ḥadīth in order to give it legal and moral meaning and purpose. For early scholars of Islamic jurisprudence, not only that which God says has significance, but also His verbalization of the enunciations has great importance as well.[23] For this reason, Islamic law cannot be successfully and accurately appraised outside the ethical and moral discourse.

Determining God's Position

In Islamic law, intent plays a double role. On the one hand, the intention of the actor (or subject; that is, the person subjected to the law) determines the applicability of the law and establishes the consequence of violating it. On the other hand, the Lawgiver is seen as giving significance to acts (*af`āl*) by the way a case is addressed. In other words, Muslim scholars believe that the style of speech indicates God's position on any given human act.[24] Subsequently, it is not only how a particular event impacts the subjects; rather, how much disapproval, approval, or pleasure with events initiated by the subjects is shown by the Lawgiver. Therefore, Muslim scholars meticulously gleaned God's position vis-à-vis any given act or event from His "speech."

Arguably, the Qur'ān is not a monotone narrative. Rather, it is a complex document that rarely finishes telling a single story before jumping to a different topic. For instance, some chapters consist of a uniform style and focus on a specific theme. Other chapters however, adopt varying style and syntax and recount a complex content with varying moods. Early Muslim scholars perceived the changing characteristics as signaling God's position on the topic discussed in any given verse or chapter.

After deliberate examination of the primary sources of law and practice, and during the systematization of Islamic law and jurisprudence,[25] five categories of the Qur'ānic speech were recognized: (1) positive imperatives (*amr*), (2) negative imperatives (*nahy*), (3) neutral narratives (*khabar*), (4) positive preponderant narratives (*istiḥbāb*), and (5) negative preponderant narratives (*karāhah*).[26]

Positive imperatives refer to the sections or verses of the Qur'ān that are stated as commands. Scholars considered this category of speech to imply obligation (*wujūb*) wherein the subject must perform whatever was asked of him or her to perform, feel, or think. Not doing so would result in punishment either in this world or in the Hereafter. Sometimes, the consequence or the form of atonement of not acting on this command is also explicitly stated. Most of the times however, the consequence is not mentioned at all.[27]

Similarly, negative commands are statements that order the subject not to undertake a particular activity (proscription = *taḥrīm*) be it in the form of words, acts, or thoughts. If one were to disregard such a direct negative command, a form of punishment in this world or the next (or both) would ensue.

Neutral statements (*khabar*), which are statements that do not express any moral inclination or judgment, do not carry any legal or ethical obligation or prohibition. In other words, neutral statements refer to permissible acts (*ibāḥah* or *nadb*). This category of speech is different from the negative or positive preponderant narratives, which express an inclination in the Lawgiver that either indicates encouragement (*istiḥbāb*) or contempt (*karāhah*), respectively. While preponderantly negative narratives discourage the subject from undertaking the acts therein described, there is no negative consequence if he does. However, refraining from such undesired acts is rewarded (in the Hereafter). Similarly, preponderantly positive narratives sanction no penalty for the subject's failure to act; yet, if he or she does act on the encouragement, he shall then be rewarded.[28]

In primary and secondary literature on Islamic law and jurisprudence, the system of the so-called legal judgments or legal categories (*al-aḥkām al-khamsah*) is described as the fivefold system or what I called herein the "pentarule declarations." Such nomenclature might give the impression that there are five and only five rules for any given event or case. That understanding, warranted as it might be due to lack of clarity and elaboration in existing publications, is nonetheless somewhat reductionist and simplistic.[29] A closer look at the Islamic literature dealing with these legal categories and judgments would show the intertwined nature of law and morality and would bring to light a more expansive system beyond the often discussed five rules and five acts.

To begin with, it must be noted that the pentarule declarations were not clearly established during the first Islamic century; rather, they were defined and used in legal arguments not earlier than the formative period of Islamic jurisprudence (not Islamic law whose formation and existence emerged with the Prophet Muhammad and continued with the Righteously Guided Caliphs). In other words, once the discipline of Islamic jurisprudence became more or less systematized, more differentiations that did not exist during the early formative period emerged signaling the complexity and intricacies of keying the rules to the legal proofs. Subsequently, it is argued by some Muslim scholars that acts in themselves are of ten categories, which are in turn tagged to the five rules, wherein the list of acts depends on their intrinsic nature. The first kind of acts consists of those that are purely virtuous (*dhā maṣlaḥah*). In other words these are the acts that consist of no blameworthiness (*mafsadah*). Inversely, an act is also fully blameworthy with no merit of goodness whatsoever. In both cases, the inherent goodness (*maṣlaḥah*) or badness (*mafsadah*) could be so strong to the point that it necessitates obligation or prohibition upon the subject, respectively. Stated differently, it can be said that the goodness of an act is so great to the point that the Lawgiver "loved" anyone who acquires it and therefore wanted everyone to act on it; hence, making it an obligation (*farḍ*). Similarly, the badness of an act can be so appalling to the Lawgiver to the point that it is made illegal. In the case where the inherent goodness and badness are weak compared to the previous instances, no obligation or prohibition will ensue; rather, desirability or undesirability will be recommended. The preceding, together with acts that consist of no inherent pure goodness or pure badness, form the five classes of acts that are governed by the five rules of judgments.[30]

Another category of acts consists of those containing an amalgam of badness and goodness at the same time. In such a case, the rules are determined based on the degree of goodness when compared to the degree of badness in the same act. The greater the difference between the badness and goodness in the same act, the more likely the rule (*ḥukm*) will reach prohibition or obligation respectively. In the case where badness and goodness are equal, permissibility becomes the rule. Subsequently, the above category becomes the branch of another five different acts that can be tagged by the same system of five rules.[31]

In order to summarize the ten acts and how they are judged, let's simplify the possibilities by laying out the following formulaic definitions (see Figure 2.1):

Let A be the ensemble of acts,
Let S be the purely good acts (*fi`l ṣāliḥ*),
Let F be the purely bad acts (*fi`l fāsid*),
Let Φ refer to the absence of purely bad and good acts, and
Let greater (>) and greatest (>>) refer to quantifying badness/goodness of S/F.

1. $A = \{S\}$; if S is $>> \leftrightarrow$ A is obligatory.
2. $A = \{S\}$; if S is $> \leftrightarrow$ A is Desirable.
3. $A = \{F\}$; if F is $>> \leftrightarrow$ A is Proscribed.
4. $A = \{F\}$; if F is $> \leftrightarrow$ A is Undesirable, Contemptuous, detestable…
5. $A = \{\Phi\}$; $\leftrightarrow$ A is Permissible.
6. $A = \{S + F\}$; if $S >> F \leftrightarrow$ A is Obligatory.
7. $A = \{S + F\}$; if $S > F \leftrightarrow$ A is Desirable.
8. $A = \{S + F\}$; if $F >> S \leftrightarrow$ A is Proscribed.
9. $A = \{S + F\}$; if $F > S \leftrightarrow$ A is Undesirable.
10. $A = \{S + F\}$; if $S \equiv F \leftrightarrow$ A is Permissible.

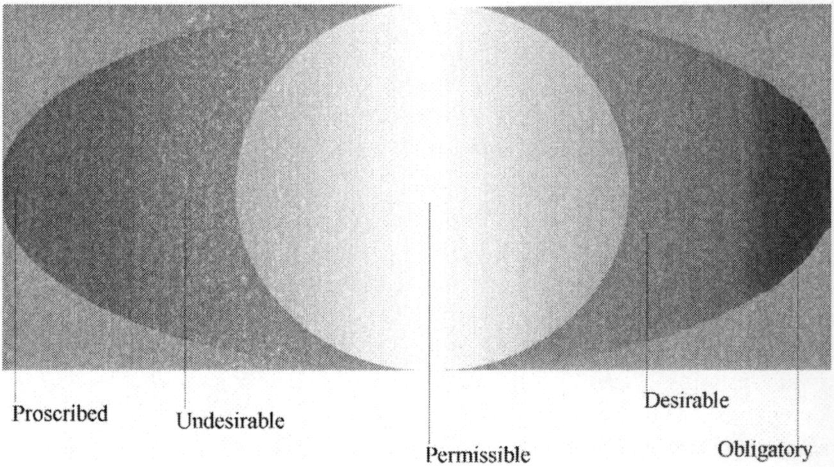

FIGURE 2.1: ISLAMIC LEGAL RULE: CATEGORIZING HUMAN ACTS

Understanding Figure 2.1: Islamic legal rules are generally presented as static "categories" where each category represents a list of acts that are prohibited, undesired, permitted, desired, or obligatory. The above illustration deconstructs that understanding and replaces it by one showing a legal system of rules that progressively slides toward prohibition or obligation. This characteristic of Islamic jurisprudence allowed Muslim jurists and judges (seen as truth seekers rather than referees) of the classical era to be flexible not only within the legal framework but also within each category (or range) of any one of the five rules. In other words, a judgment concerning a particular act (in an actual legal case) might differ based on the specific circumstances; hence, it is only in theoretical cases (mostly *iftā'* cases) that judgment is fixed.

The above analysis and the closer examination of some legal and ethical cases reveal that the system of judgments is more of a spectrum[32] that consists of an infinite number of possible judgments or rules (not just five). In such a system, not only do different cases fall on different locations of the spectrum of judgments, but also even the same case may fall on different locations depending on the circumstances. For example, under normal circumstances; divorce is deemed "extremely contemptuous" (*karāhah ilā darajat al-taḥrīm*).[33] That is to say that divorce in Islamic law is asymptotically illegal without achieving proscription (*taḥrīm*) per se. It is possible, nonetheless, that even divorce under certain circumstances might be desired or obligatory given the keying of certain legal obligations or proscriptions to ethical and moral norms. For instance, an abusive parent whose presence in the household is deemed harmful to the well-being of the children and who is not a good role model in the family will be grounds for making the divorce obligatory in the view of many Muslim jurists.[34] The fluidity of Islamic law is underscored by a number of other legal cases and legal doctrines beyond those mentioned herein; but the few cases from family and business laws mentioned here should suffice in supporting the claims I have made concerning Islamic law being a combination of social discursive and normative ethical discourses.

Core and Marginal Sanctions

The above jurisprudential system shows a fundamental difference between legal systems that are based on the triad of obligation, prohibition, and permissibility (as is the case in Common Law) and the *sharī`ah* system, which is anchored by pentarule declarations. In order to bring to the forefront the differences and emphasize the specifics, it can be argued that in the Islamic system, moral virtues are spread across a spectrum of judgments only three of which are visible to the human legal mind. The rest of the acts that are not deemed proscribed or obligatory are judged by the Lawgiver since they constitute moral and ethical norms and not laws per se. With that said, it becomes necessary in such a system that before passing judgments on any event, certain conditions must be satisfied before an event is declared permissible, proscribed, or obligatory. However, any given event can be judged satisfactorily if and only if the intent of the Lawgiver and the intent of the subject are ascertained. Consequently, more events fall into the zones of the contemptuous or desired. Even then however, these zones are not clearly defined as the number of variables in determining any circumstances of a case is so large that any given event can be placed anywhere on the zone as a result.[35] For instance, marriage can be determined to be obligatory upon the Muslim granted that she or he is physically, economically, mentally, and socially able to marry.[36] However, if the person is challenged by wealth and health circumstances, marriage in such a case becomes proscribed. It must be noted that many of the circumstances are difficult to ascertain without full and honest cooperation of the subjects. For this reason, one could argue that the concept of probity (*`adālah*) becomes a central component of the entire legal system.[37] Does that mean that there are no moral absolutes in such a fluid system?

Indeed, in a mechanical legal system that is seen to be based on these principles, it will be very difficult, in terms of logical reasoning, to make a strong case for the presence of moral or legal absolutes. For this very reason, I would argue, Islamic jurisprudence emphasizes the ethical and moral obligations on the one hand, and the degree of certainty and authenticity in terms of legal proofs (*al-adillah al-shar`iyyah*) on the other hand. In other words the question becomes, How does the Lawgiver achieve a balance between an obviously fluid and dynamic legal system and the need to exert the maximum social controls needed to achieve compliance? In my view, the answer to this question is found in the ethical and moral basis that sustains Islamic law; and that basis is essentially a system that communicates to the subjects through their vulnerabilities, insecurities, fear, and passions. In other words, it targets the psychology of the subject in order to achieve compliance. It is true that a legal system based on the goodwill of subjects is prone to abuse, and abuse prevailed in many cases. However, when the human goodwill is shaped by shocking threats and enticing incentives, compliance from a sufficient number of the populace is almost assured. As it will be shown from surveying the primary sources and legal proofs, motivation and compliance in Islamic law are achieved by way of communicating to humans' innermost selfish desires and paralyzing fears.

Emotion and Law in the Qur'ānic Discourse

Threats, Incentives, and Piety

The Qur'ānic matrix reflects three fundamental elements all of which act on and affect emotions: piety (*taqwā*),[38] enticement (*wa`d*),[39] and threat (*wa`īd*).[40] Among the three, piety is the one most difficult to define. It can be argued that its complexity reflects its importance and centrality in Islamic law and ethics. The aforementioned tripartite system of piety, enticement, and threat is best summarized in verse thirty-five from the Qur'ānic chapter titled "the thunder" (*al-ra`d*):[41]

> As a metaphor for the paradise that was promised (*wu`ida*) to the pious (*al-muttaqūn*) persons: imagine a garden full of running streams, its fruits are everlasting, and so are its shades. That is the reward for those who acted in accordance to piety (*al-ladhīna ittaqū*). The reward of those who reject faith (*kāfirūn*) is hellfire (*al-nār*). [Q13:V35]

The nexus between legal imperatives and human emotional dispositions is unmistakably expressed in a similar Qur'ānic passage:

> Fighting has been foreordained upon you whereas it is a detestable thing to you. However, it might be the case that you hate something whereas it is good for you; and similarly, you might love something whereas it is harmful to you. In that, God knows and you know not. [Q2:V216]

If moral and ethical arguments are generally designed to work on the emotional level in order to motivate the subject to act, then the Qur'ānic discourse truly mastered that art. The heritage of the Prophet and his Companions propelled that same approach even further. First, it was the Qur'ān that made the extraordinary declaration establishing Muhammad as a person of superb character.[42] Exegetes thereafter portrayed the Prophet as the personification or exemplifier of the moral values of the Qur'ān.[43] To put it in emphatic terms, the Prophet was sent with the single mission of perfecting ethical norms.[44]

The link between the Qur'ānic ethics and the practice of the community is established by the living example of the Prophet. In other words, the Muslim community sees in Muhammad's preferences and dislikes the humanized desires, likes, and dislikes of God. It should be noted also that the link between the Qur'ānic ethics and the practice of the Prophet Muhammad is not only a logical necessity that follows the belief in Muhammad as God's Messenger, but it is also a response to the deity's verbalization of its own emotions and position in regard to humans' actions. For instance, a close survey of all the Qur'ānic passages that brusquely express legal obligations or proscriptions shows that they are immediately followed by a moral statement stamped with emotions. For instance, some negative commands are not only expressed using the usual tag such as "do not" [*lā*]; but most of such passages are concluded by expressing the emotional value denoting dislike (*lā yuḥibb*) without the use of a direct Arabic word for it, such as "he hates" (*yakrah*):

> Do not seek to spread corruption and mischief on earth; surely God loves not mischief doers (*lā yuḥibbu al-mufsidīn*). [Q28:V77]

> Believers! Do not proscribe the goods that God has made legal for you and do not transgress; indeed God loves not transgressors (*lā yuḥibbu al-mu`tadīn*). [Q5:V87]

> Worship God and do not associate anything with Him. Do good deeds to your two parents, to the blood relatives, the orphans, the poor, the near and far neighbors, the far friends, the traveling strangers, and those who are under your ownership.[45] Indeed, God loves not those boasting full of arrogance and megalomania (*lā yuḥibbu man kānaṭmukhtālan fakhūrā*). [Q4:V36]

Similarly, most of the Qur'ānic positive commands are followed by expressing God's approval in terms of emotions:

> Donate for the sake of God but do not risk your own well-being and do good deeds; indeed God loves the doers of good deeds (*yuḥibbu al-muḥsinīn*). [Q2:195]

> Do not enter such a mosque (*masjid al-ḍirār*); for a mosque founded on piety from the first day is more worthy of your attendance; in it, there are men who love ritual purity (*al-mutaṭahhirīn*). [Q9:108]

In most instances of positive and negative imperatives instructing the believers in matters of law and ethics, the deity expresses its approval or disapproval by way of qualifying its own emotions. In the Qur'ān alone, the pattern of using the value of love repeats itself more than fifty-six times.[46] Furthermore, there is no Qur'ānic reference to mankind loving God; rather, it is piety and faith that is used to reciprocate for the divine love to humans. In other words, it would appear from the examined Qur'ānic passages that humans are asked to act and behave in a particular way because God tells them how He feels about those who do so. However, it is not clear how humans themselves feel about those acts. In fact, from the Qur'ānic discourse again, it seems that humans do not know what is really good and what is really bad for them.[47] The gap in consciousness and knowledge is bridged by faith and belief: in the Qur'ānic discourse, humans are not asked to love God or even love certain acts and dislike others; rather, they are asked to have faith.[48] It could be argued then, that once the person becomes willing to adopt a belief system, securing compliance in matters of acts and behavior becomes less of a challenge. The evidence gleaned from the Qur'ānic and traditional texts shows that the principle of linking emotions, faith, and acts is fundamental to establishing a compliant community. The individual (as the subject of Islamic law) is first asked to love his fellow men and women as a proof of his or her faith. Once the subject is emotionally vested, the belief system will then rely on threats of torturous punishment and enticing incentives in order to secure compliance with legal ordinances. Subjecting any individual to these conditions over an extended time period will ultimately produce that settled disposition of piety as outlined in the following section.

Crime and Punishment

Moral and legal obligations and prohibitions, in any religious tradition and not just Islam,[49] are enforced by way of threats and promises of good rewards. Not only purely religious ordinances are supported by such a system; but also mundane or civil laws are backed by threats of physical punishments and acts of violence that are seen as a just way of seeking redress and reestablishing the boundaries (*ḥudūd*). According to Islamic traditions, the family of the victim, the community, or the state is authorized to carryout that threat of punishment.[50] During the lifetime of the Prophet, and during the early Caliphate, private citizens participated in carrying out the legal orders. With time, many of the crimes and punishments were slowly transferred to state jurisdiction. But even now, many legal cases are still exclusively addressed in private religious "courts" and voluntarily enforced by the litigants and by members of the community. In all cases however, the role of violence and punishment in securing compliance is very prominent.

In the light of this understanding, the concept of piety (*taqwā*) would consist of a double meaning. On the one hand, piety thus conceived is a settled disposition of emotional fear that serves as deterrent (*wā`iz*) in the mind and soul of the subject. In other words, it has the meaning of seeking shelter or shielding oneself from imminent violence.[51] On the other hand, piety is a settled state of mind acquired through habit and custom that trains the subject to be at any given moment mindful of the ethical and legal norms. In either of these cases and in the rooting of compliance in a framework that operates on the level of emotions and faith, the Islamic legal system as either overcoming the deficiencies of secular legal powers or supplementing the limited effectiveness of the state-sponsored legal apparatus. The ethical and emotional dimension of Islamic law is further underscored by the legal doctrine known as "oath" (*yamīn*).

In terms of legal procedure in classical Islamic law, the burden of proof falls on the plaintiff, and the defendant's acquittal can be achieved through oath (*`alā al-mudda`ī al-bayyinah wa-`alā al-munkir al-yamīn*). For example, in a case where plaintiff A claims that the employer B promised him X amount of money upon the completion of a certain task; and B disputes that claim arguing that he agreed only to half that amount (X/2); and the plaintiff could not provide a definitive proof or reliable witnesses; in this case, B could swear by God that he agreed to only X/2 and the judge must rule in his favor. Of course A cannot take the oath in order to be awarded a judgment for the full amount X; because the oath cannot be used as evidence.[52]

It could be argued therefore that oath, as a legal principle that is designed to settle disputes in the absence of irrefutable evidence, derives its power from the fear that must be experienced by those who knowingly lie and take the oath.[53] The power of the oath stems from Qur'ānic threat that "promises" a person who lies while under oath extreme torture in the Hereafter. Those who honor oaths by telling the truth on the other hand, are spared such treatment and offered good reward.[54]

The qualification of judges and lawyers as persons of probity is another element that shows the role of ethics and morality in the subjects and the interpreters of the law alike. The *qāḍī*, *mujtahid,* and *mufti* must all be seen as possessing a high degree of justice and unshakable sense of fairness for them to be part of the system.[55] Furthermore, even litigants are bound by ethical directives to select only persons of probity to settle their disputes as argued in Shi'ite and Sunni scholarship.[56]

The mechanism by which Islamic law achieves the balance between fear and piety is not satisfactorily clear. Admittedly, not enough research has been done in order to explain the space between fear, as a legal means, and piety, as a state of mind. However, this lagging behind is by no means specific to theories on Islamic law. In fact, the function and place of emotions in the legal and moral processes even in modern Western legal tradition is yet to be seriously debated and analyzed despite its reliance on similar, albeit less explicit, systems of threats and incentives.[57] In the case of Islamic law, an examination of the system of crime and punishment ought to shed more light on the role of threats, incentives, fear, and piety in securing compliance, generating deterrence, and developing acceptance in terms of law and morality contexts.

In classical Islamic law, there are only six crimes for which the Lawgiver had established specific punishments. They are known as boundaries (*ḥudūd*) crimes, which consist of (1) adultery (*zinā'*), (2) nonconventional sexual practices (*fawāḥish*),[58] (3) slander (*qadhf*), (4) theft (*sariqah*), (5) highway robbery (*qaṭ`* *al-ṭarīq*), and (6) apostasy *(irtidād)*. The punishment for most of these crimes is in the form of physical harm such as a set number of lashes or stoning.[59] Given that the Lawgiver in this case determined the law and the punishment at the same time, it could be argued that this category of crimes is enshrined upon a principle that is founded on norm and consequence. In other words, the consequences are directly keyed to the crimes and the punishment could be justified, in the view of Muslim scholars, by the subject's disregard of warnings and proscriptions.

Many other crimes such as falsifying evidence or testimony (*tazwīr*), usury (*ribā*), drinking wine (*shurb al-khamr*), monopoly (*iḥtikār*), and malicious character assassination (*ghaybah*) have no fixed punishment that is predetermined in the Qur'ān.[60] This category of crimes falls under what is known as *al-ta`zīr*. They are crimes the punishment of which falls under the jurisdiction of judges, leaders (*imāms*), and rulers (*ḥukkām*), which may range from the same punishment for *ḥudūd* crimes to subjecting the accused to shaming or rebuking (*tawbīkh*). The reason the Lawgiver did not determine the punishment for crimes of this category is not satisfactorily addressed in the legal literature. In studying the punishments for these crimes that Muslim communities have devised throughout their history, one could form a good understanding of how Muslims interpret the keying of punishment in the first category of crimes.

The third kind of crimes is redressed by way of reciprocity (*qiṣāṣ*). Redress for these crimes is especially relevant to the topic of this study because it presents a dissimilar compensation for men and women; hence, an example of inequality before the law. To be sure, murder (*qatl*) and crimes resulting in dismembering or wounding the victim (*al-a`ḍā' wa-'l-jurūḥ*) are dealt with by authorizing the family of the victim to kill or wound the perpetrator under the Qur'ānic principle "an eye for an eye."[61] The family of the victim however, might choose to forgo the *qiṣāṣ* and ask instead for material compensation (*diyah*) or, in some other cases, imprisonment. Mitigation and forgiveness is encouraged in the Qur'ānic discourse and those who do so are promised good reward in the Hereafter.[62] This category of crime relies on arbitration in order to solve conflicts that are in direct violation of the body. It is not clear why crimes that involve murder and wounds are considered private claims that are settled through private institutions. One possible explanation is to argue that crimes of murder and wounds (at least in the context of the early Arabic way of life) are restricted to a small number of people who, one way or another, are related (by blood or by residence) and they are better prepared to deal with the conflict than the government. Crimes such as usury and monopoly, on the other hand, are seen as a class of crimes that affect the larger community and therefore require state intervention in order to prevent the harm.

In all cases however, ignoring an obligation or trespassing a proscription results in physical punishment (*`iqāb*) that amounts to possible physical or psychological harm in this world, and threats of sure torture by fire in the Hereafter.[63] The inseparability of ethics and law in the Qur'ānic discourse is similar to the duality of worldly and nonworldly reward and punishment (*al-thawāb* and *al-`iqāb*) that is promised therein. In order to have a better appreciation of the extent of the psychological dimension of Islamic law, one must consider the above categories of crimes in the context of the concept of punishment as seen by Muslim scholarship. Before doing so, a prelude about modern thought will be helpful in placing such matters in the proper perspective.

In modern Western thought, the debate goes on regarding the function and justification of punishment. As far as definition is concerned, a broad and nonnormative one could summarize legal punishment as *the imposition of something that is intended to be restrictive or painful, on an offender for a crime, by an entity that claims the authority to do so.* In order to justify punishment, some modern scholars have argued for distinguishing between the "general justifying aims," the principles of deciding on the subject of punishment, and the manner and amount of punishment that should be inflicted on the subject.[64] They further argue that such a punishment is necessary in order to prevent crimes that cause harm. This view is shared among scholars belonging to the so-called school of pure consequentialism.[65] Some objected to this theory and called for a "side-constrained consequentialism"[66] that will abolish punishment in order to prevent possible harm to the innocent. A third school of thought contends that punishment is ultimately the only possible "deserved response to crime" because criminals grab unfair advantage over law-abiding persons. It is argued that this retributive justification is supported by humans' emotional responses to crime.[67] Finally, another school of thought holds the view that crime must be managed through mediation and reconciliation programs that bring together the victim, the offender, and other interested parties in order to restore the harm done and initiate a process of reparation. The proponents of this "restorative justice" theory argue that such an approach will bypass punishment altogether.[68]

In contrast to the above, the Qur'ānic discourse does not explain the function and extent of punishment in general terms. Some Muslim scholars, however, have proposed a definition arguing that "punishment is a deserved harm resulting from disregard and disrespect."[69] From this definition, punishment is recognized as a "harm," but it is a harm that is deserved by way of undertaking an act that is blameworthy or refusing to act on obligation. Given that badness and goodness of acts are theoretically designated based on their impact on the subject not on the Lawgiver, it is concluded therefore that the harm is a form of deterrent "grace and blessing" (*luṭf*).[70] In most cases, nonetheless, the punishment could be fully or partially removed by way of repentance (*al-tawbah*), victims' forgiveness (*al-`afw*), or intercession (*al-shafā`ah*).[71] If none of these events happens, and punishment was to be adjourned to the Hereafter, the punishment is described as more severe and certain. In that regard, both the Qur'ānic and exegetical descriptions of the punishment after death are graphic and frightening and nothing short of torture.[72] For instance, in addition to the fact that such punishment will be eternal, according to the Qur'ānic "promise," feeling and experiencing pain is also assured by preserving the integrity of the sensory organs. In other words, in order for the subject to "feel" and live through pain and punishment, the Qur'ān makes it clear that when the subject's skin is destroyed, a new skin will be grown back on so that he or she would feel the torture (*`adhāb*).[73] Such description of harsh punishment is matched only by the enticing portrayal of the great reward for pious people. In the Qur'ānic discourse as well as in the commentaries and tradition literature, those who have faith and the pious men and women are promised a paradise that is full of all that is good. In the words of Muslim scholars, paradise is a place of unimaginable goods (*fīhā mā lā yakhṭur bi-bāl*).

When these forms of punishment are seen against the backdrop of the categorization of crimes in the Islamic legal system, one would be able to see the comprehensiveness of such a system that not only employs theories of deterrence, reparation, and adjudication of punishment and settlement to various entities, but also fuses the forces of social institutions with the instinctive and emotional agencies in order to secure compliance. This complex mechanism that relies on communicating legal and ethical norms through the "language" of emotions might explain the phenomenon of parallel legal systems[74] in many Muslim communities and more importantly, the desire of many Muslim minorities (who live in non-Muslim countries) to live by their own "personal" legal and moral codes even in the absence of an Islamic state.

Returning to a declaration that was made in the introduction to this chapter, it should become clear by now why one could not or should not legislate morality. There are at least two reasons for arguing for that point of view. Firstly, there is the practical aspect of attempting to legislate moral issues. Unless the state takes the responsibility for rewarding citizens who act on nonobligatory—yet desirable—matters and who avoid nonproscribed—yet undesired—matters, it will be very hard to establish consensus in choosing one or more institutions, in a society that is diverse in terms of cultures and religions, that will sustain the purely moral obligations and proscriptions.[75] In Islamic law, that problem was resolved by relying on a religious system of reward in another lifetime. In such a system, the purely legal cases are punished and rewarded by the society in this world in addition to the punishment and the reward to which one might be subjected in the next world. Secondly, the nature of Western states as social institutions that are built on the principle of separation of church and state makes it difficult to interject religious or "natural" morality without jeopardizing the doctrines of secularism. In attempting to do so in a society wherein many religions, cultures, and value systems exist, one will run the risk of undermining the law as is.

Based on the examined data and the various explanations of crime and punishment in the context of Islamic law, one could argue for a new kind of theory that explains especially the Qur'ānic discourse. Such a theory is founded on the idea that Islamic law's power is necessarily rooted in its vision of what I would call *communicative justice*. It is a system that does not necessarily deliver the kind of mechanical justice that will alleviate the pain of the victim or redress the harm inflicted upon the innocent; rather, it is a system that communicates through humans' emotions of fear and joy a simple message of self-restraint. Such a result is achieved by way of making the subject believe that no amount of pain or pleasure in this world will be even close to what will be experienced in the Hereafter. The success of this approach is thus dependent on whether or not the subject believes such a "promise." For that reason, faith and practice become the corner stones of developing the ideal worldly Muslim society. Obviously, for the nonbelievers, none of the promised torture and rewards is of any substance. For the believer on the other hand, the threat of extreme torture and the promise of satisfying reward are just as real as God; they are all communicated to the subject through the same conduit: emotion, which motivates to the point of establishing an unshakable disposition of piety.

Despite the examination of primary and secondary sources dealing with Islamic law, it should be clear at this point that more work is needed in order to better understand the interplay between fear, faith, and piety in Islamic legal and ethical thought as well as in broader context of legal traditions in general. It is not clear yet where fear ends and where piety begins, how fear contributes to faith and how faith can result in piety, or what role human emotions have in shaping ethical codes of conduct and human compliance with legal enunciations.

It is possible to conclude, nonetheless, from this very limited contribution to the topic that there is a complex relationship between the concept of fear and piety in the Islamic legal discourse. This relationship is underscored by the fact that the same word when used in Arabic, *taqwā*, could mean both: piety inasmuch as it is resulting from fear; and piety that is resulting from faith in a sovereign being. In the first instance, piety is induced by threats of wanton torture in the Hereafter that far exceeds any form of physical punishment in this world. In the second instance, piety is instilled by promises of unimaginable rewards in the form of physical gratification of one's desires to experiences of incessant psychological pleasures. In both instances however, the subject must either develop a repulsive loathing to pain or an enticing love for pleasure, or both.

It is these characteristics of Islamic law and jurisprudence that provide the debate on the status of women in Islam with its outer boundaries and inner tools. The outer boundary is that only the sovereign (God) is in a position to provide humanity with a neutral definition of what is just and what is fair as well as the remedies when the guidelines are violated. The inner tools consist of the processes and mechanisms of bringing human clarity and human understanding to God's will. To my mind, it is in identifying these inner tools and the selecting of authorities who can use them where rights are lost and fences are built to keep the privileged few in and the rest out.

Ultimately, Islamic jurisprudence, as a system that employs human emotions to achieve social order and individual compliances with desired societal norms, communicates its message to both men and women. However, with modern research suggesting that men and women react differently to emotional manipulations, it may be the case that women react differently to religious teachings that rely on emotional agencies. Furthermore, in the area of reciprocal justice, the doctrine "an eye for an eye" does not apply to persons without regard to their social status. In fact, the doctrine emphasizes difference as a basis for achieving justice:

> People of faith! The law of reciprocity (*al-qiṣāṣ*) is prescribed to you in cases of murder: the free for the free, the slave for the slave, the woman for the woman. But if the relative of the slain forgives, then grant any reasonable demand, and compensate him with handsome gratitude. This is a concession and a mercy from your Lord. Beyond this, whoever exceeds the limits shall be punished with painful torture. People who understand will see that there is in this law of reciprocity a way for life saving; and that they may reach piety by acting accordingly. [Q2:V178–9]

This doctrine establishes that the life of a free person is equal to that of a free person, the life of a slave is equal to that of a slave, and the life of a woman is equal to that of a woman. Theoretically, if a man kills a woman and then disappears, and the family of the victim insists on retribution (*diyah*), she can only receive the worth of a woman of her status not the worth of her killer. If, on the theoretical and philosophical level, women are presented as different from men, it becomes an easy task to translate the difference into unequal entitlements to men and women. Although the Qur'ānic rulings regarding inheritance rights are subject to debate, the basis for inequality is present in the legal philosophy of the Qur'ān.

This chapter was meant to provide the reader with a broad view of the legal and jurisprudential system in Islam. Armed with that understanding and knowledge, the reader should find it easy now to make the transition to navigate the literature dealing specifically with women in the Islamic and modern discourses. I will focus on two important cases, which are representative of Islamic laws dealing with women's rights. If, after the analysis of these cases, the above assumption stands the test of reason and logic, it should be constructive to expand the analyses and conclusions to other branches of Islamic law.

3

Basis for the Practice of Polygamy

On the Methodological and Historical Assumptions

In the preceding chapter, I have introduced an outline of the major features and principles of Islamic law and jurisprudence. In this and the following chapters, I will apply those general principles to the specific cases that have an impact on the social, economic, and psychological well-being of women. In the following chapters and whenever it is necessary, I will introduce specific legal doctrines, jurisprudential principles, or methodological elements that apply to the laws being analyzed. In other instances, a reference to explanations in the previous chapters will suffice.

I will start this chapter by an analysis and a critique of the specific case of the practice of polygamy followed by a normative and analytical treatment of property rights emanating from Islamic inheritance laws. In the view of Muslim scholars, classical Islamic law and ethics are the ultimate authority that sanctions practices such as polygamy and what is apparently unequal distribution of inheritance.[1] I will treat these two particular cases in order to bring to the forefront the nature and methodology of legal and ethical theories and the reasoning that maintains the status quo. In contributing a clearer understanding of Islamic ethical and legal mechanisms and logic it will be possible to rethink the status of matters beyond polygamy and property rights that are highlighted in this study.

My aim in undertaking these tasks is to further the debate on women's rights in modern times. Whenever improving the well-being of women and minority groups is possible from within or from without any given culture and/or religious tradition, I contend that those efforts aimed at bringing about the desired change ought to be explored. If the ultimate goal of any social movement (including the ones informed by religion) is to produce, protect, promote, and implement fundamental human rights and universal principles of justice and equality, then it is only reasonable that any conduit leading to that goal is explored and enabled.

One of the concerns (and legitimate criticisms) of what I propose to do and accomplish is that some of my methods and end-results are possibly dictated and informed by an alien Western discourse.[2] Be that as it may, I would argue firstly that my basic methodological assumptions are ultimately found in the very heart of classical Islamic hermeneutics and jurisprudence. Secondly, as social beings, we (as humans) are influenced by the language, methods, and values of the sophisticated civilizations in which we live and with which we have contacts. Throughout the history of the Islamic civilization, Muslim scholars have borrowed, appropriated, and/or assimilated the works and discoveries of other communities that preceded them, as well as that of communities that shared time and space with them. Modern scholarship is universal in its reach and in its scope and it is reasonable to assume that all scholars' work and approaches are informed by a Western methodology and assumptions. However, that by itself should not be a basis for dismissing arguments that appeal to the same logic and purpose of Islamic law and jurisprudence.

It is not my intention to propose or impose a particular rereading of legal proofs in order to produce a new and radical legal ruling (*ḥukm*) regarding polygamy and women's inheritance. Rather, I treat these cases as examples that will show that classical Islamic law and ethics are posited ideas: ideas that are rooted in religious tradition but produced by men (and some women) in order to satisfy social and cultural needs for specific communities.[3] In starting a conversation regarding the meaning and application of notions such as justice (*ʿadālah*),[4] fairness (*qisṭ*), and welfare (*maṣlaḥah*), the outcome can serve as a springboard for considering other matters of fundamental rights and entitlements that ought to be protected and cherished in any civil society.

We, as humans, are in a new and different situation relative to the situation from that where Islamic laws regarding polygamy and inheritance were formulated. It might be the case that these laws made sense at that time because of the social order and historical circumstances that existed.[5] The logic that justified polygamy then ought to be extended now to argue for different approaches to the laws dealing with polygamy in modern times. Chief among these changing circumstances is the fact that we are in a situation in which membership in the global community comes with the expectations of recognizing and seeking to uphold certain basic human rights, including women's rights to be treated as beings with unalienable dignity and honor. In a human rights era, and also consistent with the best insights of Islam, scholars of Islam are morally required to reexamine the historical causes and legal reasoning for traditional practices that injure women's well-being.

If we can show that polygamy and some unfair inheritance laws do injure the well-being of many women, it would follow that the principles of justice and fairness explicitly stated in the legal proofs ought to be activated to undo the harm. It is true, as some would argue, that perhaps some women find that the practice promotes their well-being, but it is also true that many find that it does not. Minimally, at this point, those who find it beneficial and those who find it injurious need to be included in conversations concerning how best to form legal and civil institutions today in accordance with the recognition of basic human rights.

The two cases chosen for this study will highlight the ethical, philosophical, and legal aspects of the debate on fundamental rights, justice, and fairness. Polygamy, for instance, might have a positive impact on the well-being of some women. Taken together with other Islamic legal rulings such as inheritance ordinances, the institution of polygamy shows that it directly compromises the principles of equality and fairness that were supposed to be upheld by the letter and spirit of the law as argued by traditional Muslim scholars. When considered in the same context, polygamy and inheritance laws make a strong case for rethinking the traditional views on justice, equality, fairness, and human dignity in some Muslim countries.

Methodological and Disciplinary Precedence

In the previous two chapters, I provided an overview of the various disciplines that informed Islamic law and practices. I also introduced a theoretical analysis of the aims and intents of the framers of the Islamic legal system. Before I discuss the specifics of polygamy laws in Islam, I shall further identify which legal principles and doctrines are used in the cases of polygamy and inheritance laws.

One of the most instructive suggestions in reaction to a preliminary draft of this chapter was an inquiry by a colleague who wondered whether there is an acceptance (or what I refer to herein as precedence) to my methodology and assumptions by traditional Islamic scholarship. If there is none, then my work is either a "straightforward hermeneutic of suspicion," or a downright projection of assumed universality of methods and values which I apply to communities that neither share the aforementioned (methods and values) nor coexist in the same place and time. In other words, before suggesting an alternative interpretation of the legal proofs and the primary sources of ethical and philosophical values of the Muslim community, one ought to show that the discourse adopted herein resonates with the norms and ideas of the historical subjects and actors who are parties to this extended debate. In order to satisfy these conditions, I have refined the second chapter in order to place the general premise of Islamic law and jurisprudence in the background of this analysis. Additionally, I will summarize the methodologies and logic of Muslim scholarship from the formative time period to the codification era of classical Islamic law and ethics. Moreover, I shall recreate the historical contextualization of the cases of polygamy and inheritance then and now in order to engage Muslim scholars in a debate according to the terms, methodologies, and reasoning that guided them throughout history.

One of the earliest disciplines that were used in order to assign meaning and authority to the legal proofs dealing with polygamy and inheritance is a direct interpretive approach (*tafsīr*). Muslim scholars from main Sunnite and Shi'ite denominations invariably recognize at least three kinds of interpretive methods:

(a) tradition-based interpretation (*al- tafsīr al-riwā'ī*), (b) reasoned interpretation (*al-tafsīr al-ra'yī*), and (c) implicit (or tacit) interpretation (*al-tafsīr al-ishārī*).[6]

While tradition-based interpretation is restricted to statements taken from the explanatory Qur'ānic verses (where the Qur'ān is used to interpret the Qur'ān) and the explanation by the Prophet Muhammad and his Companions,[7] the last two kinds of interpretive methods depend more or less on reason. In other words, in both of those instances, scholars rely on informed reason (*ijtihād*) in order to discover or extract that which might have been implied in any given ambiguous Qur'ānic enunciation. Moreover, it is an established fact that Muslim ethicists and jurisprudents relied on linguistic and philological approaches in order to understand the primary sources of law and practices and in order to extract the proper legal rules and findings.

Classical Islamic law is indeed the product of the above-mentioned disciplines, but it is also the product of a sophisticated and elaborate system of verification, authorization, canonization, and codification. At first, Islamic jurisprudence and practices were informed and influenced by the early theological discourse (*kalām*). Upon the failure of the scholarship in this discipline to articulate an acceptable dogma, Islamic theology was dismissed in favor of religious ethics (*uṣūl al-dīn*). With time, religious ethics matured as a branch of knowledge and branched out to give rise to jurisprudential philosophy (*uṣūl al-fiqh*), which constituted the foundation of legal tradition (*fiqh*). In summary, all four disciplines relied heavily on informed reasoning, to which the term *ijtihād* was coined.

By the end of the formative period (third Islamic century), Islamic law was able to adapt to changing circumstances due in part to its adoption of the so-called informed reasoning, a methodology that is founded on at least four pillars: (a) analogy (*qiyās*), (b) instinctive inclination (*istiḥsān*), (c) forward certainty (*istiṣḥāb*), and (d) informed assumptions (*istiqrā'*). Obviously, these are technical terms that are coined to mean specific things for Muslim scholars.[8] For that reason, I will take some space to explain these doctrines and principles in order to show that my assumptions and conclusions are warranted, since they are founded on the same principles and logic developed by scholars of Islamic ethics and jurisprudence.

(a) Analogy refers to the process of juxtaposing a case whose legal ruling is unknown against a case whose legal ruling is known.[9] Analogy applies only when the two cases being measured against one another share the same legal justification (*al-`illah*). For instance, if it were to be determined with certainty that wine was proscribed because of its intoxicating effects, a jurist would then extend the prohibition to cover beer since it is also intoxicating. Sometimes however, the legal justification is made specific upon the declaration of the legal ruling. Other times, the legal justification is implicit, in which case the jurist or ethicist must determine it first before using it as a template for other cases.

(b) Instinctive inclination is just that: a gut feeling experienced by the jurist because of his experience and the sense he develops after working with similar cases over extended time. This instinctive inclination is enough of a legal proof in the absence of an explicit one.

(c) What is meant by forward certainty is the jurist's assumption of the continuance of a circumstance (on which one was certain), which would imply the continuance of the ensuing legal ruling. This principle is very complex and requires longer qualification. However, for our purpose, an example should suffice. Let us take the example of a home that is owned by a person who has lived in it for an extended time period. Lets say, however, the owner disappears for a month. A relative claims that the owner might have died (just because he was not seen occupying the premises) and demands that the ownership be transferred to him. Short of absolutely finding that the owner is in fact dead, a judge must dismiss this (hypothetical) case on account of what I called "forward certainty." In other words, the judge must override the claimed (uncertain; *mashkūk*) demise of the original owner with the certainty (*al-thābit yaqīnan*) of his being alive that was established by virtue of knowing him to live in the house.

(d) Finally, the notion of informed assumptions refers to the process by which a judge relies on the limited survey in order to issue a general legal ruling. For instance, if we were to observe that a random number of people from a particular city speak in a specific language and dress in a specific way, it is acceptable to generalize and conclude that all the people of that town speak the same language and dress in the same manner.

All the notions and methodologies in the fields of jurisprudence and ethics were anchored by a plethora of broader guiding principles that furnished the legal and ethical justification (*al-`illah al-shar`iyyah* and *al-`illah al-akhlāqiyyah*). Guiding principles such as (1) prevention of harm (*lā ḍarar wa-lā ḍirār*), (2) suspension of proscriptions due to necessities (*al-ḍarūrāt tubīḥ al-maḥḍūrāt*), and (3) promoting inherent well-being (*al-maṣāliḥ al-mursalah*) were portrayed as the core of the spirit and letter of Islamic jurisprudence.[10] In other words, the purpose of laws was essentially to remove discomfort (*daf` al-ḥaraj*), redress injury (*mu`ālajat al-ḍarar*), and realize justice (*taḥqīq al-`adālah*).[11]

Finally, my analysis and conclusions are rooted in and supported by the five-fold system of legal and ethical rules (*al-aḥkām al-uṣūliyyah*). This intricate and elaborate system is another proof that law in Islam must pass the test of morality before it becomes binding. Unlike the tripartite modern Western system that normatively categorizes human actions as obligatory, illegal, and permissible; the Islamic matrix incorporates (and fuses) morality and legality in a system that judges the acts of the person as (1) obligatory (*wājib*), (2) recommended (*mandūb*), (3) neutral (*mubāḥ*),[12] (4) contemptuous (*makrūh*), or (5) proscribed (*ḥarām*) as explained in chapter 2. Furthermore, there is enough evidence that would suggest that these five rules are only thresholds in a moral spectrum.[13] In other words, every action one undertakes falls somewhere on a scale whose center refers to neutral (or permissible) acts and that progressively expands toward either prohibition or obligation. Toward one end and moving away from the neutral zone, acts are gradually categorized as morally discouraged, the extreme of which are acts that are irrevocably proscribed. Toward the other end, acts are gradually categorized as encouraged concluded by the acts that are irrevocably mandatory. In such a system, I would suggest that polygamy ought to be seen as extremely contemptuous, a view that is not registered in classical Islamic law. This judgment makes polygyny an ethical matter and not a legal one. This point is essential and will be discussed in chapter 5.

In summary, all these methods, processes, and principles are the stated methodologies that empowered Muslim scholars to interpret traditions and clarify ambiguous legal proofs. We will now explore the degree of commitment of Muslim scholars to these principles as they applied to polygyny and inheritance cases.

Polygamy in the Historical Context

When addressing the issue of polygamy, religion and religious beliefs automatically become part of the conversation. Religion is used either to justify the practice or to challenge its validity as a social innovation that has no place in the religious ethical discourse. To oppose polygamy requires that the practice is framed in a cultural and political set of circumstances that necessitated it. Historical and religious records nonetheless show that polygamy has always been practiced in Semitic societies.

In the view of Muslim scholars, the Arab people are a branch of the Semitic people whose genealogy takes them back to Abraham, the Hebrew Patriarch, through his son Ishmael. Arguably, before Abraham and Sarah had Isaac, the desperate couple, fearing that Sarah was past her fertile years, agreed to have Abraham father a son with the maiden girl, Hagar, offered to them in Egypt. But when both Sarah and Hagar finally gave birth, to Ishmael and Isaac, the former (along with his mother) is pushed to the arid central land of the peninsula (known today as Arabia) while Sarah and Abraham continued to live in the Fertile Crescent. With time, Ishmael becomes the patriarch of the Arabs while Isaac becomes the patriarch of the Israelites.

As far as polygamy is concerned, historical and religious data firmly and convincingly show that the Hebrews (hence, the Jews) in particular and the Semites in general have a well-established tradition of polygamy. According to biblical and Talmudic (and even Islamic) literature, Abraham, Esau, Jacob, Saul,

David, and Solomon—to name a few—all were involved in polygamous marriages. According to Jewish scholars, it is said that although there is an implied limitation on polygamy, instances of unrestricted marriages whereby one man is married to many women are not uncommon:

> R. Tarphon, both priest and tanna, betrothed unto himself three hundred maidens in order to feed them out of the priestly heave-offering. Rabbi Judah the Prince sponsored twelve levirate marriages for one poor Israelite and helped to maintain that large family. Of two famous amoraim, Ra. and R. Naḥman, it is told in the Talmud that they had their wives at home, but contracted new marriages on their visits to new communities.... Josephus informed the Roman world long before: "It is the ancient practice among us to have many wives at the same time." In theory at least, the Talmud assumes polygamy as the marriage rule without question. The co-wife (*Ẓarah*) is a prominent figure in tannaitic discussion of the levirate law.[14]

As in Judaism, in early Christianity polygamy was either permitted or tolerated:

> Probably during the early centuries, Christian teachers were fully aware that no prohibition against polygamy could be adduced from apostolic writings.... It is not surprising therefore that history records polygamous unions on the part of Christian dignitaries in earlier as well as in later times, and often with the consent of Church and clergy. The Council of Trent in 1563 was still troubled with those insubordinate, critical minds who taught that "polygamy was permitted to Christians and was not prohibited by any divine law," and, seeking to make an end to this teaching, legislated by the full authority of the Roman Church an unequivocal prohibition of polygamy, pronouncing a ban upon those who might teach otherwise.[15]

From historical accounts, it is evident that people's attitude toward polygamy was shaped by the cultural, social, and economic conditions of each society. Subsequently, religious authorities tended to interpret religious texts and religious laws fully mindful of the circumstances of the community. The discussion of polygamy in the Islamic discourse is not different. From the emergence of Islam until today, social, economic, and cultural conditions have informed the debate on polygamy. Before considering the topic in the exegetical and legal contexts, a brief overview of the environment in which early Islamic thought emerged is in order.

The arid environment and harsh conditions in which the pre-Islamic Arabs lived could neither confer hope for a long life nor allow the inhabitants to aspire to an eternal life. When one is challenged every day and barely survives, the possibility of a longer life, let alone an eternal one, ought to be frightening to say the least, because a future eternal life could be just as horrible. Fatalism was the norm. As a result, the human life was merely a price for another life, and the human worth was consequential only inasmuch as it was needed to redeem another.[16] There is no doubt that the early Arabs were among the most violent peoples; the massive occurrence of murder and revenge transcended every other practice to the point that it turned into a "trade." These appalling practices and conditions are neither the invention of the imagination nor an exaggeration.[17] In fact, the literature and historical reports that talk about the pre-Islamic Arabs do indeed confirm the existence of the numerous enterprises of death and the ensuing institutions. The *jāhiliyyah* poetry glorified killing, wars, and violence. Early harsh Qur'ānic condemnation of infanticide,[18] murder, revenge, and disregard for human life underscores the decadence and depravity of the state of affairs of the Arabs of Mecca and Yathrib of that era.[19] The fact that the Mad_nah Charter, which was drafted to establish peace among the tribes living in what was previously known as *Yathrib*, references blood-money obligations in almost every article also indicates that this epidemic of willful killing was chronic and pervasive. Such a culture of violence affected both men and women. Men in general were the perpetrators and the victims of murder, homicide, wars, and revenge, but women especially suffered the burden of being transformed into a means of entertainment for the few surviving and privileged men. In an environment like the one we are describing, the ratio between women and men could easily be something close to three to one.[20] Polygamy, servitude, and other enterprises that cater to men would undoubtedly flourish given the circumstances.[21] It would appear that even the Qur'ān, an early advocate of the rights of the poor and of disenfranchised people, recognized the weight of the reality of the institution of polygamy[22] but avoided addressing it immediately.[23] That hesitant treatment and ambiguous wording of the texts dealing with the issue in early Islam appears to have solidified a status quo and eternalized what is an incidental and circumstantial reality. Regardless of how one looks at the Qur'ān (revealed or authored by Muhammad), Muslim and non-Muslim scholars agree that the Qur'ān is context specific. For non-Muslim scholars, every invention (in this case the Qur'ān) is informed by the environment and context in which it is conceived. For Muslim scholars, the Qur'ān was revealed on occasions that gave it context. There is an entire category of literature that chronicles those occasions of revelations known as *Asbāb al-nuzūl*.

The Philology of Polygamy

In this section, I will examine the interpretive and normative tradition regarding the Qur'ānic verses that addressed polygamy and then present a rereading of the text in order to see if there is room for an alternative interpretation that disengages women from a *stare decisis* that could be a result of erroneous interpretation or temporary allowance.[24]

In Islam, polygamy is ostensibly legalized by the following Qur'ānic verse:

> If you fear that you are unable to deal justly (*tuqsiṭū*) with the orphans, then marry other women of your choice: twos (*mathnā*), threes (*thulāth*), and fours (*rubā`*). However, if you fear that you cannot deal justly (with them) (*ta`dilū*), then only one or (captives) that your right hands possess. That will be more suitable to prevent you from doing injustice. [Q4:V3]

Firstly, it must be noted that the Qur'ān and the tradition of the Prophet (*Sunnah*) contained many injunctions regarding the status of orphans in general. This would only underscore the preponderance of the phenomenon of violence that resulted in the deaths of large numbers of men, many of whom could be fathers; this led to the existence of an entire class of orphans that required special legal intervention. It is my contention that the aforementioned verse is just one of the enunciations in regard to the rights and status of orphans. This time, the Qur'ān speaks specifically about the case of female orphans.[25]

The meaning of the Qur'ān is not generally determined by the direct reading of the text. Rather, it is fixed by the contextual circumstances and the oral interpretations that are inherited from recognized authorities.[26] Primarily, it is the practice (*`amal*) of the Prophet that will assign the final and decisive understanding of any given verse. Alternatively, authoritative traditions inherited from the Companions are used to fix the meaning and scope of the Qur'ānic injunctions.[27] In this case, polygamy is determined based on two reports: one from the Prophet and the other from his wife `Ā'ishah.

One Prophetic tradition is invariably cited in the collections of *ḥadīth* but it is mostly concerned with the limitation of the number of wives to four without addressing the case of orphans mentioned in verse [Q4:V3]. It is reported that when Ghaylān Ibn Salāmah accepted Islam with his ten wives, the Prophet asked him to choose four of them and let go of the rest.[28] Apparently, this tradition has settled the peculiarity arising from the ambiguity of the terms used in verse [Q4:V3], which are not explicit about the prohibition of being married to more than four wives at the same time.[29] This ambiguity does not explain the fact that the Prophet himself was married to at least nine wives at the same time. In order to reconcile this Prophetic undertaking with the established cap on polygamy, Muslim scholarship came up with an exclusionary rule arguing that the Prophet had the license to go beyond the cap but no other Muslim has such a permit.[30]

The particulars of marriage and the options available for the orphans are determined by a series of traditions inherited from `Ā'ishah, `Umar, and other Companions (the disciples of the Prophet).[31] However, `Ā'ishah's analysis appears to be the one adopted by Sunni scholarship (*jumhūr*), and it would suffice to elaborate on that tradition in order to explain the effective laws in this case.

It is reported that `Urwah Ibn al-Zubayr asked `Ā'ishah to explain to him the Qur'ānic verse [Q4:V3] on which she commented saying:

> It was the custom of the Arabs who had under their custody beautiful and rich orphan girls to marry them without offering them their fair dower. This verse (referring to [Q4:V3]) was then revealed to terminate that practice and make it compulsory that either orphan women are offered their fair dower or they are left alone.[32]

Similar traditions were reported, all of which basically advocated that (a) a man may marry up to four orphans and nonorphans provided that he treats them justly and fairly (*yuqsiṭ*), (b) a man cannot marry orphans at all because of fear of being unable to treat them justly and may instead marry up to four nonorphans, or (c) a man could marry up to just four orphans provided that he treats them fairly. The above were the only mentioned interpretations of the verse and related traditions.

Clearly, being an orphan woman did not make a difference in terms of the legality of marrying them when considering these three divergent yet acceptable interpretations. In this understanding, it must be noted also that, according to Muslim scholars, the question of fairness is in relation to pecuniary matters not necessarily to fairness in treatment and respect.[33] However, according to yet another tradition reported in al-Qur ubī's *Tafṣrī*, the principle of *qisṭ* may extend to cover the moral and sexual needs (excluding justice in love as discussed later) of the wife even if she is not involved in a polygamous marriage.[34]

To sum up, the only substantial break from past practices in the institution of marriage is the fact that the interpretation of verse [Q4:V3] yielded an absolute prohibition of one man marrying more than four wives simultaneously.[35] As to the status of the orphans and the rights of women in general, it is clear from the interpretive legal and religious tradition that men's interests and marriage "rights" were preserved while those of orphan women were limited. Moreover, it could be argued that orphans' marriage rights[36] were in effect revoked since one view at least prohibited men from marrying them. If marriage is to be seen as a universal right, then clearly, prohibiting men from marrying orphan women is more of an unfair limitation on women than on men since men could still marry up to four other women as long as they are not orphans. Classical Islamic literature does not reflect any women's voices on this matter,[37] which is due in part to the fact that in this particular debate, male scholars dominated this discourse and no input whatsoever was sought from or provided by women.[38] In other words, the status inherited from the pre-Islamic times continued to influence and to guide the understanding and practices of marriage. The elite-dominated interpretive discourse of the Qur'ān did not see the relevant verses from the point of view of the need for social justice and did not consider the changing circumstances. It was seen within the context of the dominant culture of that time and apparently polygamy was part of the culture. When one brackets-in the fact that polygamy was seen by some then as an act of "goodness" toward women, it becomes clear why limited polygamy (four wives) was in itself a major achievement. It is doubtful that these verses were ever intended to permanently fix the status of women given the extraordinary circumstances in which they were living during the emergence of Islam.[39] This ambiguity can now be exploited to rectify an arrangement that was not meant to be permanent. In order to do so, a fresh look at these verses and a consideration of the alternatives are in order.

Regarding the status of orphans, it would seem that verse [Q4:V3] proscribes polygamy, but does not prohibit marrying orphans.[40] I would argue that this Qur'ānic passage prohibits polygamy involving orphans even if a man thinks that he could establish justice (*qisṭ*) but mandates monogamous marriages to orphans. In other words, the language of verse [Q4:V3] suggests that even if a man is capable of being fair and just, he nonetheless may enter into a polygamous marriage with nonorphans who have family members who can defend them and support them in case he fails. It only allows monogamous marriages involving orphan women. It does not stand to reason for a man to take a chance with orphans who lack paternal support, but at the same time it did not prohibit men from marrying orphan women.

As it were, in Islamic law, it is argued that orphan girls are protected by way of prohibiting men from marrying them. For instance, some scholars hold the view that if a man wishes to marry more than one wife, then he should be able to do so as long as none of the wives is an orphan. But even this view is not shared among all scholars, since some of them do indeed permit a man to marry up to four orphan wives, as reported by al-Ṭabarī and al-Qurṭubī in their commentaries on verse [Q4:V3]. Notwithstanding the lack of consensus, that limitation[41] on men can be hardly regarded as a protection of orphan women's interests. After all, it is more of a limitation than a protection, since barring men from marrying them only adds to the difficulties of finding a suitable husband as the pool of potential mates is restricted by that stipulation. A more reasonable reading of the verse then allows men to marry orphan women on the condition that the husband entering into such a marriage with orphan women does not marry a second, third, or fourth wife regardless of the status of the additional three women. This reading of verse [Q4:V3] is more in harmony with the grammatical, syntactical, and moral context of chapter *al-nisā'* as a whole and the Qur'ān in general. In other words, I only applied the accepted jurisprudential principles (1), (2), and (3) that I mentioned at the opening of this chapter.

For instance, al-Ṭabarī reports that some legal scholars insist that the Qur'ānic passage ([Q4:V3]) that places justice as a condition (*fa'in khiftum allā tuqsiṭū*...) in fact means from of marrying orphan women (*falā tankiḥūhunna*).[42] I would argue that if that was the intended meaning, then it would make more sense linguistically and grammatically to structure the conditional and response clauses as follows: If you fear that you would not establish justice among the orphans, then marry *whomever* you desire from other women: twos, threes and fours. However, in the passage the term *whatever* (*mā*) was used instead of *whomever* (*man*).[43] That word choice implies that the emphasis in the verse is on the number of wives rather than on the category of women. It would follow from this logic that men could marry orphan women provided that such a marriage is monogamous. Marriage to other women would remain subjected to existing polygamous practices, but even then, a man ought to marry only one woman for fear of being unjust. This understanding would explain the need to repeat the condition for *fairness* and *justice* twice in the same short passage. This interpretation is also in conformity with the acceptable interpretive approaches (b) and (c) that I introduced earlier in this chapter.

It is curious that this understanding of the verse (prohibiting polygynous marriages involving orphans in favor of monogamous marriages) was never presented by classical Islamic legal and exegetical scholars despite the fact that it can be easily derived from the simple reading of the Qur'ānic text. This is especially curious because the text, word choice, and style of verse [Q4:V3] do indeed distinguish between *al-yatāmā* (orphans) and *al-nisā'* (women, ladies) as two different groups or classes of women as some exegetes admit.[44] In retrospect, the existing (pre-Islamic) polygamous arrangement ought to be limited to the pool of women who enjoy the family and paternal support. For the rest of the verse, although the language of verse [Q4:V3] does not necessarily establish a cap on the number of nonorphan wives, it nonetheless concludes that it is preferred to marry just one wife. If verse [Q4:V3] were to be taken in the context of verse [Q4:V129], which states "You (men) will never be able to establish justice among women even if you try hardest," it would become clear that establishing justice between multiple wives is a hopeless endeavor; hence, polygamy is undesirable (*makrūh*).[45] Again, this analysis is merely the application of interpretive method (a) (previous discussion), which allows for the explanation of the Qur'ān by the Qur'ān.

The suggestion by some Muslim scholars that a man ought not to marry orphans if he wishes to maintain a polygamous lifestyle is in itself an admission of potential harm unfairly inflicted on orphans who are entering into a polygamous marriage. In other words, these scholars accept the general premise that was advanced by the Qur'ānic verse that qualified polygamous marriages (at least those involving orphan women) to be injurious. To remedy the situation, some scholars concluded that, in order to deal with the moral and ethical problems raised by the Qur'ān, men are barred from marrying orphan women. However, this solution is clearly benefiting men and placing orphan women at a disadvantage since a man gives nothing of his so-called rights but orphan women will be rendered "unmarriable."

This arrangement, I would argue, came into existence due to the fact that the interpretations of the Qur'ānic enunciations were generally conducted by members of the elite class that was dominated by men. A number of women were part of this elite class as well; hence, there is a lack of ordinary and disadvantaged (orphan) women's perspective. It is reasonable to suspect then that the outcome is biased especially when taken in the context of an Arabic society that had regarded honoring custom and established norms as an essential virtue in men and women of that time period. As a patriarchal society, the final decision apparently was left in the hands of males. Regarding, men who determined, for themselves and by themselves, that they lacked the capacity to establish justice, all that was required of them, per this determination, was to leave orphans alone, unmarried, and marry as many other women as they wished (*mā ṭāba lakum*).[46] In the event of a surplus of unmarried women such arrangement would hardly qualify as a fair solution for orphan women. Not only are they now lacking the paternal support that is needed in a male-dominated society, but they also become undesired by men for marriage due to their status.

Some have argued that the prohibition of polygamy involving more than four women was due in part to the fact that the Arabs in the pre-Islamic times used to marry many wives, which resulted in creating very large families with large expenses. Subsequently, when the heads of the household, who are men, exhausted all their personal wealth as a result of that practice, they would resort to usurping the money of the orphans who were under their care.[47] Theoretically, this same argument could be used by Muslim reformers and propose further restrictions on polygamous marriages given the changing circumstances. Moreover, the above argument is founded on a jurisprudential principle that allows jurists or Muslim leaders to curb, permanently suspend, temporarily suspend, or abrogate a legal ruling if the welfare of a person or the welfare of the community requires it. There are numerous instances like these where the Caliph `Umar is said to have suspended the punishment for theft after a long drought and harsh economic conditions. It is also `Umar who prohibited temporary marriages, according to Muslim exegetes and historians.[48]

Scholars familiar with the Islamic exegetical collections know that they are generally inclusive and comprehensive. Exegetes, in order to appear authoritative and aware of all arguments, list all traditions and interpretations even if such traditions are contradictory. Al-Ṭabarī is known for this practice to the point that his work was seen as being more encyclopedic and less normative because of the multitudes of divergent points of view he includes. In order to give an authoritative aspect to his work, he generally concludes his discussion of any topic by making a statement in favor of one position or simply stating his personal inclination toward one of the stated views. In other instances, he proposes his own ruling on the matter. Despite this richness in perspectives and inclusiveness in points of views, there are curious gaps and an absence of discussions of possible interpretations of the verses on polygamy. Some terms were excluded from the linguistic and legal analysis despite their relevance and centrality to laws on polygamy. One such case of omission is the lack of explanation of the peculiar use of the terms *mathnā*, *thulāth*, and *rubā`*.

Also unexplained is the absence of the term *āḥād*.[49] It is possible to argue that the monogamous option was left out because it is linked to the content of the first clause of the conditional sentence. That is to say that the intent of verse [Q4:V3] has restricted marriage to an orphan to one (*āḥād*), but left the door open for polygamous practices to effect only nonorphan women. In other words, the language, the syntax, and the choice of words all support the view that that verse mandates monogamous marriages with orphans but does not take an explicit legal action on polygamous marriage if it did not involve orphan women. Moreover, even a polygamous marriage with nonorphans was discouraged.[50]

The traditional Muslim discourse on polygamy has been static. It continues to protect the interests of the elite class and ignore the rights and interests of disadvantaged women despite mounting evidence and changing circumstances that support flexibility in interpretation. The existing rigidity cannot be due to the meaning and intent of the Qur'ānic enunciations, since we have demonstrated that textual analysis could, and indeed did, yield different reading of the verses dealing with polygamy.[51] The rigidity and inflexibility could be the result of unyielding control exerted by an elite-dominated exegetical discourse informed by social practices. These practices defined what is proper and what is not but no original reading of the legal proofs was undertaken. Moreover, if the legitimizing principle behind polygamous marriages was indeed the imbalance in number of males and females in early Arabia due to the conditions described earlier, how could one explain its continuation now in places like Saudi Arabia where the ratio of men to women is no longer skewed by the wars and violence that existed in the distant past?[52]

There are at least two areas that require further research. The first relates to the position of the Qur'ān in regard to polygamy. Contrary to Muslim exegetes' conclusions that identified three possible interpretations of the verses on polygamy, there is linguistic and normative evidence that suggests that the Qur'ān did not take a definitive stance on the matter and more specifically did not recommend an explicit binding legal ruling. Minimally, one could argue that there is at least a fourth possible understanding that was not addressed or recommended by Muslim interpreters: The textual analysis of the legal proofs shows that the Qur'ān took a firm position prohibiting polygamous marriages involving orphan women but did not actually prohibit marrying them. In the Islamic commentaries, however, there is no prohibition on marrying orphan women in polygynous marriages and when restriction is necessary, most scholars prohibit marrying orphan women. This peculiar understanding that clearly does not advance the interests of orphans and their rights to marriage is expressive of a position dominated by the elite; hence, it did not challenge the established practices that favored men and ignored the weak. The position I take in understanding the verses dealing with polygyny was not explored in classical and modern legal and ethical literature.

The second area that needs to be further examined by scholars of legal and cultural studies is the nature of the interpretive process and its impact on legal determinations and issues of social justice. In other words, would it be sufficient to include representative voices in the interpretive process or must there be abstract determination of the meaning and scope of the concepts of justice, fairness, and equality?

4

Women in Islamic Law of Inheritance

During pre-Islamic times,[1] the Arabs passed their wealth to able men who could protect their honor and their family.[2] It was a common practice then for men to enter into agreements with other men, assuming they lacked male progeny, whereby if a man died, the other would be his heir and also marry his wife to protect his honor and his family.[3] With this kind of social order in place, marriage practices were, to some extent, a form of business transaction. It was common for a man to enter into such an agreement with another person of his choosing. If he did not make that choice before his death, other members of his family would be responsible for the arrangements of paying his debt or disposing of his wealth and looking after his family.[4] In this social order, it was also common for a son to marry the wife (or wives) of his father after his death, or for a brother to marry his brother's wives upon his death. These practices might explain the Qur'ānic prohibition of interfamily marriages.[5] The prohibition of marriages to family members is unusually detailed, suggesting that incest and marriages to nearest of kin were common in pre-Islamic Arab society.

Given that marriage was a form of sponsorship that depended on agreements similar to political treaties, customary tribal inheritance laws closely reflected the social and psychological dimensions of members of the community. In that regard, when a father died, his wealth (and debt) is automatically passed to his able son who can "carry the sword."[6] There are no reliable records that show a deviation from this pattern. Even wealthy women (such as the Prophet's first wife) do not seem to have been the recipients of any inherited wealth from their fathers or any uterine relatives. In fact, in the case of Khadījah, it is clear that she accumulated her wealth through inheritance from two wealthy husbands who died and did not leave male descendants.[7]

The clarity of the Qur'ān in prohibiting marriages to close relatives is only matched (in details and specificity) by its explicitness in assigning portions (shares) of the deceased's estate to specific heirs. Undoubtedly, the unusual clarity can be explained by the relationship between marriage and property rights. But it could be also signaling customary practices that were no longer acceptable to the emerging Muslim community. Notwithstanding the radical changes brought forth by the Qur'ānic legislation, the later development of

Islamic law did not reflect the spirit and intent of the Qur'ānic moral and legal code. The documents that I have examined for this study show a pronounced dichotomy between the rulings in classical Islamic law and the explicit text of the Qur'ān.[8] Subsequently, many modern Muslim reformists find ample room in the space between Qur'ānic and Islamic law to launch a critique of the practices that affect the economic, social, and political rights of women.

Like the laws preserving polygamy, Islamic laws on inheritance are understandably seen by human rights thinkers and activists as another area that sanctioned discrimination against women in Muslim communities. The basis and the logic for the continued support for the practice of polygamy was introduced and critiqued from the point of view of the reasoning and purpose of the law in the Qur'ān. I shall adopt a similar approach with the laws of inheritance in order to examine the rootedness of classical Islamic law rulings in the legal proofs as suggested by Muslim scholars. Moreover, I shall apply grammatical, normative, and interpretive reasoning in order to explore alternative views that were at various points held by some Muslim scholars throughout the history of the Islamic civilization. By way of relying on objective interpretation of the verses on inheritance, the data will show that what many Muslim scholars propose as a matter of consensus is in fact a corpus of legal rulings that stem from precedents rather than universal understanding (consensus-based understanding) of the meaning of said verses.

The Qur'ānic and Interpretive Dichotomy

Muslim scholars argue that Islamic law, per Qur'ānic enunciations, fixed the portions of inheritance for each of the heirs.[9] Scholars familiar with the Arabic text of the Qur'ān would concur that for the Qur'ānic discourse, which is known for its vagueness, the verses dealing with inheritance rights are unusually deliberate and explicit. Verses [Q4:V11–12] decree that each of the members of the family of the deceased inherits a specified share (*farḍ*). The primary legal proofs (*adillah*) supporting of classical Islamic laws of inheritance are found in no more than four Qur'ānic verses. For the purpose of clarity and specificity, I shall provide herein a translation of all these verses.

> For men a predetermined share from that which the two parents and the relatives leave behind; and for women a predetermined share from that which the two parents and the relatives leave behind: be it a large or small amount, there is a fixed ordained share. [Q4:V7]

> God advises you regarding the inheritance of your children: for one male a share equal to that of the two females. If they are women more than two, then, they (women) shall receive two-thirds of what the deceased leaves behind. If she was one woman, then she shall receive the half. For each of the deceased's two parents

one-sixth if he leaves behind a child. If he does not leave behind a child and he was inherited by his two parents, then his mother shall receive one-third. If he has brothers, then his mother shall receive one-sixth. These shares are received after paying off any debt or specific will that he may have left behind. You know not whether it is your parents or your children who are more beneficial to you; and these are God's ordered shares, indeed God is wise and all-knowing. [Q4:V11]

To *you* (*lakum*; husbands) half of what your wives leave behind if they have no child. If they have a child, then you shall receive one-fourth of what they leave behind after paying off any debt or bequests that they might have left behind. To *them* (*lahunna*; wives) one-fourth of that which you leave behind if you have no child. If you have a child, then they shall receive one-eighth of what you leave behind after paying off any debt or bequest that you may leave behind. If the deceased is a man or a woman who has no children and no parents, and he or she has a brother or a sister, then each of them shall receive one-sixth.[10] If they are more than one brother and one sister, then they shall share one-third after paying off any nonexploitative (*ghayra muḍārrin*) debt or bequest that the deceased may leave behind. This is God's will and indeed God is all-knowing and all-kind. [Q4:V12]

They ask of you a formal declaration; say God will offer you a formal declaration concerning *kalālah*.[11] When a person dies and he has no child and he has a sister, she shall receive half of what he leaves behind. He shall inherit all of hers if she has no child. If he has two sisters instead, they shall share two-thirds. If he has brothers and sisters together, then they will inherit from him whereby each male shall inherit a share equal to that of two females. God explains to you so that you don't go astray, and God has the knowledge of everything. [Q4:V176] (*Emphasis* on *you* and *them* mine; see discussion of the topic of patriarchic language in chapter 5.)

Before considering these verses in the legal, philosophical, and hermeneutical context, it is imperative that the above translation is further clarified by an explanation of the grammatical and syntactical elements that may not be obvious from the English translation.

It is possible that Arabic is the most specific of all major living languages. As a result, grammatical analyses of the language of legal proofs are necessary in order to derive the intended declaration of the Legislator. For example, in classical Arabic (the language of the Qur'ān), there are fourteen pronouns as opposed to just six or seven pronouns used in modern English. The large number of pronouns allows the speaker (author) to be more specific since there are pronouns not only for singular, dual, and plural designations but also for feminine and masculine forms of the singular, dual, and plural pronouns. For instance, there are two pronouns for the second person singular (you; *anti/a*): one for feminine and one for the masculine subjects. The same applies to the dual (*antumā/antumā*) and plural (*antum/antunna*) pronouns. Furthermore, there is an established convention for the choice of pronouns: for singular impersonal subjects, the default pronoun is the third person (he; *huwa*). Similarly, for plural subjects that are mixed (feminine and masculine), the masculine third person plural (they; *hum*) is used. In other words, the only instance where the third person plural feminine (they; *hunna*) is used is when the designated subjects are all women and not even one man is among them.

The specificity of the Arabic language is not only reflected in the pronouns but also in verbs, nouns, and adjectives. One could learn a great deal about the intent of the Legislator from the choice of words used in the legal proofs. In the English translations of Arabic texts, the specificity is shown in the added insertions sometimes added in parenthesis, brackets, or within the main text as extra wording. For example, one may wonder why I added the word "two" before "parents" in the translation of verse [Q4:V11]. The clue for doing so is found in the Arabic word "*abawāh*" which means "his two parents." Also the beginning of verse [Q4:V11] has a nominative sentence starting with the verb conjugated with the feminine plural pronoun to form (*kunna*), which signals that the subject of that sentence refers only to the female heirs who are possibly sharing an inheritance with one or more males, as will be discussed in the next section.

The Legal and Exegetical Treatment of the Verses on Inheritance

Admittedly, in Islamic law, legal rulings are derived from the direct reading of the primary legal proofs when the text of legal proofs is explicit.[12] Ibn Rushd for instance held the view that explicit verses ought to be taken for what they say while ambiguous verses ought to be left for philosophers to determine their meaning.[13] Theoretically, Muslim scholars argue that if there is an explicit Qur'ānic basis for a particular argument, then the Qur'ānic determination should prevail over all reasoned and *ijtihādic* finding. All Qur'ānic references to inheritance are translated above. The divergent points of view therefore are a result of interpretation and precedent and not necessarily stemming from other legal proofs.

By looking at the verses and the precedent established by the Prophet and his Companions, Muslim scholars were able to develop a "system" that eventually created a hierarchy of heirs and accommodate individuals and entities not mentioned in the Qur'ān. For our purposes, we will introduce the general principles inasmuch as they are relevant to the topic of this study: to understand the rights of women to inheritance.

According to the majority of Muslim scholars, a person has the right to inherit if she (or he) is related to the deceased by way of (1) marriage (*nikāḥ*), (2) true kinship (*qarābah*), or (3) guardianship (*walā'*).[14]

A woman with a valid marriage contract is entitled to inherit from her husband even if the marriage was not consummated. Furthermore, she is entitled to her Qur'ānic share even if the husband dies while she is in her waiting period of a revocable divorce (*ṭalāq rij`ī*).[15] Furthermore, one must keep in mind that, in Islamic law, a marriage contract is not necessarily an official paper signed by the spouses, witnesses, and an official. In fact until recently, marriage contracts have been more or less similar to what is known in the West as "Common Law marriage." An Islamic marriage is valid with the declaration of the offer (*ījāb*) and acceptance (*qabūl*) before an adequate number of qualified witnesses. As such, it is essentially an oral contract. The binding nature of oral contracts in Islamic law raised the status of the spoken words. Specifically, certain phrases became binding once uttered even if they were uttered in jest. According to Islamic tradition, the effects of uttering the formulae for marriage, divorce, and emancipation (of a slave) are automatic. It should be noted that this rule applies to actions that would impact the status of persons who have been historically members of the oppressed class (women and slaves) and it seems that it is meant to discourage actions that relativize the dignity of a human being.

True kinship is defined in Sunni Islamic law as the relationship due to birthing (*wilādah*). It is further divided into "original affinity" like parent and grandparents and "descendantal affinity," like children and grandchildren. Heirs belonging to this class of heirs are distinguished from others—such as uncles and aunts and brothers—by the fact that they are related to the deceased directly (not by intermediaries). Heirs directly related to the deceased are of three classes:

(1) The first class includes individuals who inherit "fixed shares" (*farḍ*) and they are ten: (a) three males (father, grandfather, and the maternal brother) and (b) seven females (mother, grandmother, daughter, the daughter of the son, sister, paternal sister, and maternal sister). According to Sunni Muslim scholars, individuals belonging to this class have priority regardless of their gender, in theory.

(2) The second class of heirs (*`aṣabah*) consists of those who inherit an "estimated share," which is generally the remainder of what is left of the estate after the heirs of the first class receive their fixed shares. This class consists of four subclasses: (a) the deceased's offspring (son and son of the son and however lower), (b) the deceased's ancestors (father and grandfather and however higher), (c) the offspring of the father of deceased (full or half uncle and however lower), and (d) the offspring of grandfather of the deceased (great, full and half uncles and however lower).

(3) The third class consists of relatives who inherit neither a mandated nor an estimated share such as the son of the daughter, the daughter of the brother, the son of the sister, and paternal and maternal aunts.

The rights of all the heirs mentioned above are guaranteed according to Muslim scholars but following these guidelines is a matter of compliance rather than enforcement.[16] The compliance of the believers is assured by the threat and enticement expressed in the verses immediately after the ones assigning shares and as discussed in chapter 2:

> Those are the boundaries established by God: Whoever obeys God and His Messenger will enter gardens full of water streams and in it they will live eternally; and that is the great success. Those who disobey God and His Messenger and trespass His boundaries will enter hellfire; therein he will live eternally and to him there will be humiliating punishment. [Q4:V13–4]

Before presenting specific cases, a few clarifications are in order. In Islamic law, the term "fixed sharers" (*aṣḥāb al-furūḍ*) is often used to suggest that these individuals have their inheritance predetermined in the Qur'ān. As it is clear from the translated verses dealing with inheritance, that implied characterization is in fact inaccurate. For instance, the granddaughter, grandfather, and grandmother are not mentioned in the Qur'ān nor was there a specific share designated for them. The females (daughter, two daughters, three daughters, mother, sister, and wife) were specifically mentioned in the Qur'ān but were not part of the customary tribal law. Generally speaking, when considering the legal opinions of jurists belonging to all Sunni and Shi`ite schools of thought, it becomes impossible for any "system" of ranking heirs to emerge. In fact, even within Sunni jurisprudence, any attempt to generalize a particular system of ranking is immediately undone by counter examples. For example, while some jurists may speak of "fixed sharers" as the individuals who have a predetermined portion of the legacy, other jurists from another Sunni school of thought may dispute the said share on the basis that it is not mentioned in the Qur'ān. Similarly, while some Sunni and Shi`ite jurists speak of a "priority-based" ranking of heirs, such a ranking is usually challenged by the lack of reference in the Qur'ān to some of the so-called higher priority heirs. On my part, I will try to be as consistent as possible by calling Qur'ānic heirs or sharers as referring only to those individuals specifically mentioned in the Qur'ān. Other heirs are assigned shares by the power of Islamic law and not by Qur'ānic enunciations.

In order to have a better understanding of the way Sunni scholars read the verses dealing with inheritance, it is imperative that we consider specific cases. Given my focus on women's rights, I will restrict my inquiry to cases dealing with female heirs.

According to the majority of Sunni jurists, in classical Islamic law, daughters inherit according to three precedents:

(1) The daughter shall inherit one-half of the estate by way of fixed share (*farḍ*) if she is the only child and there is no brother who will cause her share to diminish. If the father of the deceased is alive, he shall inherit the remainder by way of "estimated share" (*ta`ṣīb*).

(2) Two daughters or more shall inherit two-thirds by way of fixed share (*farḍ*), in the absence of a full brother or half brother. If they have full brother, they will inherit by way of *ta`ṣīb*. If there is a half brother, he will share the estate with them on an equal basis: that is, the daughters' share will be diminished

to one-half so that the other half goes to the son of their father. This rule clearly violates the notion of explicitness (being overriding to interpretations) since the Qur'ān does not state that the shares of daughters is diminishable to one-half.

(3) If one daughter is competing with one or more brothers, she shall inherit only by way of "estimated share" (*ta`ṣīb*) according to the rule 2X = Y after the heirs of "fixed shares" receive theirs.[17]

While the inheritance of one and more than two daughters is explicitly mentioned in the verses dealing with inheritance, the shares of two daughters is not found therein. For that reason, Muslim scholars rely on the following tradition to determine their inheritance:

> According to Jābir, the widow of Sa`d Ibn al-Rabī' came to the Messenger and complained: "Messenger of God, these are the two daughters of Sa'd who died with you during the battle of Uḥud. Their uncle took everything and they will not be able to marry without money." The Messenger said: "God will decide regarding that matter." After that, the verse dealing with inheritance was revealed so he told the brother of Sa`d: "Give the two daughters of Sa`d two-thirds, one-eighth to their mother, and whatever remains is yours."[18]

In a similar fashion, Muslim jurists have determined the inheritance of the sister as follows: (1) one sister, in the absence of anyone who will demote her (causing her to inherit by way of *ta`ṣīb*), shall inherit one-half as a fixed share. If there are two or more sisters, then (2) they shall share two-thirds in the absence of other, higher heirs. (3) She shall inherit by way of *ta`ṣīb* if there is a full brother according to the rule 2X = Y. If she is competing with one or more daughters of the deceased, then (4) she shall share the remainder with them if there were other true heirs. If the true heirs inherit the entire estate; then the sister is barred (*ḥajb*). (5) One of two sisters is also barred by the presence of a full brother, half brother, son of the son of the deceased, or a father.[19]

In general, and according to Islamic exegetes and jurists, the children inherit according to three distinct instances depending on their gender. They are either males (one or more), females (one or more), or males and females (two or more). If the heirs are a son and two daughters, the son will inherit a share equal to that of two daughters per Qur'ānic decree ([Q4:V11]). However, if the heirs are one daughter and one son, then the daughter shall receive one share (1/3) and the son receives two shares (2/3) according to Muslim exegetes.[20] It must be noted that this conclusion is not explicitly stated in the verses on inheritance. Similarly, if the children are a number of daughters and sons, each son shall inherit two shares while each daughter shall inherit one share. For example, if a deceased is survived by four sons and five daughters, the estate is divided into thirteen portions and distributed among them whereby each son receives two shares (for a total of eight shares going to the sons) and each daughter receives one share (for a total of five shares going to all the daughters). If the deceased is survived by sons and daughters as well as other heirs (parents and spouse[s]), the other heirs receive their predetermined shares first then the rest is divided among the children according to the rule 2X = Y.

It may be the case that the deceased is survived by a daughter (or daughters) and no sons. According to Islamic exegetes, one daughter inherits one half and more than two daughters receive two-thirds, but scholars admit that the Qur'ān is not explicit about the inheritance of exactly two daughters.[21] The case of two daughters is a highly contested case and understanding it might provide us with the key to rethinking the logic of classical Islamic law in the area of women's rights to inheritance. The majority of Sunni jurists appropriated Ibn `Abbās's position, which gave two-thirds to two daughters although the grammatical structure of verse [Q4:V11] explicitly states that the two-thirds are given to *more than* two daughters.[22]

Given that the Qur'ān is not explicit concerning the inheritance of two daughters, one must be curious as to the basis for the consensus reached by the majority of Muslim scholars. Those who hold that the inheritance of two daughters is two-thirds rely on an argument that establishes a link between the opening words of verse [Q4:V11] and the unstated share of two daughters. It is reported that Abū Muslim al-Iṣfahānī had argued that scholars know that the share of two daughters is two-thirds because it is explicitly stated that "for the male, a share equal to that of two females." In other words, if a deceased is survived by *one* male and *one* female, the son's inheritance will be two-thirds (per rule 2X = Y):

According to the Qur'ān the share of the son is equal to the share of two females. That means that if the deceased leaves behind two daughters (1D + 1D) and one son (1S), the estate is divided into four portions. Then, one portion is given to the first daughter, another to the second daughter. The remainder—which is two portions—is given to the son. If that is the case, it follows then that if a deceased is survived by one daughter (1D) and one son (1S), the estate will be divided into three portions. One portion of the three portions (1/3) is given to the daughter, the remainder—which is two portions out of three (2/3)—is given to the son. By applying the mathematical property known as "reflexivity," al-Iṣfahānī then concludes that the share of two daughters is two-thirds. In other words, if the share of one son is equal to the share of two daughters, it follows that the share of two daughters is equal to two-thirds (which is the share of one son if one daughter was competing with him for the estate).

There are numerous problems with this logic although the mathematical analysis is sound. One of these problems is that the exegetes who hold this view assumed that the rule is applicable in all cases. But the Qur'ān is explicit in stating that one daughter inherits one half and did not restrict that by the presence of a son (brother to her)—at least not explicitly. Muslim exegetes and jurists insist that it is a rule, yet at the same time when they tried to justify the ruling that awarded one son the entire estate, they argued from a linguistic approach that considered the word *awlād* to refer to mixed children (sons and daughters). If that is the case, then it would make sense to assume also that the passage "if she were one [daughter], then she shall inherit one-half" also refers to a mixed pool of heirs that might include one or more sons. But that logic is rejected and Muslim scholars insist that one daughter inherits one-half only if she is the sole heir (she does not have one or more brothers).[23] Logically speaking, if the Qur'ān is in fact speaking of the inheritance of one daughter in the absence of all other heirs (such as brothers and parents), one would question the rationale of restricting her inheritance or even taking the time to determine her share if there are no other heirs to complicate the division of the estate. It would make more sense that the Qur'ān was actually determining the inheritance of one daughter in the presence of other heirs such as her brother, a parent, and uncles who might otherwise take all or most of the legacy as was the practice during the pre-Islamic era.

Aware of the importance of inequality and the diminished share of females, Muslim scholars played the devil's advocate and tried to contest the sense of justice and fairness of the verses of the Qur'ān that they understood to award females fewer shares than males. It was specifically mentioned that, given that women are weaker and less capable than men in general, it would make sense to award the weaker party more not less. With that said, they asked, why "did God make her share half of that of the man?"[24]

Exegetes provided a number of justifications for this perceived inequality. First, they said that women did not have to fight in wars or work outside to provide for the family. Men did: They fought more and worked more and he who works more and spends more (on the family) is in greater need for more; hence, the larger share in terms of inheritance. Secondly, they argue, men are more complete and more qualified to hold religious and political positions. Additionally, the testimony of one woman is half that of one man. Therefore, he who possesses such traits is deserving of more awards. Furthermore, it was reported that when Ja`far al-Ṣādiq was asked about the reason for the male inheriting twice the share of the female he answered as follows:

> It is reported that Eve took one handful of food and ate it. Then she took a second handful of food and stored it for herself. Lastly, she gave one handful to Adam. Since she took two shares for herself and gave only one to Adam, God [later] reversed that and gave a man a share twice the size of that of a woman.[25]

From the writings of these exegetes, there are no Prophetic reports that explained the inequity in awarding inheritance and, for that reason, they relied on reason and specifically on deductive reasoning in order to justify their understanding of the verses dealing with inheritance. But it is clear that there are grammatical and syntactical issues that needed to be bent in order to bring them in conformity with what emerged as the standard of assigning shares. For example, in order to make the segment of verse [Q4:V11] sound as a rule rather than a specific case, an exegete added to his commentary the preposition and pronoun suffix "*minhum*" (from them children) to "*li-dhakarin* [*minhum*] *mithlu ḥaẓẓi al-unthayayn.*"[26] Shawkānī also saw the need for the compound (*minhum*) but admits that the Qur'ān does not state the share for two daughters.[27]

Another part of the verses on inheritance that is contested on grammatical and syntactical grounds is the one where it is said: If she is (*kānat*) one [daughter], then she receives one-half. If they [feminine pronoun] are (*kunna*) women more than two, they receive two-thirds. Normally the verb "to be" (*kāna*) when used in a nominative sentence will conjugate reflecting the subject of such a sentence and not necessarily the predicate of the sentence. If that part of the verse was addressing the inheritance of the male and female children (as stated in the opening of the verse), the proper pronoun to use is "they" masculine (*hum*). The verb *kāna* conjugated with *hum* will be *kānū*. By using *kunna* instead of *kānū*, it can be argued that the passage is talking about the case where the women inheriting with the son are now one and then more than two respectively and not necessarily just one or more than two inheriting on their own in the absence of any sons. This understanding would then remove the discrepancies associated with the absence of any reference to the two daughters. In other words, the verse could be interpreted in the light of this understanding as follows: God advises you in regard to the inheritance of your children (males and females): One son shall receive a share equal to that of two daughters. If there is one son and only one daughter, then she shall receive one-half. If there is one son and more than two daughters, then the daughters shall share two-thirds. The absence of this understanding despite it being based on sound grammatical or logical reasoning underscores the need to further examine the legal rulings on inheritance. It also invites fresh perspectives that will help us better understand the interpretive processes and appraise the claims of explicitness and implicitness of the legal proofs that are the basis of law and ethics.

Women, Justice, and Interpretation: The Principle of `Awl

Arguably, I have selected the cases of polygamy and inheritance laws to examine the concept of justice because they are present in both the Islamic and Qur'ānic discourses. When taken together, polygamy and inheritance rules provide a clearer picture of the interplay between legal proofs and actual practices. More importantly, inheritance laws are about assigning specific numbers (as shares) to specific persons (as heirs). Therefore, regardless of the clarity or ambiguity of the legal proofs, the outcome is expressed in very certain and specific figures in the form of fractions pegged to specific individuals. Given that the legal proofs and the legal rulings are both expressed in exact numbers (fractions) and named persons, the discrepancies between the numbers in the legal proofs and those in the corpus of law (legal rulings) provide us with a window into the mind of Muslim scholars: How do they understand justice? In the situation where conflict between rights of different individuals arises, whose rights are more important and what criterion is used to determine that?

The answers to these questions could be gleaned from the principle of *`awl* that emerged, according to the most reliable accounts, during the reign of the second Caliph `Umar. Since the Qur'ān does not provide an exhaustive list of all the circumstances of inheritance situations, it was clear to early Muslim scholars that the distribution of mandatory shares (*farā'iḍ*) falls under three possibilities: (a) balanced distribution (*farīḍah `ādilah*), (b) short distribution (*farīḍah nāqiṣah*), and (c) long distribution (*farīḍah `ā'ilah*). While the first refers to the situations where the number of heirs matches the number of mandated shares, short distribution refers to the situations where the number of heirs is lower than the number of shares, in which case the heirs will inherit their mandatory shares and the remainder by way of return (*radd*). Clearly these two situations do not present a challenge to jurists. It is the third situation, where the number of shares of the designated heirs is greater than the portions of the entire estate, that presents a problem for legal scholars and offers us a good case study to understand Muslims' conceptualization of justice and fairness. Inheritance cases falling under this situational category are generally resolved by the widely accepted principle of *`awl*. According to Muslim exegetes,[28] this principle was born out of the ruling of the second Caliph `Umar who was asked to distribute the inheritance of a woman who died and left behind a husband and two sisters. According to the explicit Qur'ānic determination of shares for these heirs, the husband is entitled to one-half of the estate of his wife (since she did not leave children) and the two sisters' share two-thirds of the estate. Faced with this predicament (1/2 and 2/3 overexhausting the legacy) the Caliph consulted the top leaders of the community at that time. It is reported that al-`Abbās Ibn Abī Ṭālib used an analogy to determine the proper inheritance wherein he asked the Caliph `Umar:

> What would you do if a man dies and leaves behind six dirhams but two men have debt claims against the deceased: three dirhams for one and four dirhams for the other? In this case wouldn't you divide the money into seven equal shares?

When `Umar replied to this hypothetical question that he would do so, al-Abbās then suggested that he does the same thing with the inheritance in this situation: Divide the estate into seven equal portions and then redistribute it whereby every one of the heirs inherits a lesser share than that which is mandated in the Qur'ān. Later scholars further justified this practice by arguing that since the heirs are equal in terms of entitlement to inheritance (cause to inherit), they should be equal in the effects resulting from the insufficient shares too. In other words, they did not see it as fair that one heir inherits his or her full share while the other inherits only part of the sanctioned share.

Ibn `Abbās disagreed with the principle of *`awl* but did not publicly express his dissent until `Umar passed away. When he was asked about his solution to the predicament faced by `Umar, he argued that a priority should be given to those made a priority by God and only those not a priority have their shares diminished for lack of funds. We don't know of a definitive answer regarding the list of heirs in order of priority because there are conflicting reports dealing with that part of his argument. In one, it is said that he argued that the husband, the wife, the mother, and the grandmother are the heirs for whom God gave priority. As to those with lower priority, he mentioned specifically the daughters, the daughters of the son, the full sisters, and the sisters from the father's side; all of whom happen to be women.

In another report, he argued that individuals with explicit Qur'ānic shares diminished to lower explicit Qur'ānic shares are heirs of high priority; whereas the heirs with explicit Qur'ānic shares diminished to nonexplicit Qur'ānic share are of low priority.

The principle of *`awl* is especially important because it potentially affects large numbers of cases. Generally, whenever a deceased is survived by a spouse, a parent (or parents), siblings, and children, it will be very likely that the same problem (long distribution) presents itself. For example, when the deceased is survived by a husband and two sisters, and since their Qur'ānic share is one-half and two-thirds (which exceeds the estate), the entire estate will be portioned into seven portions instead of six and redistributed and the husband now receives three portions while the sisters receive four portions. Similarly, if the deceased is survived by a husband, two sisters, and the mother, not all the heirs can be awarded the Qur'ānic shares. Therefore, the estate will be divided into eight portions and redistributed: three portions (instead of one-half), four potions (instead of the two-thirds), and one portion (instead of the one-sixth), respectively. Each portion in this case is equal to one-eighth.

From the principle of *`awl* and the cases associated with it, I highlight the following:

(1) The early generation of scholars and religious leaders (and certainly the Caliph `Umar) understood inheritance rights as entitlements and, as such, they sought to solve every problem "fairly" and "reasonably."
(2) The large number of problematic cases that required the application of the principle of *`awl* is evidence that the Qur'ānic verses dealing with inheritance were not systematic.
(3) Early Muslim scholars like Ibn `Abbās and his followers considered explicit legal proofs to be inviolable rights and on that basis they allowed the rights of those for whom there is no explicit Qur'ānic share to be "diminishable."
(4) Early Muslim scholars (such as `Umar) attempted to determine inheritance rights based on the explicit Qur'ānic legal proofs and the principles of justice

and fairness. Some saw justice preserved by adhering to the letter of the legal proofs, others (`Umar) saw it fit to adjust the letter of the law to conform to the demands of fairness and justice. It must be noted that when the principle of *`awl* is applied in any given case, none of the heirs receives his or her Qur'ānic predetermined share. When seen from the point of view of modern-day Muslims, that undertaking ought to be radical to say the least. As noted in another study,[29] the Sunnah of the Prophet Muhammad played a minor role in canonizing the laws of inheritance. It is likely that since the verses on inheritance were revealed late in his lifetime, the Prophet did not provide a comprehensive determination of the law.

With the above observation in mind, I will proceed to present some of the contested cases of inheritance and it is hoped that the above information will be useful and helpful in understanding the origins and causes of divergence. The above survey of the explanations of the verses dealing with inheritance shows the theoretical framing of inheritance claims. During the time period known as the High Caliphate (*al-khilāfah al-rāshidah*), the community leaders and their advisors applied their sense of justice and fairness in order to determine the inheritance of individuals in the light of the revelation. When cases of inheritance challenged the limited number of Qur'ānic legal proofs and the scarce guidance of the Prophetic traditions, this early generation of leaders relied on custom and cultural practices in order to solve complex cases. After the death of the Prophet, and once the civil unrest that followed his passing away was controlled, the Muslim community experienced an unprecedented period of prosperity and stability. According to historical reports, the Caliph `Umar had to create the institution of the "treasury" (*bayt al-māl*) in order to store and manage the increased state revenues. Before that, it is reported that all revenues were spent, paid, or distributed the same day they reached the Caliph. Subsequently, prosperity and stability was also marked by an increase in personal wealth and larger and healthier families whose members are now living longer and spending more. During a time like this, it is normal to find a deceased survived not only by his children, but also by spouse (or spouses), parents, and even grandparents, all of whom will be competing to inherit one person; hence, the marked complexity of inheritance cases.

Given that the legal rulings were more or less compromises established on an ad hoc basis, the corpus of such rulings consisted of heterogeneous precedents many of which exhibited antagonistic reasoning. Despite this lack of uniformity, the rulings of this generation of leaders, once implemented, were construed by later scholars as legal precedents emanating from the consensus of the Companions. In classical Islamic jurisprudence, such a consensus cannot be overturned by later consensus. Coupled with the splintering of the Muslim community into schools of thought and jurisprudence, the final corpus of laws governing inheritance and bequests consists of a mixture of theory-based rulings and consensus-based ones. For this reason, a comparative survey of Muslims' laws of inheritance will reveal a great deal of conflicting opinions, rationale, and legal determinations. The next section considers some cases in a comparative context and tests the limits of explicitness in pegging each legal ruling to the proper legal proof. This approach is essential since it is the claim of Muslim scholars that a law based on the explicit enunciations of the Qur'ān cannot be reformed or ignored. To that end, one must ask the question, How many of the legal rulings actually result from a direct reading of the legal proofs and how many are merely the preservation of men's opinions?

Explicitness, Consensus, and Interpretation

The determination of the shares to be assigned to the legal heirs is said to have been derived from the primary sources. In fact, it is said that Islamic laws of inheritance cannot be changed (to appease Western critics) because that will be a violation of explicit Qur'ānic enunciations.[30] In other words, the determination of such shares is not a subject of interpretation. If this is the case, one must wonder as to the cause of widely divergent opinions of Muslim jurists. In that, Muslim scholars had assigned different shares to the same heirs especially when we consider the rulings by jurists from the Shi`ite schools of law and contrast them to those of the Sunni scholars. If everyone's ruling is derived from the Qur'ān and if the legal proofs are explicit and present in the Qur'ān, then on what authority did each of these scholars rely for deriving the law? Stated differently, if the Qur'ānic enunciations are explicit, one would expect all jurists from all legitimate schools of thought to reach a consensus. It follows then that the lack of consensus in fact signals a lack of explicitness.

In order to put things in context, I will examine some specific examples. The cases selected here are meant to highlight the difference of opinion among Sunni and Shi`ite scholars and provide us with a reference point to start the investigation into the question of explicitness and interpretation.

Shares and Heirs in the Comparative Context

The following cases are examples of the sharp differences between these jurists suggesting the uncertainty and lack of consensus among Muslim scholars on the meaning and interpretation of inheritance verses.[31] With that in mind, the cases below (compiled by the late M. J. Maghniyyah; see his *al-Fiqh `alā al-madhāhib al-khamsah*) will highlight the inconsistencies which suggest that oral tradition and not systematic understanding (or even Qur'ānic enunciations) must have played a major role in assigning meaning and confining the scope of the Qur'ānic verses on inheritance.

Case 1: A deceased survived by a daughter and a brother on the two parents' side or the father's side

According to Sunni legal scholars, the estate is to be divided as follows:

Daughter	Brother
1/2	1/2

Imāmī Shi`ites disagree and award the entire estate to the daughter and none to the brother.

Case 2: A deceased survived by a daughter and a mother

Sunnis:

Mother	Daughter
1/6	3/6

The grandfather from the father's side shall take the remainder if he is alive; otherwise, it shall go to the brothers from the two parents' side. If they are not alive, then the brothers on the father's side shall inherit the rest.

Imāmī Shi`ites say:

Mother	Daughter
1/4	3/4

Agnates take nothing.

Case 3: A deceased survived by a father, a mother, and daughter's children:

Sunnis say:

Father	Mother in absence of a "barrer"	Daughter's children
2/3	1/3	0

Imāmī Shi`ites say:

Father	Mother in absence of a "barrer"	Daughter's children
1/3	1/6	1/2

Case 4: A deceased survived by the mother, father, and husband:

Sunnis say:

Father	Mother	Husband
1/3	1/6	1/2

Imāmī Shi`ites say:

Father	Mother	Husband
1/6	1/3	1/2

Case 5: A deceased survived by mother, father, and wife:

Sunnis say:

Father	Mother	Wife
1/2	1/4	1/4

Imāmī Shi`ites say:

Father	Mother	Wife
5/12	1/3	1/4

Case 6: A deceased survived by a father and a daughter:

Sunnis say:

Father	Daughter
1/2	1/2

Imāmī Shi`ites say:

Father	Daughter
1/4	3/4

Case 7: A deceased survived by a daughter and a grandfather on the father's side:

Sunnis say:

Grandfather	Daughter
1/2	1/2

Imāmī Shi`ites say:

Grandfather	Daughter
0	all

Case 8: A deceased survived by wife, mother, and a grandfather on the father's side:

Sunnis say:

Wife	Mother	Grandfather
1/4	1/3	5/12

Imāmī Shi`ites say:

Wife	Mother	Grandfather
1/4	3/4	0

Case 9: A deceased survived by daughter and son's daughter:

Sunnis say:

Daughter	Son's daughter
1/2	1/6

The rest goes to the residuary

Imāmī Shi`ites say:

Daughter	Son's daughter
all	0

Case 10: A deceased survived by two daughters, son's daughters, and son's son:

Sunnis say:

Daughters	Son's daughters and son's son
2/3	They share 1/3 (2X = Y)

Imāmī Shi`ites say:

Daughters	Son's daughters and son's son
All	0

Case 11: A deceased survived by daughter and a full or agnate sister:

Sunnis say:

Daughter	Sister
1/2	1/2

Imāmī Shi`ites say:

Daughter	Sister
All	0

Case 12: A deceased survived by a daughter and uterine brother:

Sunnis say:

Daughter	Brother
1/2	0

And 1/2 (the remainder) goes to the residuary

Imāmī Shi`ites say:

Daughter	Brother
All	0

Case 13: A deceased survived by a daughter and a full or an agnate uncle:

Sunnis say:

Daughter	Uncle
1/2	1/2

Imāmī Shi`ites say:

Daughter	Uncle
All	0

Case 13: A deceased survived by a brother's son and a full or agnate brother's daughter:

Sunnis say:

Brother's son	Brother's daughter
All	0

Imāmī Shi`ites say:

Brother's son	Brother's daughter
2/3	1/3

According to Shi`ites, they will share the estate based on the rule 2X = Y.

The above cases and other data examined for this study shows a pattern whereby Sunni Muslim scholars assign, in most cases, the inheritance of women as determined in the Qur'ān. However, it is also clear that they understand those shares as the maximum a woman could inherit. For example, in the first case (above), according to Sunni jurists, the brother takes the second half of the estate. Shi`ites disagree and award the entire legacy to the daughter. For Shi`ites the inheritance of the daughter is a sensitive matter for theological and political reasons, Sunni scholars do not justify the increased share of the brother of the deceased (Case 1) although the Qur'ānic determination allows him to inherit only as *kalālah*, which is understood by exegetes and legal scholars to mean "without descending or ascending immediate relatives." That is, when the deceased is not survived by a child or a parent, then his estate will go to the nearest of kin thereafter; hence, the brother or brothers and sisters (as per [Q4:V12]).

Case 6 further shows that Sunni scholars understand women's inheritance, even if mentioned in the Qur'ān, as the minimum they could inherit. In this particular case, the daughter inherits her Qur'ānic share, but the remainder is awarded to the father although verse [Q4:11] explicitly states that the parents' (mother and father) inheritance is limited to one-sixth in the presence of a child. In fact that Qur'ānic passage specifically speaks of a deceased survived by one daughter and two parents. Therefore, the increase of the father's inheritance to one-half from one-sixth while that of the daughter remains one-half suggests that women's inheritance hardly increases above her Qur'ānic ordained share whereas that of men, even if their share is not mentioned at all, increase many-fold. Case 13 is another good example where the daughter, again, inherits only her Qur'ānic share and her uncle, who is not a Qur'ānic heir who competes with the children of the deceased, sees his inheritance increase from one-sixth to one-half. Similarly, in case 7, the grandfather who is not a Qur'ānic heir is also awarded one-half while the share of the daughter was left unchanged.

The above examples should not suggest to the readers that difference of opinion in assigning shares is present only when comparing the views of Sunni and Shi`ite scholars. In fact, in modern times, the difference is present even within Sunni communities. With that said, it must be noted that some of the reforms that took place in Sunni Islam were not recognized as legitimate interpretations of the legal proofs. Nonetheless, diversity of doctrine and the process of modern reform are noted by recent scholars. N. J. Coulson found that the share of a daughter in Pakistan, Egypt, Tunisia, and Iran is one-third, one-half, three-fourths, and the entire estate respectively when she is competing with a granddaughter and a brother. Furthermore, only Egyptian law allows the brother to inherit one-third while he is barred in Pakistan, Tunisia, and Iran.[32]

In order to have a sense of the logic employed by Sunni scholars even in modern times, I have examined a recent document that was meant to direct the Egyptian courts to distribute inheritance according to Islamic law (see table 4.1). The document detailing the distribution of inheritance was first published by *majma` al-buḥūth al-islāmiyyah* (11/08/1969) and authorized and distributed by Lajnat al-Fatw of al-Azhar (01/14/1970). This document was also used to develop Egypt's inheritance law (statute 77 of the year 1943). The law is mostly derived from Ḥanafī jurisprudence.

In this and other documents, women are shown as a separate class of inheritors when compared to men. For instance, in the majority of cases, when men compete only against the Islamic State for the estate of the deceased, the State (*al-ḥukūmah al-islāmiyyah*) will be barred (*ḥajb*). Women, and under the same conditions, do not exclude or bar the State; rather, they inherit only their stated share that is explicitly mentioned in the Qur'ān; the remainder goes to the State. This peculiar arrangement has no basis in classical Islamic law. What I will show in this chapter is that women's shares, despite the fact that it is explicitly predetermined in the Qur'ān are treated as variables whereas the shares of men are fixed despite the fact that they are either implied or undetermined. It seems that the basis for this practice is not the Qur'ān but rather the practice of the early Companions and especially the determinations of shares as established by the *shaykhayn* (the first two Caliphs Abū Bakr and `Umar).

Admittedly, not all possible cases of inheritance are treated in the Qur'ān. Nonetheless, some Muslim scholars argue that all primary heirs are mentioned and those whose inheritance is not explicitly mentioned could have their shares

TABLE 4.1: EXAMPLES OF MODERN ISLAMIC LAWS OF INHERITANCE

Category	Heirs	Shares
Children	Sons	All
	The Islamic State	None (barred)
	One daughter	1/2
	The Islamic State	The remainder
	Two or more daughters	2/3
	The Islamic State	The remainder
Parents	Father	All
	The Islamic State	None (barred)
	Mother	1/3
	The Islamic State	The remainder
Spouses	Husband	1/2
	The Islamic State	The remainder
	Wife	1/4
	The Islamic State	The remainder
Siblings	Sister	1/2
	The Islamic State	The remainder
	Brother	All
	The Islamic State	None (barred)

determined by linking them to the "cause of inheritance." For example, although the inheritance of the grandson (son of the son) is not explicitly mentioned, his share is that of his father (in his absence) because he does not inherit directly but through his father. This view was shown to be inaccurate when we listed the Qur'ānic individual and classes of heirs. Even within classical Sunni Islamic jurisprudence, inheritance laws are far from being systematic. An aggregate summary of heirs and their shares as seen by the majority of modern Sunni scholars is provided in table 4.2. This summary will then be compared to data generated by way of blind survey that asked individual interpreters to determine the shares of each heir or class of heirs based only on their understanding of the text of the Qur'ān (various English translations and Arabic).

TABLE 4.2: THE HEIRS AND THEIR SHARES ACCORDING TO SUNNI ISLAMIC LAW

	Inheritor	Shares	Return (radd)
1	1 Son	All	
2	2 Sons	All	
3	> 2 Sons	All	
4	1 Daughter	1/2	1/2
5	2 Daughters	2/3	1/3
6	>2 Daughters	2/3	1/3
7	Father	All	
8	Father +	1/6	1/2
	Son	1/6	The rest
9	Father +	All	0
	Brothers	0	5/6
10	Mother	1/2	1/2
11	Mother +	1/6	0
	Daughters	2/3	Y
12	Mother +	1/6	0
	Brothers	0	5/6
13	Husband	1/2 (only)	No *radd*
14	Husband +	1/4	0
	Children	0	1/4
15	Wife	1/4 (only)	0 (No *radd*)
16	Wife +	1/8	0
	Children	0	7/8
17	1 Brother and/or 1 Sister	1/2	1/2
18	>1 Brother and/or >1 Sister	2X = Y	0
19	1 Sister	1/2	1/2
20	1 Brother	All	
21	2 Sisters	1/2	1/2
22	2 Brothers	NM	
23	>2 Brothers + Sisters	All	0

Shares and Heirs per Blind Survey

Description of Data Collection

The main data for this part of this study was compiled by providing participants in a study of the text with passages from the so-called legal proofs. The data were collected in different places and during a time period that extended from 1998 until 2006. The participants were of different national, cultural, and religious backgrounds. At the time of this writing, 908 people had participated in the study (270 Arabic speakers and 638 English speakers), among them students, friends, colleagues, and members of Muslim communities from the United States, Tunisia, Morocco, and the UAE. The English speakers were given four different translations of all the original Arabic verses dealing with inheritance. The Arabic text was given to bilingual or Arabic speakers. The participants were randomly selected from people of different ethnic, religious, and educational backgrounds. Fifty-eight percent of the participants were males. The analysis of the data however did not suggest any trends where one's ethnic, religious, or national background played a major role. Also, the level of proficiency in English (granted that all participants were fluent in English) did not appear to show any correlation. The only observed trend was along the gender lines on which I will comment in the section dealing with that topic.

The primary data consists of entries for the participants (Interpreters), their gender, the translation that each of the participants used, his or her native language, heirs (or inheritors), and the shares for each of the heirs. The participants where not asked to determine the shares for all possible inheritors. Instead, they were given a list of twenty-three individuals or groups of heirs and they were asked to assign them shares based only on the translation they were given and without looking at other sources or relying on other information they might already have. The list of heirs[33] consisted of: one son, two sons, more than two sons, one daughter, two daughters, more than two daughters, father, father and children, father and brothers, mother, mother and children, mother and brothers, husband, husband and children, wife, wife and children, one brother and/or one sister, more than one brother and/or one sister, one brother, one sister, two brothers, two sisters, and more than two brothers and sisters mixed. The original database included every answer provided by each and every participant. However, only the shares that were the subject of the greatest consensus were included in Table 4.3 (below) to save space and simplify the presentation. However, all the information was used and analyzed in order to examine the data for various trends, correlations, and specificities.

To understand the symbols appearing in the table, the following key and explanations will be helpful. The letters *NS* are used to denote "not specific." That is, if an heir does not have a share explicitly mentioned in the Qur'ān or his share is only "implied" (*IM*), the participants do not indicate the implied or "concluded" share. They were asked to indicate *IM* (for implied) or *NM* (for "not mentioned") instead. For analysis purposes, and only in some instances, I have sometimes collapsed the two categories into one *NS*. In other instances, and whenever it was significant, I have kept those categories (*NM* and *IM*) separate.

In some cases, if the participant thought that a pair of heirs receives their inheritance based on the rule 2X = Y, the combined share for such pairs was indicated by *O*. The rule 2X = Y refers to the cases where the heritage is to be distributed among males and females on the basis of the share of one male being equal to that of two females. For example, if a deceased leaves behind four daughters and two sons, that rule would mean that half the inheritance will be given to the four daughters and the other half will be given to the two sons. This particular case will be discussed in detail given the new findings of this study.

As to the texts of the Qur'ān that were used in this survey, participants relied on four different translations. Each interpreter was given one or more (in controlled processes) of the translations by Yusuf Ali, M. Pickthal, Shakir, and the author as Translation 1, Translation 2, Translation 3, and Translation 4, respectively. Speakers of Arabic were given a copy of the original verses isolated from the rest of the text of the chapter. All the participants were given ample time to look and interpret the passages but they were instructed not to rely on other sources such as exegetical works or legal documents. In other words, they were asked to interpret the text as is without relying on any other source of information as much as practical. A synopsis of the results is provided in Table 4.3.

Explanation and Interpretation of Data

Participants in the survey were given all the verses dealing with inheritance. One-third of the participants were volunteers. Two-thirds of the participants were students. Nearly half of the students took the survey as an extracurricular activity, which did not affect their progress in the courses they were taking with me or with my colleagues throughout the years. The other half took the survey as a take-home quiz with the implication that if they did not perform satisfactorily they would not receive credit. When comparing the data from all these groups, however, there was no significant difference in their results. It seems that the volunteer participants who thought that the task was too demanding simply did not participate and those who participated invested the needed time to provide as careful an interpretation as possible. In general, the student participants seem to have considered their participation important regardless of whether or not they would receive credit. The nature of the survey and the data they were interpreting also seemed to have played a major role in successful return of the survey. Since the text was assigning shares to each heir, the task could have been considered by the participants as being specific. The end result is the collapsed data in Table 4.3.

The data in table 4.3 should underscore the gap between legal determinations based on interpretation and those based on tradition. When comparing the findings of the interpreters of the legal proofs to the corpus of Islamic law of inheritance, one should be able to see the difference between theory and practice in the religious discourse. I will go beyond the data in the table to highlight some specific cases and the interpretations associated with each.

The inheritance of the son that appears to be settled according to traditional and modern scholars is highly contested by the participants (Interpreters). While 56% of all interpreters (all translations and the Arabic included) found that his

TABLE 4.3: HEIRS AND THEIR SHARES BASED ON THE CONSENSUS OF THE INTERPRETERS

Interpreters of Legal Proofs					
CASE	TR 1	TR 2	TR 3	TR 4	ARABIC
1 SON	49% (NS)	57% (NS)	58% (NS)	57% (NS)	57% (NS)
2 SONS	94% (NS)	93% (NS)	92% (NS)	91% (NS)	100% (NS)
> 2 SONS	96% (NS)	94% (NS)	96% (NS)	92% (NS)	100% (NS)
1 DGHTR	97% (1/2)	95% (1/2)	98% (1/2)	97% (1/2)	100% (1/2)
2 DTRS	80% (2/3)	57% (NS)	64% (NS)	64% (NS)	86% (NM)
>2 DTERS	90% (2/3)	87% (2/3)	90% (2/3)	91% (2/3)	71% (2/3)
FATHER	73% (NS)	74% (NS)	81% (NS)	82% (NS)	86% (NS)
F+CH	85% (1/6)	78% (1/6)	85% (1/6)	87% (1/6)	100% (1/6)
F+BRS	89% (NS)	91% (NS)	94% (NS)	89% (NS)	72% (NM)
MOTHER	91% (1/3)	86% (1/3)	92% (1/3)	93% (1/3)	100% (1/3)
M+CH	90% (1/6)	85% (1/6)	89% (1/6)	90% (1/6)	100% (1/6)
M+BRS	91% (1/6)	80% (1/6)	93% (1/6)	94% (1/6)	100% (1/6)
HUSBAND	96% (1/2)	95% (1/2)	99% (1/2)	98% (1/2)	100% (1/2)
H+CH	96% (1/4)	93% (1/4)	97% (1/4)	98% (1/4)	100% (1/4)
WIFE	85% (1/4)	89% (1/4)	92% (1/4)	96% (1/4)	88% (1/4)
W+CH	85% (1/2)	89% (1/8)	93% (1/8)	95.5% (1/8)	87% (1/8)
1BR/1SIS	80% (1/6)	82% (1/6)	86% (1/6)	89% (1/6)	100% (1/6)
>1BR/1SIS	74.5% (1/3)	72% (1/3)	82% (1/3)	86% (1/3)	86% (1/3)
SISTER	88% (1/2)	89% (1/2)	87% (1/2)	90% (1/2)	100% (1/2)
BROTHER	69% (1)	41% (NS)	40% (1)	64% (1)	100% (1)
2SISTERS	87% (2/3)	85% (2/3)	89% (2/3)	88% (2/3)	89% (2/3)
2 BRS	81.5% (NS)	83% (NS)	86% (NS)	87% (NS)	100% (NM)
>2Bs+SRs	83% (NS)	64% (NS)	63% (NS)	66% (NS)	57% (O)
	84.9	84.7	84.6	86.3	90.4

Understanding Table 4.3: M + CH (mother and children): For example, 90% of the participants who used Translation 1 (TR 1) found that the inheritance of the *mother* when the deceased is survived by *children* is one-sixth. Similarly, M + BRS (mother and brothers) refers to the inheritance of the mother (one-sixth) when the deceased is survived by brothers. The only exception is for the BR/SIS (and >1BR/1SIS), which refers to any combination of one brother and one sister (or brothers and sisters) inheriting at the same time. For further explanations, see the section with the sub-heading *Description of Data Collection*.

share is not specific (NS), as many as 28% of the Interpreters awarded him the entire estate thinking that it was implied. When considering the inheritance of two or more sons, however, the interpreters easily established the consensus that their share is not specific (NS). In one translation, as many as 66% of the interpreters have found that their inheritance is not mentioned (NM) at all. Similarly, native speakers of the Arabic language were unanimous that the inheritance of two or more sons is not specifically mentioned in the Qur'ān and 71% have found it to be not mentioned altogether.

In contrast, over 97% of the interpreters found the inheritance of one daughter to be explicitly stated as one-half. Speakers of Arabic who examined the Arabic text of the Qur'ān were unanimous that the daughter's share is one-half. A similar degree of consensus (91%) was reached regarding the inheritance of more than two daughters. The interpreters' consensus widely varied from one translation to another. For instance, 80% of those who examined Translation 1 determined the inheritance of two daughters to be two-thirds. Surprisingly, 57% of those who relied on Translation 2 thought that the inheritance of two daughters is not specific and only 32% of them thought it was two-thirds. Interpreters of Translation 3 were even more divided over the inheritance of two-daughters: 64% thought it to be not specific and among those 64%, 46% thought it to be not mentioned. Only 25% thought it to be two-thirds. Of those who examined the Arabic text, 86% thought that it is not mentioned.

Similar numbers are found when considering the inheritance of siblings. When collapsing the data of all four translations as well as the Arabic, it was found that 91% of all interpreters thought the inheritance of one sister to the deceased to be one-half. That same case is underscored by the unanimous finding of the readers of the Arabic Qur'ānic text, who also found it to be one-half. The inheritance of one brother on the other hand was unanimously found to be the entire estate only by those who relied on the Arabic text. Those who relied on the translations provided varied findings: while 69% of the interpreters who examined Translation 1 determined that one brother's share to be the entire estate, only 31% of the interpreters of Translation 2 agreed with them. On the other hand, almost the same number of interpreters of Translation 2 and Translation 3 thought the inheritance of one brother to be not specific: 41% and 36% respectively. Of those who interpreted Translation 4, 64% thought it to be the entire estate.

When determining the inheritance of two sisters and two brothers, exactly the same number of interpreters (87.6%) found the inheritance of two sisters to be two-thirds while that of two brothers is not specific.

Interpreters agreed that the shares of females are explicitly mentioned while only a few male heirs have their shares specifically and explicitly stated in the Qur'ān. In general, the shares of daughters and sisters are hardly contested and they are stated in the form of a fraction. The interpreters of all the translations as well as the interpreters of the Arabic text reached a substantial agreement (higher than 84%) in determining the inheritance of the sons and the brothers to be not specific. The only exception to this trend is the inheritance of the husband, which is as specific as that of the wife. When considering all the interpretations and all the translations and all possible cases and collapsing the data and then comparing it on the basis of the gender of the heirs only, it was found that 3437 cases of males' inheritance were not specific whereas only 629 cases involving females were so. In other words, the Qur'ānic text consistently and explicitly determined the inheritance of females in the form of ratios and fractions but left the inheritance of males either unstated or implied.

When the data for all 23 cases are collapsed, the respondents consistently were unsure about the exact shares of males than about the shares of females. Table 4.2 shows the data for the children (one daughter, two daughters, and more than two daughters; one son, two sons, and more than two sons), parents (father, father in the presence of children of the deceased, and father in the presence of the brothers of the deceased; mother, mother in the presence of children, and mother in the presence of brothers), spouses (husband and husband and children; wife, and wife and children), and siblings (one sister and two sisters; one brother and two brothers). When combined, there were 3437 cases involving males for which the interpreters (respondents) found no specific share either because it was not explicitly mentioned or because it was implied. In contrast, only 629 cases involving females were found to be nonspecific by the same interpreters.

The gap between the nonspecificity for cases related to children and parents is unmistakably clear: 1549 for sons and only 378 for daughters. The gap remains obvious for parents as well: 1146 for father and 115 for mother. However, although the nonspecificity declines sharply when considering the spouses, it is only in this specific case that the males have a smaller number of nonspecific cases than females; albeit too small to cancel out the difference in the other cases. For spouses, interpreters found 19 cases where the shares of the husband were not specified or implied compared to 73 for the wife. Table 4.4 and Figure 4.1 are intended to make this point clearer.

TABLE 4.4: A COMBINATION OF NONSPECIFIC SHARES FOR MALES VS. FEMALES

Males	3437
Females	629

FIGURE 4.2: VISUALIZING NONSPECIFIC SHARES FOR MALES VS. FEMALES

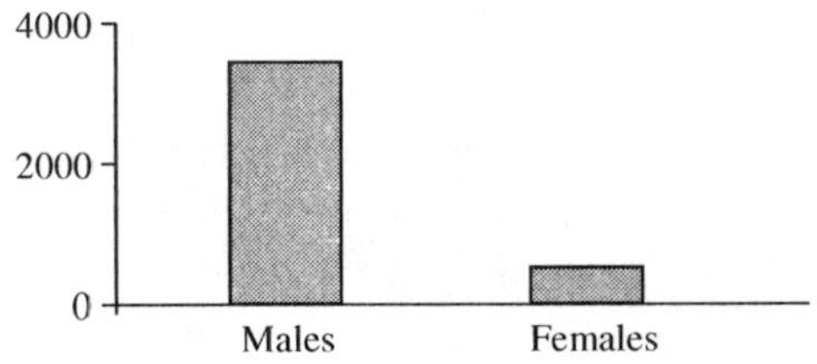

What the data shows is radically different from what is practiced in the Muslim communities and for that reason we were concerned that there might be a "sympathy" inclination by female interpreters that cause the data to be skewed in favor of females. In order to prove or disapprove such a possibility, we have analyzed the data along the gender lines in order to see if there are patterns that might help prove or disprove the theory. Table 4.4 summarizes the findings of this analysis. Each table represents the findings of all female interpreters contrasted to those of male interpreters for specific cases of male and female heirs. The comparison reveals a difference that is dubbed "consistency rate," which shows that female interpreters followed the survey instructions and interpreted the data with consistency. The result, the readers will see, is not indicative of a gender bias, but more of a gender trait where women seem to be more detail oriented than men. In other words, it seems that women consistently follow the instruction closely but most men may rush to conclusions without maximum efforts into understanding the instructions first before solving the problems. Whether that trait is biological or cultural is beyond the scope of this study.

When I compared the texts of the primary source of Islamic law (the Qur'ān) and the legal rulings (*aḥkām*) concerning women's inheritance, and when I noticed that many Shi`ite legal rulings radically differed from those issued by Sunni scholars, I assumed that these laws were the subject of scholars' interpretations. Since the overwhelming majority of these scholars were men, my initial working theory contended that, had an equal number of Muslim women participated in the deriving of laws, such laws would have been balanced. I assumed that if women were allowed to participate in the interpretive process, their voice would be more sympathetic to females or at least their perspective would produce legal determinations that are in favor of females. Similarly, even if we were to assume that men's interpretation was not skewed toward their interests, it is possible still that men's views are dismissive of women's claims to inheritance. With these suppositions in mind, this study tested them by analyzing the results of the survey, especially the cases where male and female heirs are concerned. The results of the analysis of the data are summarized in tables 4.5 and 4.6.

The comparison of the aggregate data as well as the comparison of one hundred male and one hundred female interpreters at a time (ten times, randomly selected each time) did not show that men are biased against women or interpret texts in their favor nor did it show that women are biased against men or interpret the texts in their favor. These results were statistically consistent among all the various categories represented in the pool of participants (Muslims, nonMuslims, students, Arabic speakers, English speakers, Muslims in America, and Muslims where they are majority [in Tunisia and Morocco]).

Incidentally, however, it is evident that women were consistently specific in their interpretation of the texts: If they did not see a specific share that could be awarded to the heir, regardless of the gender of the heir, women were more

TABLE 4.5: SEARCHING FOR GENDER BIAS IN INTERPRETATION: MALE HEIRS

a. One son

	IM/NM	2X = Y
Females	56%	0.40%
Males	53%	5%

The Consistency Rate: 3% more women see NM/IM than men, but no significant gender bias is noticed.

b. Two sons

	IM/NM	2X = Y
Females	95%	0%
Males	89%	0%

The Consistency Rate: 6% more women see NM/IM than men, but no significant gender bias is noticed.

c. More than 2 sons

	IM/NM	2X = Y
Females	95%	0%
Males	93%	0%

The Consistency Rate: 2% more women see NM/IM than men, but no significant gender bias is noticed.

TABLE 4.6: SEARCHING FOR GENDER BIAS IN INTERPRETATION: FEMALE HEIRS

a. One daughter:

	IM/NM	2X = Y
Females	3%	0%
Males	2%	0%

The Consistency Rate: 1% more women see NM/IM than men, but no significant gender bias is noticed.

b. Two daughters

	IM/NM	2X = Y
Females	50%	0%
Males	49%	0%

The Consistency Rate: 1% more women see NM/IM than men, but no significant gender bias is noticed.

c. More than two daughters

	IM/NM	2X = Y
Females	9%	0%
Males	8%	0%

The Consistency Rate: 1% more women see NM/IM than men, but no significant gender bias is noticed.

inclined than men to categorize the legal proofs as it did not mention the specific share to the specific heir or that the share was implied rather than explicit. However, from the representative data above and from other extensive analysis, it was not evident at all that the gender of the interpreter predetermined or influenced the way they understood the legal proofs or the law for that matter.

One other important outcome of this study, and more specifically from the data associated with the survey, is the degree of deviation that results from interpretation. The analysis of all the data that we collected shows that there is a margin of deviation in interpretation that is directly proportional to the level of explicitness of the text being interpreted. Even the most explicit text was shown to carry with it an average of 14% deviation. In other words, it can be said that only 86% of interpreters of the original Qur'ānic text are likely to agree on the meaning of verses such as those dealing with inheritance. This deviation was not only present in the data collected from the participants who interpreted our data for the purpose of this survey, but it is also evident from the comparison of the four translations: In nearly every case, one of the translators interpreted the original Arabic text in a way that was different from that of the other three translators. Similarly, for every one hundred interpreters of Translation 1, Translation 2, Translation 3, and Translation 4, there were fifteen, fifteen, sixteen, thirteen interpreters, respectively, who disagreed with them.

Assuming that this degree of deviation is accurate and holds across languages, it is likely then that interpretations that are based on second- or third-generation translations[34] may carry a degree of deviation as large as 28% and 42%, respectively; a significant margin that brings doubt to the process of relying on translated materials.

5

Women in Modern Times

Discussion

Linking Polygamy and Inheritance: Disadvantaging Women by the Numbers

In a spirited defense of the permissibility of polygamy, a Muslim scholar writes:

> One ought to not forget that acting justly before all wives also includes the laws of inheritance without exception. In that, the inheritance of wives is equal, the husband does not have the right to deny anyone of them because acting justly is mandated by God.... "Indeed God commands that you act righteously and that you give to the relatives; and He ordained that you avoid lewdness and wickedness. [*al-naḥl*: 90][1]

It is true that the wives equally share one-fourth or one-eighth (depending on whether or not the deceased is survived by a child). However, that is only relative justice. If we consider the rights of a wife in a monogamous marriage and compare her inheritance to that of a wife who is part of a polygamous arrangement, the difference is obvious. Specifically, and in the case where a childless husband dies and leaves behind a wife, she inherits one-fourth of what he leaves behind.[2] According to Muslim jurists, however, if the deceased leaves behind more than one wife, then they are partners in one-fourth. Similarly, if he is survived by a child, one (or more) wife shall receive (or share) one-eighth respectively.

By applying these rules of inheritance, it becomes clear that polygamy impacts women beyond the social roles that were seen as the justification of polygamy. Considering that Muslim scholars have already argued that the justice (*qisṭ*) of which God speaks in the passage related to polygamy concerns only material justice and fairness,[3] it becomes impossible to be fair to a woman by imposing on her a polygamous marriage, since doing so will diminish her inheritance by a factor equal to the number of wives to which her husband was married. For example, if a husband dies and leaves behind an estate worth $800,000 and no children, the wife's inheritance is $200,000. However, if her husband was married to three other wives besides her, she would only receive $50,000. Obviously, if the right to inheritance is a divine right as expressed in the Qur'ān, it can be argued that it is a natural right that cannot be violated, diminished, or delegated. However, clearly the husband's right to enter into a polygamous marriage directly affects the incidents of marriage and creates a conflict with the rights of the wife. The wife then, by virtue of her entitlement to the incidents of marriage, must be consulted and her consent must be sought as a matter of law. That is not the case in practice or in law according to scholars in some schools of thought.

The segment of verse [Q4:12] that sanctions the terms of inheritance for the spouses uses the same verb forms and the same noun structure (plural) when addressing both men and women. The husband has been favored to inherit one-half or one-fourth of his wife's estate depending on whether or not she has children. The wife, on the other hand, is said to inherit one-fourth or one-eighth under the same conditions. However, when the possibility of a polygamous marriage is taken into consideration, women's shares would diminish even further, fourfold, although the Qur'ānic language does not suggest that, either by explicit statements or by distinguishing the language referring to husbands and wives. Therefore, the fear of failing to establish justice (*qisṭ*) in the context of polygamous marriage is not imagined or hypothetical; rather, it is real and necessary.[4]

Discussing the Status of Women

Although this work focused primarily on two cases (polygamy and inheritance), one should not expect that by solving these two cases the status of women will improve. To the contrary, the path to full inclusion of women in society is a long one; this applies not only to the Muslim community but also to the Western world.[5] Many Western countries are yet to elect their first female head of state, and in many other areas of life women are still underrepresented despite the fact that they form more than half the population. This only points to the pervasiveness of the problem of social justice as a universal challenge. In most world communities, women are either active or passive participants in preserving a social order that has disadvantaged them. As the literature dealing with the topic of the status of women suggests, even when the laws governing the above two cases are reformed or abrogated, women still face other challenges, most of which resulted from the top-down legal reforms imposed mechanically. Thereafter, the culture of oppression and discrimination against women and minorities persists. For this reason, I will expand the discussion to cover related topics that show the way women have been used to preserve an elitist worldview whose main concern is to uphold the interest of the privileged class.

In a previous work and subsequent lectures, I argued that polygyny ought to be proscribed. Since then, I have unearthed additional sources, read more materials, conducted more research, and talked to more people. I no longer feel that criminalizing a practice such as polygamy would necessarily promote human rights and preserve human dignity. To me, human dignity is nonnegotiable and, as such, it is worthy of our attention not *only* when the greatest number of people are affected by abuse and discrimination. True human rights norms are settled commitments in society and cultures to honor the dignity and life of every human being even if we disagree with him or her. As long as the actions of a person are not egregiously harmful and injurious to herself or to other members of the community, one must find ways to accommodate the actions of such an individual. Equally important to this recognition of individual rights, I am also cognizant of the danger of some taking advantage of legal allowances in order to maximize their interests and pleasure with full disregard to the impact of their actions on society at large. I remain convinced that polygamous marriages have been used in most cases to benefit men and rarely to the benefit of women. Rare as it may be, a few women might find the practice of benefit to them, and these few women ought not to be deprived of a venue that promotes their well-being as they (women) see it. In other words, since polygamous marriages negatively impact women (at least financially as I have shown above), the practice ought to be an option for women and not a "right" of men. I am also aware that my position requires a shift in cultural practice and a transformation in the language and meaning of marriage for it to materialize. For that same reason, I identify the nature of the problem as a question of meaning and societal structure. With that said, I believe that the conversation on women's rights in the area of polygamous marriages and inheritance laws will benefit most from allowing a variety of voices to speak out about these issues. In that regard, I hope that the presentation of perspectives of members of the modern Muslim community who hold conflicting views on the subject will accomplish such a goal.

Other Contested Perspectives

In the preceding four chapters, I have adopted normative, analytical, and quantitative approaches to examine the Islamic ethical, jurisprudential, and legal traditions in order to establish the background and the context of ordinances and practices that have impacted, negatively and positively, the well-being of Muslim women. However, the criticisms and reactions thereto must be understood in the global context: Women are human beings with inviolable rights to equality, dignity, and respect. The status of Muslim women becomes an appraisal of the status of women regardless of their ethnic or religious affiliation. In other words, we are looking above and beyond the specific identity markers in order to formulate the conditions that transcend religious and ethnic boundaries. Subsequently, Muslims' reactions tend to compare the condition of Muslim women to their counterparts in other societies and stress the specifics in order to deflect direct criticism. Similarly, outsiders point out the progression toward universal values that liberate and empower women regardless of their historical background. In this chapter, I will introduce some of the issues of contention. I will allow space for the various voices and points of view so that we understand the origins and scope of the claims and counterclaims.

The legal and economic status of Muslim women, like that of women in the West, has become a main theme in the feminist discourse. Generally speaking, women's political and ideological movements emphasize the overhaul of the institutional and intellectual framing of the debate. There are many eloquent and articulate arguments that have situated the fight for women's rights either within the cultural environment of each community or have sought to globalize it and disentangle it from the ideological and political standpoint that sees secularism and liberalism as prerequisites for true change in peoples' attitudes toward women and their issues. Some would argue that women's rights cannot be secured if such rights are sought under the premise of group rights. In fact it is said that "group rights are used to subordinate women."[6]

Some self-proclaimed feminists see their success in promoting women's rights to be contingent on framing the movement in the secular and liberal discourse. It is argued that only in the secular framework could Muslim women achieve their goals. Clearly, this is a direct response to some Muslim women who are working within the Islamic system to reform it. Many Muslims who are active in the struggle for equality and justice for women remain convinced that practiced inequality and discrimination are the result of passive participation by educated Muslim women in the various domains of education, politics, and scholarship. Those holding this view argue that it is more practical to work within the system and reform it than to adopt alien ideas and methodologies.

The view of Muslims working for the amelioration of the status of women from within the existing systems reflects the history and special circumstances that place women living in Muslim countries under totally different conditions. For instance, Western women will not find resistance to the call of liberalization and secularization of the society since it is from that secular heritage that Western communities in general and Western women in particular earned their rights after years of abuse and neglect. However, in the Muslim world, which fell under the direct control of the Western occupiers for nearly a century, it is understandable that one remains skeptical of the stated and unstated goals of the colonial powers. The memories of an occupation that was pretexted as an act of "civilizing and advancing" the backward communities but which brutalized and victimized the natives are still vivid in the memory of the generation that has lived that past as well as in that of the first generation of descendents. As a result, the mere use of the language of the West is a shameful reminder of occupation, subjugation, and exploitation.[7]

Even if a woman were to call for equal treatment based on the teachings of the Qur'ān, but relies on the language of Western feminism, her call would be immediately dismissed as an alien intrusion. Many Muslim peoples still feel that they are under proxy occupation. Arab and Muslim intellectuals still write about the cultural and ideological occupation and such a discourse resonates extremely well with the Arab and Muslim masses.[8]

On the other side of the equation, Western feminists charge Muslim women with undoing the achievements of the movement by succumbing to the demands of religious institutions and religious authorities. It was argued that, by accepting the framing of women's struggle within the Islamic discourse, Muslim women are legitimizing the limitations and restrictions imposed on them in the name of religion.[9] Doing so would also isolate Muslim women from their "sisters" around the world, thereby subjecting a global cause to cultural relativism and undue limitations.

It is undeniably the case that abuse of and discrimination against women all over the world is real. Cultural and societal norms should not be used to relativize abuse and subjugation of women and minority groups. Having said that, one ought to understand the context and history of women's struggles for equality: In the case of modern Western women, their achievements and successes is accredited to their deliberate choice to fight for rights and respect within the framework of the secular discourse. Their goal was not to reform the religious tradition to which they belonged; rather, it was to present their historical grievances in the name of common sense and civility that were preached since the Enlightenment. Religion and historical past were marginalized; the better days for Western women are here and now and possibly in the future, and there was no need to look back.

Muslim women, on the other hand, are part of a civilization whose peak and whose "Enlightenment" era is in the past; a past where religion is perceived to have played a major role in their liberation from society's negative restrictions.[10] For this and other reasons, many Muslim women do not feel the need to completely rescind the past and adopt Western values. Many Muslim women scholars today compare their status under Islamic law and practices to that of their counterparts under Judaic-Christian traditions and conclude that their situation is better than that of their counterparts'. However, they seem to be unaware that, today, Judaic-Christian traditions do not play as much of a *public* role in deciding for women as Islam does in Muslim communities. This point of view is reflected in the work and activism of the late Zainab al-Ghazali.

Zainab al-Ghazali, an Egyptian and the daughter of an Azhar-educated father, was an organizer of women and an activist. Early in her youth, she was an active member of the Egyptian Feminist Union, founded by Huda al-Sha'rawi in 1923. Al-Ghazali resigned her membership to protest the ideas and ideals of the women's liberation movement. At the age of eighteen, she founded the Muslim Women's Association. Her vision for Muslim feminism is summarized in an audio recording:

> Islam provided everything for both men and women. It has given women everything: freedom, economic rights, political rights, social rights, and public and private rights. Islam gave women's rights in the family granted by no other society. Women may talk of liberation in Christian society, Jewish society, or pagan society, but in Islamic society it is a grave error to speak of the liberation of women. The Muslim woman must study Islam so she will know that it is Islam that has given her all her rights.[11]

Al-Ghazali is an example of female elites who was instrumental in helping the male elite preserve polygyny and other legal rulings that are disadvantageous to women.[12] Her position on such issues cannot be distinguished from that of male scholars such as Yusuf al-Qardawi, who argues that marrying more than one wife is permitted in Islam, but it is not mandatory or desirable. In fact, he continues, polygamy is undesirable for any man who has a wife that satisfies him and who has no reason to take a second wife.[13] He contends that, short of necessity, taking a second wife amounts to placing oneself in harms way. In order to make his point clearer, he quotes a widely reported *ḥadīth*: "Whoever is married to two wives and he favors one over the other, he shall be resurrected with half his body crooked."[14] As it can be seen from the language of this opinion, polygamy is a man's right and the only thing that will prevent him from marrying a second, third, or fourth wife is the absence of a "reason." This view literally invalidates all the justifications that considered "surplus of women, women's need for male support, and the effects of war" as the primary grounds for the "legalization" of polygyny.

To be sure, Muslims' reaction to criticism focusing on polygamy combines half denials, casuistic justifications, and counteraccusations. For instance, some argue that polygamy rarely happens and it is never the rule; rather, it is the exception.[15] It is further contended that, even when it happens, it usually happens for valid reasons such as the first wife being sterile, has chronic illness, disability, disfiguration, or psychological and sexual abnormalities.[16] Additionally, it is suggested that men generally have stronger sexual drive than women and for that reason they need two, three, or four wives or else they may fall to the evil of illicit sexual acts. In fact, some of these scholars see Western immorality (sexual relations out of wedlock, fornication, adultery, etc.) as a direct result of their rejection of polygyny. From this perspective, the West stands charged with hypocrisy: Polygamy is criminalized; yet, too many men have more than one girlfriend, have lovers while they are married, and have numerous affairs.[17]

The above justifications of polygamy are contested by both academicians and practicing Muslims.[18] Most recently, Amina Wadud, a devout Muslim and scholar of Islamic studies, argued that the "three common justifications given for polygamy" are not sanctioned in the Qur'ān and that the conditions that allowed the practice then no longer apply today.[19] She stresses that the Qur'ānic verses dealing with polygamy are primarily concerned with justice and not with maintaining the status quo that benefited men:

> In fact, as far as they [proponents of polygamy] are concerned, the only measurement of justice between wives is material: Can a man equally support more than one wife? This is an extension of the archaic idea of marriages of subjugation, because fairness is not based on quality of time, equality in terms of affection, or on spiritual, moral, and intellectual support. These general terms of social justice are not considered with regard to just treatment of wives.[20]

Despite the affects of polygyny practices on women's inheritance rights, Wadud, like many other Muslim scholars, does not provide a detailed appraisal of the laws of inheritance other than to stress the fact that Islamic law (or the Qur'ān) does not allow females to be disinherited. She elaborates on the rule of 2X = Y saying that other parts of the verse show that the rule is limited to siblings and there are cases where a female inherits a share equal to that of a male (probably referring to the parents inheritance).[21] Muslims' reluctance to explore inheritance laws in a critical manner is typical and shows the degree of difficulty in challenging the legal proofs. Religious authorities often justify practices rather than critique them and, in that regard, Muslim scholars are not alone in arguing for the protection of institutions that discriminate against women in the name of the greater good for the greatest number of people. Here is a similar voice:

> Is it more Christian to have organized prostitution, marital infidelity with impunity, a rapidly growing divorce rate and increasing number of illegitimate children, than polygamy? Is it more Christian for young women to become prostitutes, call girls, or mistresses than to become the second or third wife of a respected member of the community?[22]

Although these justifications seem to be based on some sort of "science," most authors who adopted this defense fail to address the basic problems of double standard and contradiction: If the purpose of Islamic law (and the religious discourse in general to include other religious traditions) is to establish and preserve equality, equity, fairness, and justice, then why aren't women granted the same considerations? Is it not the case that women too can find themselves in relationships with impotent men, sterile husbands, disfigured persons, or psychologically or mentally abnormal individuals (not to mention abusive and violent men)? When one factors in the fact that in classical Islamic law, divorce is primarily in the hands of the husbands,[23] it becomes clear that women are legally and socially in a position of weakness.

I have established the complexity and the inherent injustice of polygynous marriages when inheritance laws are also as predetermined as they are in Islamic law. But that issue is ignored and Muslim scholars hardly link the two topics (polygyny and inheritance). That avoidance places the proponents of the traditional system at a comfortable position from where they can defend each separately. They justify polygyny on social grounds and they praise inheritance laws as a system that guarantees women's rights to own property. Since the traditional view appears to offer a male a smaller share than that of a female of the same degree of affinity to the deceased, proponents of the system, as is, rely on peculiar logic to justify the established rules:

> What women sometimes lose [due to the unequal distribution] of inheritance will be more than replaced by the system of dower. For example, let's suppose that a man dies and he is survived by a son and daughter. The daughter will receive (50) and the son will receive (100). After that, the daughter will receive (25) or more from another man when she gets married and the son will pay (25) to another woman when he gets married. In the end, each of them will end up with an equal amount (75). Furthermore, while the son will further spend more on her and on the children, she will not be under any obligation to spend her money.[24]

The above logic is a common line of defense but its commonality should not take away from its inaccuracies and misleading assertions. The above scenario is not representative of real life for the following reasons:

(a) The dower is not a fixed amount and under no circumstances is it said to be as high as one-fourth of a person's worth (or estate);
(b) The dower is usually a small amount or symbolic object and rarely a sum of money that will enrich a person; and
(c) Even if a woman inherits a large sum and receives another large sum as a dowry, she rarely, if ever, keeps it to herself, declining to spend it on the family. What kind of a mother will she be if she keeps her money while the children are in need? Even in an ideal situation, the above scenario is almost impossible to materialize.

Readers of the writings of modern Muslim proponents of polygamy would easily note the degree of fervor and certainty by which they justify polygamy. On the one hand, polygamy is principally justified in their eyes on the ground that it provides a social "good" for women. As I mentioned in the opening of the chapter on polygamy, Muslim scholars explain that the practice was necessary because, during the early days of Arab (and early Islamic) society, women were dependent on the support of men. But since the number of men then was considerably smaller than the number of women due to wars and violence, it was very unlikely that a monogamous lifestyle would have helped women who outnumbered men. Hence, one can understand the need and necessity of polygyny as a solution that benefits women more than it benefits men. Indeed, this explanation seems reasonable. What is not reasonable, however, is the continued practice despite the fact that those conditions are no longer applicable. If one were to look for a reason, one would soon discover that, despite claims to the contrary, men desired polygyny more than women. In fact, the language used by scholars who support its continuation suggest that it was men's wish to preserve the practice that legitimized polygyny. In fact, throughout the history of the Islamic civilization, the language of the defense of the polygynous lifestyle showed it to be a right of men and their exclusive prerogative:

> Indeed it should be known that the justice mentioned here is not a condition for marrying more than one wife. Rather it is a ruling for the man who wishes to marry a number of wives that he must observe in the event of marrying more than one wife, and an exhortation to restrict himself to one wife if he fears he will not be able to deal with them justly.[25]

As the language used by an-Nabhani indicates, polygyny is to preserve men's interests and even the perceived restrictions are there *for* the man (choosing polygynous marriage) so that he is guided to the proper path. The language, then and now, speaks for men. If a man wants more than one wife, so be it. According to Muslim scholars, God "has permitted polygamy without restrictions, conditions or any recourse to any justification. Rather, every Muslim is given the right to marry two, three, or four wives of his choice."[26] With this kind of understanding, it becomes clear that the debate about polygyny is in fact a debate about entitlement: men's entitlement to marry up to four women. While some modern Muslim scholars are inclined to look into the causes and reasons behind the "permissibility" of polygyny, more traditional scholars dismiss that approach altogether, arguing that no reasons for or against the preservation of polygyny ought to be presented because doing so amounts to violation of Islamic law:

> Consequently, it becomes clear that it is not allowed to justify polygamy with reason (*Illa*) since no *Illa* is to be found for it in the speech of the Legislator. An *Illa* has no value in making a ruling into a Shar'a ruling except when it is found in the speech of the Legislator.[27]

In other words, in the conservative Islamic discourse, it is almost a moot point to argue whether the stipulation of justice is a condition that limits the rights of men. However, the pressure exerted by women's rights proponents is forcing many Muslim scholars to address these concerns and answer to the charges of violating the principles that the Qur'ān is said to uphold. After all, when the religious authority is preserved in a written document such as the Qur'ān, it becomes accessible to all. When that happens, the understanding of the enunciations is no longer reserved to the religious scholars. Everyone cites the same source and it is for each camp to contest the reasoning and logic of the other. In that context, Nawal al-Sa'dawi's analysis of the verse dealing with polygamy and her citation of Abduh's interpretation forced a reaction (of the same category [logical and analytical]) by religious scholars. That much progress has been made at least.

The reliance on logic to justify inheritance laws or the practice of polygyny is a sign of a passionate debate taking place within the Muslim community. Even Arab feminists not known for their approval of religion-inspired laws use the reasoning and the tradition of the religious discourse to argue against polygyny. Al-Sa`dawi for instance, argues that the Qur'ān itself does not permit polygamy; rather, it prohibits it in a way that leaves no room for doubt since the Qur'ānic verse explicitly states that "if you fear that you establish naught justice, then one woman," which proscribes polygyny on the ground of failing to establish justice—justice that is impossible according to the Qur'ānic verse "and you shall not be able to act justly among women even if you try your hardest." She insists that there could be no clearer and more explicit reference in the Qur'ān prohibiting polygyny. She contends that it was these same verses that were used by major juridical schools that proscribed polygyny in many Muslim countries, such as Tunisia,[28] and used by reformist Muslim pioneers such as Shaykh Muhammad Abduh who called for the prohibition of polygyny more than sixty years ago in order to protect the Muslim family and prevent the disintegration and the abandonment of mothers and children.[29] A similar line of argumentation that contested the practice is advanced by Faridah al-Naqqash:

> Despite that al-Imam Muhammad Abduh has decreed, in the beginning of the century [twentieth] in Egypt, as did al-Shaykh Mahmoud Shaltut, in its middle, that polygamous marriages are not valid; and despite that Tunisian law also prohibits the practice; yet, some juridical schools of thought that are relying on medieval opinions continue to defend polygamy and consider any attempt to annul it an assault on the *sharī`ah*.[30]

Other Muslim scholars and activists from around the world have used the same argument to defend the position of some states that prohibited polygamy in their national laws and to encourage other scholars to speak against the practice since it is harmful and injurious to women. Their call is usually answered by a consistent reaction from scholars who oppose the prohibition of polygamy on religious grounds. Although the voices are many, the gist of the argument is generally the same. In the interest of brevity, I will rely on representative arguments such as the ones proposed by Abu Ghaddah, al-Kurdistani, and a limited number of representative modern Muslim scholars.

Abu Ghaddah refers to the same statement by Muhammad Abduh, but instead of emphasizing the passage where he restricts polygamy by the condition of establishing justice, he highlighted "*al-sharī`ah al-Muḥammadiyyah*" which, according to him, "has permitted a man to marry four women." He cites the entire passage by Abduh where he was reported to have said "*al-sharī`ah al-*

muḥammadiyyah has permitted a man to marry four women, on the condition that he knows for himself that he is able to establish justice among them," but he focuses only on the part that says "*al-sharī`ah al-muḥammadiyyah* has permitted a man to marry four women." Because of that part of the statement, he rejects the idea that Abduh advocated the prohibition of polygamy because, to Abu Ghaddah, polygamy is part and parcel of Islamic law that "is supported by the Qur'ān, the Sunnah, and practice of the Companions, and that of the entire Ummah."[31] He agrees with the view that contends that "Islam does not oblige a man to marry more than one woman, but it permits him to do so (*yubīḥu lahu dhālik*) if he sees that his life is in need of that."[32] In other words, polygamy is the prerogative of men and only men as suggested by Abu Ghaddah and al-Sha`rawi. As to the stipulation of justice as a condition, it was left to al-Sha`rawi to accuse the opponents of polygamous practices of misunderstanding the verse. He suggested that the part of the verse, "you shall not be able to establish justice even if you try hard" cannot be understood without the continuation of the same verse which states "so do not be fully inclined in favor of one wife [*falā tamīlū kulla al-mayl*]." When the verse is taken in that context, al-Sha'rawi argues, it becomes clear that polygamy is permitted in Islamic law, otherwise, how can one be "fully inclined toward favoring one" if there is no other wife?[33] Proponents of polygyny argue that even if we concede to Abduh or other reformists that polygamy ought to be proscribed, their decision is invalid because "scholars do not have the freedom to legalize or proscribe anything that runs counter to the principles of the *sharī`ah* no matter how knowledgeable a scholar is. Only God legislates."[34] The position that considers the legislative function to be the prerogative of the only sovereign, God, makes the need to examine the claim of explicitness in the Qur'ānic enunciations even more important. For this reason, I introduced the quantitative method that examined the explicitness of the verses dealing with inheritance and I hope that other endeavors would follow.

Concerning the justifications of practices such as polygyny and unequal distribution of inheritance, and when all arguments are not enough, it is usually the case that Muslim scholars appeal,[35] as did al-Ghaddah in the work quoted below, to the supremacy of the Qur'ānic explicit determination. It was shown by the examples, however, that the supremacy of the Qur'ānic enunciations is subjected to reason and context by the early Companions and the first generation of jurists. As a result, many of their rulings were not in conformity with the explicit verses of the Qur'ān.

The critics of polygamous marriages have not justified their contempt to the practice on legal and religious grounds alone. Indeed, many have argued that polygamy ought to be proscribed because it is injurious and demeaning to women. In that regard, Nawal al-Sa`dawi echoes the voices of many other women when she argues that, in polygamous marriages, women and children are physically and mentally injured:

> Indeed the protection of the family and the children is the highest virtue.... Could members of the family life with a sense of security and stability knowing that a member of such a family is able, at any given moment, and for no other reason than one's pleasure, abandon them and threaten them...? Surely, there is no stability and no security in the life of the Muslim family for numerous reasons. The first is the exclusive right of men to marry more than one wife without any restrictions.... For this reason, it is imperative that limitations on men's prerogative to divorce and marry at will are imposed in order to protect the family from disintegration. Indeed, threats of divorce or taking another wife might be more harmful to the well-being of women and their children than the actual occurrence of either. As the proverb states, the occurrence of harm is more bearable than anticipating its happening.[36]

In response to the above issues, Muslim scholars offer a mixed message. On the one hand, they admit that some men have, do, and will abuse their "prerogative." On the other hand, they hold women responsible for causing their husbands to seek another wife:

> We see the protection of the wife is that for which she herself is responsible. That is for them to learn how to be righteous wives who, through her commitment, makes her husband prefer death over marrying another woman even after her death.... Wives could further protect themselves by teaching other women to stay away from men and to dress properly for they are guilty of making polygamy attractive to men since it is they—women—who make themselves available for marriage to a men whom they know to be married.[37]

Abu Ghaddah goes on to argue that moral decadence is ultimately a result of some societies' efforts to curb polygamy. He suggests that there is clear double standard when the West allows "sexual polygamy" but prohibits polygamous marriages. By sexual polygamy he refers to Western societies' legal tolerance of people with more than one sexual partner. As an example of the so-called sexual polygamy, he cites the case of former U.S. president Bill Clinton who had an affair with an intern. Abu Ghaddah finds it appalling that "he was impeached for lying under oath, but not charged and tried for adultery."[38] Although the defense of winning by default is universally recognizable as flawed and fallacious, it is often used by cultural and religious apologetics with the hope that if they can prove that the other side is in worse situation than they are, they would see their side as winning for lack of any real practical solution.

Debating the merits of polygamy and strict distribution of inheritance is not a novelty nor is it the result of Muslim's contact with alien cultures and ideas. The religious discourse that is founded on conserving and preserving religious thought and practices is always confronted by changing circumstances. When that happens, even the same community will be forced to rethink or rejustify established rules. The issues do not have to impact a large segment of the society for people to start debating them. Polygamy is practiced by less than 4% in Egypt, 9% in Mauritania, and is highest in Sudan at 17%. Nonetheless, these figures are used by both proponents and opponents to make their respective cases. Those who wish to proscribe polygamy say that it is a practice that is degrading to women and is undertaken by a small percentage of the population and therefore it ought to be banned as it serves only the whims of a small minority. Proponents counter by saying that that small percentage would revert to illegal and illicit practices to satisfy their needs were we to ban polygamy.[39]

Just like when slavery was declared inhumane,[40] some scholars have come to a similar realization regarding polygamy and have asserted that "polygamy is contrary to the Law of Nature and Justice, and to the Propagation of the Human Race."[41] However, it must be noted that slavery and polygamy were not only justified by the economic and social conditions that made such institutions necessary; rather, some have argued that slaves and women are only fulfilling their natural role.[42] In other words, morality and ethics have served as a double-edged sword in the discourse on human rights when we consider the history of moral philosophy on this matter.

The opening paragraphs in the chapter on polygamy suggest that the historical circumstances may explain the initial indifference toward unrestricted polygamy and the lack of ardor from the part of the Qur'ān to deal with the phenomenon more forcefully. In a sense, one might argue for a social function that legitimized the existence of this institution. However, it is reasonable to ask for the reason women alone are expected to carry the burden of the consequences of this unfair environment that was produced by society as a whole, if not by men exclusively. Subsequently, one might say that polygamy was an unjust solution to unfair social, economic, and political circumstances. Once those conditions have changed and improved, the practice ought to cease to exist as well. However, even in communities that have evolved beyond that practice, there are some voices that would rather see it come to force once more.[43]

The suggestion that polygamy can solve social ills as suggested by some scholars is untenable to say the least. I am not aware at this point of any significant study that has determined that conditions and circumstances (similar to the ones that legitimized it in the past) exist today to the extent that it is necessary that the institution of polygamy in modern society be preserved.[44] There is also the view that attempted to explain the need for polygamy by invoking the very nature of men and women. It is argued for instance that men were allowed to enter into a polygamous marriage because they are by nature jealous (*ghīrah*). Women on the other hand, do not experience jealousy; rather, they are prone to envy. For that reason, men are allowed four wives, but women are allowed only one husband.[45] In addition to these reasons intended to be used to permanently justify and universalize polygamy, there are studies that attempt to explain polygamy in terms of social, political, and economic functions.[46]

Some of the functions highlighted in the studies of Asian and African communities practicing polygamous marriages emphasize the economic and social needs but neglect to mention that women in this kind of arrangement are turned into laborers.[47] Moreover, there is no real integration of women's voices in any debate on the subject, and any solution or recommendation in regard to this matter is suspected to take into consideration only the interests and desires of men and the protectors of religious traditions. One of the aims of this study is to suggest, in the light of these and other more recent findings, that the interpretations of the Qur'ānic legal proofs ought to be reconsidered in the context of economic, cultural, and religious backgrounds with full and direct participation of all parties, especially disadvantaged women.

For instance, the very verse that is used as a legal proof (*dalīl*) to legitimize polygamy begins with warning against failure to establish justice or fairness: "And if you fear that you shall not establish justice among the orphans; then, marry other women."[48] The direct reading of this passage suggests that it is not necessarily concerned with protecting men's rights for polygamous marriages; rather, it is interested in the need for protecting the rights of orphans. This doctrine of *qisṭ* (justice, fairness, equity) was downplayed in order to maintain the status quo; but the very logic of fairness and justice requires that the point of view of all parties affected by such an arrangement is taken into consideration. There is no indication that the interpretive exegesis (*tafsīr*) had factored in the natural rights and interests of the two parties of this equation equitably. This misstep was not necessarily caused by an acquired bias of the interpretive process but was more the direct result of the dominance of traditional interpretive exegesis on the way the Qur'ān was understood. In other words, the text of the Qur'ān was at that time period understood contextually and not rationally. For example, if scholars were to find a tradition from the Prophet that was perceived to be contextualizing a particular verse, the understanding and application of the verse will be necessarily fixed by such a tradition, even if the particular tradition was not intended to permanently fix the meaning and application of Qur'ānic enunciations. There is no evidence that shows that the contents of the Prophetic traditions were critically evaluated to determine what was divinely inspired and what was purely *ijtihādic* (independent reasoning), even though Muslim scholarship admit that the Prophet has exerted his personal *ijtihād* on occasions and when it was shown to be wrong, he rescinded his opinions that were based on such personal *ijtihād*.[49] Additionally, the Islamic materials contain numerous references to instances where the Prophet issued particular rulings (based on his personal *ijtihād*) that were overturned by the Qur'ān.

Despite the historical indicators used to argue that the surplus of women necessitated polygamous marriages, or the psychological and ethical needs that are used to legitimize it today (as contended by some modern scholars), polygamy in the Qur'ānic context is simply predicated on fairness and justice (*qisṭ*). As such, if women during the early years of Islamic civilization saw it as advantageous for them to be involved in polygamous marriages, then so be it. However, the principles of justice and fairness should not and cannot deprive other generations of women, and women from other communities, of the right to decide for themselves what is fair and just for them. With the changing circumstances, it becomes imperative that the demand for justice, stipulated in the Qur'ānic verse dealing with polygamy, through the eyes of disadvantaged women is considered. In other words, the assumed impartiality of the Islamic legal and ethical proofs (as sources of law and morality) ought to be tested by allowing (and listening to) the voices that speak to women's interests. More importantly, disadvantaged women's voices will enrich the discourse of human rights and ensure the honoring of human dignity when education is guaranteed and dissent is respected. Without education, it might be the case that women's voices will not add to the pool of ideas since it will be informed by the cultural and social discourse, which could be the medium that preserves discrimination.

Education is fundamental not only for teaching rights and responsibilities but also, and most importantly, for teaching critical thinking. Educated critical thinkers analyze the issues without cultural and societal restraints. With that skill at hand, men and women will be able to go beyond the ordinary and explore the possibilities of meaning and function of concepts and practices that affect their lives. Subsequently, the status of women ought to be appraised in the context of the meaning and power of the principles of justice, fairness, and impartiality. It is true that such principles are ultimately social and linguistic constructs that are always manipulated to conform to the dominant discourse. I would argue, nonetheless, that the broad and full participation of *educated* women would and should ensure that the conceptualization of rights takes into consideration the voices of all concerned parties.

In order for this to happen, the limits of impartiality ought to be first recognized and then reconstructed anew. In the case of Islamic law and practices, the boundaries for concepts (such as justice) were drawn by the declarative norms of the early Companions. In other words, later Muslim scholars' understanding of the meaning and function of justice, fairness, and equality was shaped by the historical—not the logical or the reasoned—definition of such terms. Stated differently, modern Muslims' sense of justice is conceived along the same lines as the sense of justice of the earliest generation of scholars who lived during the formative years of Islamic jurisprudence and ethics. Muslim Religious scholars are not only limited by the inherited tradition but also by the specific school of thought from which they operate. It is not common that a Shi'ite scholar offers formal legal opinion for Sunni Muslims and the reverse is also true. Despite the claims that highlight the role of reason and well-being of individuals and groups, classical Islamic law and traditions are only representative of the reasoning and the well-being of the people of the time of the Companions. Muslim scholarship must either demonstrate and prove that that historical reasoning and logic is absolute and immutable (an almost impossible task without appealing to belief systems), or accept its limitations and revisit and reexamine the concepts of justice, fairness, and equality under the faculty of reason and common sense.

In the case of the modern Western discourse, the limits of impartiality are drawn along the boundaries that favor the secular discourse. The secular discourse is perceived as the neutral space that guarantees real justice, fairness, and equality. However, this claim that has been championed by the secularist of Turkey and France has been challenged by the reality on the ground. The ban on headscarves created an environment that discriminates against Muslim women who *chose* to practice a belief system that requires them to wear such garments. Muslim women who adhere to what they see as religious obligations are prevented from education (a human right per universal declarations, treaties, and international law) and from work in government institutions. Conservative Muslim governments have been rightly pressured and denied membership in some world forums on account of their discriminatory laws that coerce women to wear headscarves; yet, France and Turkey are not held to the same standard for legislating laws that discriminate against women wearing headscarves.

It is undoubtedly the case that the ban on headscarves in France is in fact a violation of the international norms and conventions (CEDAW, ICCPR, ICESCR), in the same way that polygamy is a violation of the women's rights when it is imposed on them. However, the silence by some Western scholars on this gross violation of individual and group rights greatly undermines the efforts to reach out to Muslim women and support their cause. The French ban on the headscarf in the name of secular values ought to be a humbling experience for secular activists and cause them to look beyond labels and ideological boundaries and apply impartial justice instead.

Ultimately, Western civilization perceives its values and laws as universal, just as did the Islamic civilization when it formulated its views on justice, fairness, and equality. Thus I submit that humanity stops making progress in creating a better world for everyone when a civilization arrogantly believes that it has discovered absolute truths. We leave some of us behind and we abuse others when the limits of impartiality are no longer challenged due to our fictitious monopoly on absolute values regarding the cases of polygamy and women's inheritance. These cases show the need to examine and rethink classical Islamic law and ethics as a whole. In starting a conversation regarding the meaning and application of notions such as justice (*`adālah*), fairness (*qisṭ*), and welfare (*maṣlaḥah*), the outcome can serve as a springboard for considering other matters of fundamental rights and entitlements that ought to be protected and cherished in any civil society.

We, as humans, are in a new and different situation relative to the situation in which traditional Islamic laws regarding polygamy and inheritance were formulated. These laws made sense at that time because of the social order and historical circumstances that existed. The logic that justified polygamy then ought to be extended now to argue for different approaches to the laws dealing with polygamy in modern times. Chief among these changing circumstances is the fact that we are in a situation in which membership in the global community comes with the expectations of recognizing and seeking to uphold certain basic human rights, including women's rights to be treated as beings with unalienable dignity and honor. In a human rights era, and also consistent with the best insights of Islam, scholars of Islam are morally required to reexamine the historical causes and legal reasoning for traditional practices that injure women's well-being.

If we can show that polygamy and some unfair inheritance laws do injure the well-being of many women, it would follow that the principles of justice and fairness explicitly stated in the legal proofs are activated to undo the harm. It is true, as some would argue, that some women find that the practice promotes their well-being, but it is also true that many find that it does not. Minimally, at this point, those who find it beneficial and those who find it injurious need to be included in conversations concerning how best to form civil institutions in accordance with the recognition of basic human rights.

The two cases chosen for this study highlight the ethical, philosophical, and legal aspects of the debate on fundamental rights, justice, and fairness. Polygamy, for instance, might have a positive impact on the well-being of some women. Taken together with other Islamic legal rulings such as inheritance ordinances, the institution of polygamy compromises the principles of equality and fairness that were supposed to be upheld by the letter and spirit of the law as argued by traditional Muslim scholars.[50] When considered in the same context, polygamy and inheritance laws make a strong case for rethinking the traditional views on justice, equality, fairness, and human dignity.

Bespoke Justice versus Tyranny of Majoritism

Since the publication of a journal article dealing with polygamy in Islamic law, I have talked about the same topic in small and large gatherings and seminars and I have benefited from these exchanges. I have learned from them and many of the original ideas have been revised for this book. Current events and the renewed interest in this topic make it one of the most dynamic themes not only for academicians but also for activists and politicians in the Muslim world and in the West alike. The increased interest might be the result of the universality of the culture of marginalizing specific groups within society. To be sure, it can be argued that no specific culture is more prone to abuse women than others. Historical documents show that each community had its record of abuse of minorities and women. The United States of America, the exemplar of Western civilization, regarded women as a subclass of citizens, legally and practically, until very recently.[51] One must recall that American women had to fight long and hard to earn many rights including the right to vote (which was secured as late as the 1920s) or own property in their own name. That is not necessarily the case with women of the Islamic civilization: Muslim women participated in the political process and owned property much earlier than the 1920s. For this reason, the status of women ought to be taken in its global context, for purposes of discussion, but resolved locally in order to allow for a closer examination of the particulars of each culture and each society.

What is of paramount importance is the degree of subjugation of women by the state (hence the legal discrimination) and by society (hence the cultural devaluation of their sense of being). Having established that, it might be helpful to look at the legal processes and how they impact personal freedoms and individuals' privacy. Such an approach ought to be inclusive in that it synthesizes the legal and social phenomenon without regard to borders. In fact, by looking for examples from a comparative and international point of view, it will be possible to gain a broader and more realistic assessment of the status of women and other social groups.

By way of example, in the United States, a series of recent events (legal measures, city ordinances, and court decisions dealing with family and family laws) have brought to the forefront many of the practices and issues associated with personal statutes including polygamy, which has been banned for nearly 130 years. The basis of the ban is succinctly summarized by Jonathan Turley[52] in an opinion piece published by *USA Today* (10/3/2004):

> In its 1878 opinion in *Reynolds vs. United States*, the [U.S. Supreme] court refused to recognize polygamy as a legitimate religious practice, dismissing it in racist and anti-Mormon terms as "almost exclusively a feature of the life of Asiatic and African people." In later decisions, the court declared polygamy to be "a blot on our civilization" and compared it to human sacrifice and "a return to barbarism." Most tellingly, the court found that the practice is "contrary to the spirit of Christianity and of the civilization which Christianity has produced in the Western World."

Turley further argues that "contrary to the court's statements, the practice of polygamy is actually one of the common threads between Christians, Jews and Muslims." He points out that "Old Testament figures such as Abraham, David, Jacob and Solomon were all favored by God and were all polygamists. Solomon truly put the 'poly' to polygamy with 700 wives and 300 concubines." He cites studies that "have found polygamy present in 78% of the world's cultures" and suggested that "as many as 50,000 polygamists live in the United States." He concludes by admitting that he detests polygamy but that he "would rather have a neighbor with different spouses than a country with different standards for its citizens." He charges the ban on polygamy as an act of hypocrisy.

Contextually, his arguments came in the aftermath of the high court's 6–3 ruling in June 2003 in the *Lawrence v. Texas* case, which brought national attention to the issue of same-sex marriage and the legal reconsideration of the laws proscribing sodomy.[53] That same ruling, however, is seen by at least one Christian group as precedent that would ensure that polygamy becomes "the next civil rights battle." In fact, six months after the *Lawrence* decision, three members of the Church of Jesus Christ of Latter-day Saints[54] applied for marriage licenses (of a polygamous nature), and when they were turned down by the Salt Lake County clerks, they started the process of appealing the law, which might take their cases all the way to the U.S. Supreme Court. The end of that path is hard to predict. Ordinarily, the freedom of religion, right to privacy, and the principle of no proscription on acts that do not harm or injure would make it difficult for the court to ban polygamy. Justices might argue that the Constitution protects the free exercise of religion when the religious practice does not injure a third party or cause some public danger, which would make polygamy within the legal limits. But it is also likely that opponents of polygamy could try to justify the ban by citing the hardship of configuring property rights and benefits between multiple spouses—an argument I advanced when I considered the impact of polygamous marriages on women's rights to inheritance and property ownership.

One of the reasons I have chosen polygamy and inheritance laws as case studies for exploring the status of women is because I see a clear numerical link between the two: Polygamy could potentially take away from the value of the estate that would be inherited by the wife in case of the death of the husband. If there is only one wife who is the husband's heir, she will inherit whatever the laws of that society will allow her to inherit. If she is party to a polygamous marriage, she would be forced to share the inheritance with other wives. Even in communities where the rules of wills and bequest are more relaxed than those in Islamic law, the potential for diminished shares is present. In Islamic law where the spouses' shares are predetermined in the Qur'ān and standardized in the law, there is little room to adjust the diminution of shares even by way of bequeathing more property since wills and bequests are limited to a maximum of one-third. Furthermore, some Muslim jurists prohibit any adjustment by will or bequest if a bequest were to benefit the beneficiary of a legally mandated heir.

It is true that adults ought to be able to make any arrangement they choose as long as it is not harmful to others and to society, but one must ask the question whether such choices are actually made after knowing all the facts and all the inherent rights. In an environment where critical education and awareness are lacking, it might be the case that choices are informed more by ignorance than by deliberation. In order to protect the rights and dignity of every person and combat the lack of education at the same time, more emphasis ought to be placed on creating and preserving civil institutions whose mission is to teach, raise awareness, and advocate for the less fortunate and less educated persons.

Whatever the case may be, it is now clear that the examples I have presented show the pervasiveness of the issues of polygamy and property rights in all cultures regardless of religion and ethnicity. It also shows the difficulty of classifying any given practice as being a right or an encroachment on individual rights. Polygamy could be seen as an enslavement of women but, for consenting adults in Western societies, it is now seen by some individuals and some civil rights organizations as a civil right. It may be the case that the courts determine that the ban on polygamy is unconstitutional. These events and the emerging literature dealing with these issues show us that there is much to be done in terms of research and exploration of social issues and matters of social justice in general.

When I first wrote the article dealing with the issue of polygamy, I argued that the cause of the skewed understanding of the legal proofs that legalized the practice is primarily the exclusion of women from the interpretive process. During the classical Islamic law era, the laws on polygamy and inheritance were a case of men writing from their own perspectives. I contended then that if women were allowed to participate in reading and canonizing the rules governing their economic and social status, the laws that we see today might be friendlier to women and more reflective of their interests than they are now.[55] A similar conclusion was presented by Barazangi when she suggested that educated women's input might be enough to rectify the skewed interpretations that are the product of males' input:

> In this conclusion I would like to emphasize the central issue that still challenges not only Muslim women but also other religious scholars and practitioners: *Why has the authority to interpret "religious" texts been exclusive to male religious elite?* I would suggest that unless we recognize women as having such an authority, nothing will change.[56]

While I maintain that the classical understanding of the legal proofs dealing with women's rights is biased and favoring men, I have now come to recognize that women's participation alone might not have changed the outcome. Even if an equal number of women authorities participated in the codification of laws governing family and property rights, there is no strong indication or evidence that would suggest that such participation would have rectified the deficiencies in the corpus of law.

This correction is based on the additional research and extensive testing of the initial theory. The data that were introduced in chapter 4 clearly indicates that women interpreters will not necessarily, consciously or subconsciously, interpret the legal proofs in a way that furthers their interests. The only pattern that was observed is that women paid more attention to details and more closely followed instructions than men did. Beyond attention to details, these data confirm what other researchers in the field of psychology and sociology have suspected: Women tend to be more law-abiding citizens than men. It is true that being more detail oriented, remaining within the confines of the instructions given by authorities, and staying within the boundaries of the law make an ideal citizen.

However, if society does not provide the justice and fairness that benefit the ideal citizen, being an ideal citizen will necessarily disadvantage law-abiding citizens who are treated unfairly and unjustly by society and by the established laws.

The data and its analysis in chapter 4 suggest that for women, being female did not encourage them to be more sympathetic to females to the extent that they will interpret the data in a way that furthers women's interests. Another implication of this finding would suggest that values and legal rulings are understood through the lens of the culture and practices of the time and the gender of the "interpreter" does not necessarily guarantee new perspectives or new understanding. It is culture and society that established the parameters of processing information.[57]

As it stands now, and in the light of the recent findings, I argue that the skewed understanding of the legal proofs on polygamy and inheritance is not necessarily the result of the dominance of men over the interpretive, judicial, and executive processes and institutions but, rather, as *a result of the social patterns and the prevalence of discriminatory language* during the formative period of Islamic law and ethics. In other words, the prevalence of any given understanding or practice could be explained by the connection between society and meaning (language), on the one hand, and human natural resistance to radical "change," on the other hand. That is to say that society is the actual and ultimate criterion for fixing meaning and assigning rights and privileges. One of the appealing functions of religion as a social institution is its power to map out the individual and communal life that causes society to exhibit the appearance of stability and long-term predictability. Once a religious practice or customary rule is implemented, it will be hard to radically revise it even by those who are disadvantaged most by its effects. In a sense, it seems that the uncertainty of the unknown is more frightening than the unfairness of the known and therefore people are willing to sacrifice hopeful possibilities for practical realities.

There are many implications for this conclusion. Firstly, since it suggests that even if women had participated in large numbers in the institutions that were involved in formulating the various legal rulings, there is no guarantee that the outcome would have been responsive to their needs. After all, like men, they would have seen as right that which was established by society to be so and see as wrong that which was seen by society as wrong. Fairness and justice are relative concepts determined by traditions and customs. People of any given society demand only some degree of fairness and justice, not absolute fairness and justice. As it were, a society that sanctioned slavery for example, does not see the use and abuse of slaves as a morally appalling and abhorrent act. Similarly, in a society where women are part of a social order that favors men, even women will see the rules that maintain that paradigm as a "fair" and "just" arrangement.[58]

The idea that law and morality are social constructs that condition both men and women to judge things in a similar fashion is underscored by independent research. A study was undertaken during the month of March 2000 to survey the opinion of Palestinians in the West Bank and Gaza Strip in order to gauge the status and need to reform Islamic family laws. Researchers interviewed a random sample of twelve hundred people over the age of eighteen regarding a number of issues. Most telling was their response to questions about the need to change some specific laws to make them more responsive to women's needs. When they were asked if they would like to see a law enacted that allows women to file for divorce, 68% of the males said no, but 63% of women also said no.[59] Given that Islamic law affects women differently than men, one would assume that there would be a pronounced difference in the degree of aspirations and views of men and women. The actual results did not prove that to be the case. This, in my view, underscores the role of society in shaping and informing an individual's sense of fairness, especially in regard to issues of social justice.

Secondly, by arguing for a society-based conceptualization of justice, fairness, and equality it is necessarily implied that a radical change in circumstances and function requires a revision of the legal and moral rulings governing the rights of men and women. Moreover, to suggest that the concepts of justice and fairness are social constructs is not to argue for relativism, cultural or otherwise. Instead, it reenforces the notion that human beings are the product of their environment, which is constantly changing. With that change comes the need for new understanding and new interpretation of the legal traditions. The relationship between fairness and justice and the specific circumstances has been already introduced by classical and modern Muslim scholars and can hardly be contested. What have not changed are their interpretation and understanding of the legal proofs. For instance, al-Kurdistani speaks for many other Muslim scholars when he suggests that the obligation of bridal dower, spousal and child support, and help to the needy parents and relatives justify the unequal distribution of inheritance (see chapter 4). If this is really the case, does that mean that Muslim scholars would then call for a change of these rules if they were to be shown that none of these circumstances apply in a given society or for a given family?

As is the case with most religious traditions, interpretation is an essential tool not only in assigning meaning to ambiguous passages but also in fixing meaning to explicit and simple ones. In the case of Islamic law, practice and implementation are what elevate dormant pronouncements and give them power and authority. The jurisprudential and linguistic tools are secondary to the pronouncements and decrees of living authorities. This reality was played out repeatedly during the lifetime of the Prophet and the early Companions. The way these individuals understood the enunciations of the Qur'ān informed the way justice and fairness was defined. With that said, it must be noted that in the case of inheritance, at least, the verses dealing with heirs and their shares were revealed during the last several years of the Prophet's life and the lack of tradition relating to the implementation of these verses is proof of that. For that reason, the interpretation of these verses was governed by the practice of the Companions and Caliphs rather than by the practice of the Prophet.

Be that as it may, the verses dealing with polygamy and inheritance are understood in the context of preserving the status quo rather than in the context of revolutionizing the way society treated women. For instance, the style of the Qur'ānic passages addressing polygamy is neither expressive of positive commands nor preponderantly favorable narratives. That would rule out obligation and desirability as possible legal rules. At best, and as suggested by most Muslim scholars, the language would only support neutrality (*ibāḥah*). However, verse [Q4:V129] clearly states that men will fail to establish justice between more than one wife even if they try their hardest. That is the classic definition of preponderantly contemptuous narrative that entails undesirability.

In regard to inheritance verses, the analysis of the data and the examination of all the verses dealing with the rights of heirs show at least three basic trends: (1) There is no general rule dictating that a woman inherit a share equal to one-half of that of a man; (2) the shares of women heirs are explicitly mentioned and specifically determined but not those of male heirs; and (3) it is possible, based on the direct reading of the legal proofs, that a female heir inherits a bigger share than a male counterpart. In other words, the Qur'ānic verses on inheritance are more concerned with the rights of women and less with devising a system. These verses established minimum standards that ultimately had shifted focus from the rights enjoyed by men and guaranteed a "fixed" share to women. Lastly, there is enough evidence to suggest that the Qur'ānic logic in distributing inheritance takes into consideration the number of female heirs and awards shares accordingly. For example: one daughter inherits one-half but any number of daughters above three will share two-thirds. The same applies to one sister and more than three sisters. More research needs to be done in order to understand the reasons behind this logic.

The Islamic and Qur'ānic discourses are adamant about the place of justice in protecting society, preventing chaos, and preserving human dignity (*karāmah*). The preservation of individuals' dignity and life is premised on the Qur'ānic proposition that humans and all that with which humans are endowed are borrowed gifts that belong to God. Therefore, it is not a matter of debate to preserve and protect the life and dignity of persons. However, a problem arises when balancing the protection of society and preventing chaos, on the one hand, and preserving the life and dignity of the persons that make up such a society. Furthermore, when society is taken in a global context, further contestations emerge. It is because of the competing claims and multitudes of contexts that the Islamic and Qur'ānic discourses employ a variety of approaches and reasoning in defining, promoting, and upholding justice.

The diversity of approaches and reasoning are present in the language the Qur'ān uses when addressing issues of women's rights. For instance, the verse on polygamy ([Q4:V3]) uses three different terms related to justice: *qisṭ*, *`adl*, *`awl*. The word "*qisṭ*" is used in the beginning of the verse when talking about orphans: "If you fear that you do not act fairly (*allā tuqsiṭū*) among orphan women..." Arabic language scholars provide a number of meanings for the word *qisṭ*: justice, fairness, equity, rightness, correctness, measured acts, and completeness. In modern Arabic, the same word was coined to refer to "measured payment of equal portion installments." All modern and classical exegetes commenting on the word *qisṭ* understand it to mean "acting justly and fairly."

In the middle of the verse, another word is used: "... if you fear that you do not act justly (*allā ta`dilū*), then one woman..." Similarly, scholars of Arabic explain the word "`*adl*" as: straightness, straightforwardness, impartiality, probity, honesty, and uprightness. This same term is used in the legal context to refer to the character of individuals to be trusted on important matters like serving in public office, being a religious leader or scholar, or serving as a witness. All Muslim exegetes and legal scholars agree that the term refers to acting justly and fairly.

The two-line verse concludes by using yet a third word, "`*āla*": "that is the least you ought to do so that you do not act toward women unfairly (*allā ta`ūlū*)." According to grammarians, the word "`*āla*" means to deviate from the right course, to oppress, to deviate, and to distress. Muslim exegetes argue that the phrase (*allā ta`ūlū*) recommends against polygamy so that the man is not inclined to love one wife more than the other or because he may not be able to provide equally to all wives.

The repetition of words that mean almost the same thing is either an emphasis on the concept of justice or an enumeration of the reasons for discouraging the act. The first word "*qisṭ*" can be understood to refer to the financial injustice done to orphan women were they to be taken by men in polygamous marriages. The second word "`*adl*" refers to the social and moral risks to men involved in polygamous marriages as it might result in the loss of their character of *probity*, which is required for every important social role. Lastly, the word "`*awl*" connotes the loss of emotional equilibrium that will cause men to veer and deviate from the designated course of morality and lose the ability to provide equitably to his family. When these meanings are taken together in the social context of justice as being the prevention and undoing of injustice (*ẓulm*); one will be able to see the importance and complexity of the concept of justice in Islamic thought.[60] As seen in the context of the Islamic religious discourse, justice has significance when taken in the contexts of providence, reciprocity, and intent. For Muslims, one does not lay a claim to just treatment on the ground of deservedness, but, rather, on the basis of intention before and during the act. This mode of justice is internal and therefore it is judged and rewarded by what I called *communicative justice* expressed in the Qur'ānic discourse. There is also a sort of vertical justice and that is the kind of relationship between God and His adherents: God provides His subjects with tools and knowledge on how to live a righteous life and behave justly. In return, the adherents are not held responsible for acts that may have undesired outcomes but for which they have no foreknowledge. In the instances where either intentional or unintentional acts negatively affect the community or individuals, the laws of reciprocity are used to redress the wrong and restore justice. The redress system is ultimately governed by the social roles for each member of the society and for that reason the concept of justice in Islamic discourse is determined by social status, part of which is determined by gender. Be that as it may, the concept of justice, like many other concepts tied to social behavior, is fluid, flexible, and dynamic. In the context of Qur'ānic discourse, justice and fairness is circumstantial and predicated on the judgment of the parties involved, and for that reason, justification and interpretations are especially important in determining the legal rulings for cases involving polygamy and inheritance laws.

Nonetheless, inequity in polygamy and inequality in inheritance laws was initially justified by the exegetes of the classical period by a logic that not only separated people based on their gender, but clearly saw a difference in role and biology of men and women. Exegetes of that time period saw the inequity as a matter of fact in a civilization that established itself in a worldview accredited for its rise. They were not embarrassed by and did not apologize for the perceived and real difference in inheritance and marriage rights. In modern times however, and as was shown in chapter 5, the position of Muslim scholars now comes during a time when their worldview is challenged by a dominant Western one that preaches fairness and equality from a different context and outside the social roles traditionally associated with Islamic society. For that reason, modern Muslim scholars tend to justify polygamy and inequity in inheritance rights by "tweaking" mathematics (see al-Kurdistani) in order to make it look like a fair and just arrangement. In other words, the defining of justice and fairness is not inclusive of the Western view. However, given that Islam, for many, still provides a worldview and a comprehensive system, adjusting one pillar of it, or one concept, leads to a collapsing of the entire system in the eyes of the adherents. Polygamy and inheritance laws are a minor component of the Islamic system, but systems are founded on building blocks. If the building block is defective, it automatically causes the collapse of the system. That is another way of looking at concepts such as justice, fairness, and equality as social constructs that have greater significance than being merely a single item in a multitude of unrelated issues.

Today, more Muslim men and women are initiating the process of rethinking issues related to human rights not necessarily because the abuse of human rights has reached a critical level; rather, because there is a global culture of examination of the impact of political and cultural systems on the lives of individuals, minorities, and women. Therefore, by virtue of being members of this emerging global community, Muslims are also looking at their own societies through the lens of modern discourses. It has been established by many studies including this one that classical Islamic law (and the cultures attached to it) is, to put it neutrally, different from other contemporary systems. Be that as it may, this perceived or real difference must be explained and either accepted for what it is or brought in line with the dominant worldview.

Some modern Muslim scholars are seeking justice and fairness in the name of equality; a concept that is either outright dismissed by other Muslim scholars or downplayed as a concept that is foreign to Islamic teachings and practices. In a lively discussion on the merit and place of equality in the Qur'ānic discourse, a number of Muslim women (`A'isha `Abd al-Rahman, Amina Wadud, Asma Barlas, and Nimat Hafez Barazangi) discuss this topic.[61] While `Abd al-Rahman and Wadud reportedly maintain that a claim of equality, gender equality that is, cannot be an effective tool to improve the status of Muslim women, Barazangi argues that equality, as a human value that was proposed by what she sees as "the revolutionary Qur'ānic discourse," ought to be the basis of seeking equitable and fair treatment.

> While wishing to maintain the neutrality (with regard to gender, class, race) of the principles and in the text of the Qur'an, these two scholars and others who share a similar understanding may have overlooked the fact that these principles were intended to change the practice and its underlying assumptions *exactly because* the practices were keeping the considerations for cultural-specific prescriptions (of how to function according to one's sex) at the same level of Qur'anic guidance.[62]

Ostensibly, Barazangi rejects the idea that the Qur'ān recognizes the "difference" between men and women, an opinion that is held by `Abd al-Rahman and Wadud according to Barazangi.[63] Barazangi, on the other hand, suggests that the Qur'ānic discourse does not support such discriminatory language and, in her view, the revolutionary discourse of the Qur'ān could be used to eliminate the wrong interpretation that informed classical Islamic law. She identifies the problem of understanding as a "lack of strategic pedagogical deficiency." In other words, if women are better educated on *how* to read and understand the Qur'ān, the problems of inequality and injustice will be resolved. To summarize the position of these three Muslim women, one could suggest that the similarity between them ends at their recognition of the Qur'ān as a common denominator. While `Abd al-Rahman and Wadud accept some of the traditional interpretation of the Qur'ān, Barazangi however, sees in classical Islamic law a process that preserved the Arabic discriminatory cultural discourse and pegged it to the Qur'ān. Her approach is therefore geared toward a reformation project where proper education in the area of reading the Qur'ān is central:

> How could al-Hibri expect to change the patriarchal view of Islamic law—her professional venue—when she does not recognize the shortcomings of such solutions and interpretations despite their apparent validity? . . . these female thinkers have not read the Qur'an perceptually, as Fazlur Rahman (1982) suggests. Perhaps that is because they were limited by their professional disciplinary views, by the social limitation, by the rush to prove to non-Muslim feminists that Islam is on the

side of women's human rights, or by the confusion between Islamic legal law and Qur'anic law as Maysam al Faruqi (2000) explains.[64]

It is possible that Barazangi's theories regarding the reason behind what she sees as erroneous positions are contested by Wadud, `Abd al-Rahman, and other women and men who share their reformist views. Additionally, since Barazangi does not subject any of these theories to testing, the opinions of the scholars she is criticizing remain as valid as her own assertions that proper education on how to read the Qur'ān is the only way forward. For all that we know, even a new "pedagogical" approach to reading the Qur'ān will be informed by the assumptions, culture, politics, and professional training of its authors, be it Barazangi or others. Furthermore, even if such an approach were to be proven sophisticated enough to advance the well-being of women today, we cannot be sure that such an approach will not intrude on future generations who might very well have different needs, disparate problems, and unique circumstances. Nevertheless, it is possible that the participation of more individuals, regardless of their gender and their social or economic class, could contribute to the amelioration of the status of persons affected by social norms in different ways. Having said that, wider participation should not be construed to mean radical reformulation of legal norms and legal rulings. The existence of laws on the books does not necessarily translate into more or strict protections of the rights and dignity of persons. Additionally, in modern societies, laws are applied asymmetrically to persons of different social, economic, or gender background. A poor person may not benefit from a law enacted on his behalf if she or he does not have the resources. Similarly, a rich person may escape the limits imposed by a law if he or she pays for the resources to contest such a law. Therefore, strengthening the emergence of civil institutions that will provide the support mechanism to individuals impacted by unfair social limitations or government restrictions should have priority over enacting new laws or reforming the existing ones. To me, the process is more important than the end result; and that process is the perpetual generation of civil and civic institutions that are more efficient in providing specific services to individuals. Civil society institutions can provide not only the services, but also the education that instill awareness. To be sure, this was not my initial position; indeed my new position was the by-product of involvement in public discourses on the subject matter through the venues of civil institutions such as educational organizations, watchdog entities, interest groups, private clubs, faith-based institutions, professional associations, and advocacy societies just to name few. Hence, there emerges the undeniable power of the civil discourse, among people who do not necessarily share the same position on a particular social issue or the same experiences and backgrounds to generate diverse points of view, which enhances inclusiveness and diversity in society.

Barazangi is not the first or last Muslim female scholar who makes the claim that the Qur'ānic discourse is egalitarian when it comes to the rights of men and women and that interpretation is the cause of the problem.[65] Leila Ahmed also concluded that although the Qur'ān's ethical vision "was stubbornly egalitarian, including with respect to the sexes," the meaning of such ethical values were restricted by the social practices of the communities of the time. She argued that women's status was not necessarily determined by the enunciations of the Qur'ān but, rather, by the cultural negotiation between the Muslim framers of Islamic law and "an urban Middle East with already well-articulated misogynist attitudes and practices."[66] To focus her comments on the themes of this book, it ought to be noted that she contends that when "licensing polygamy, concubinage, and easy divorce for men, originally allowed under different circumstance in a different society, Islam lent itself to being interpreted as endorsing and giving religious sanction to a deeply negative and debased conception of women."[67] The accretive nature of the legal and religious traditions can hardly be contested.[68] In the Islamic discourse, legal precedents all but assured that early Muslims' visions of society are preserved. In the context of the Semitic and Mesopotamian cultures, religious customs were transmitted and preserved in and by Jewish and other local practices and were then passed to Islamic communities.[69] That much Ahmed and other scholars have established thus far. However, the implications and the recommendations that might be employed in the practical sense are not yet articulated as a matter of consensus. There exists a wide gap between the identification of the problems and the recommendation of effective solutions. Nonetheless, the fact that Muslim and non-Muslim scholars are now engaged in this lively debate about the status of women worldwide is indeed encouraging.

It was during public speaking events, which included spirited exchanges like these that I learned to be less emphatic about my conclusions and theories and more cognizant of the possibility that there might be others who see things in a fundamentally different light. For instance, it is undoubtedly the case that each of these scholars (Wadud, `Abd al-Rahman, and Barazangi) holds a view that each of them sees as compatible with the belief system to which she adheres. However, that which might be acceptable for one could be unacceptable to the other. In my view, `Abd al-Rahman and Wadud are right in that there is legal "neutrality" in the Qur'ān regarding gender. To focus on the themes of this study, I concur that conclusion applies specifically to polygamy. The language of the Qur'ān does not take a clear stance on the issue and I have explained that in chapter 3. I do not think that Barazangi can escape the fact that the Qur'ān contains many instances of legal neutrality and in many locations adopts purely patriarchal language.[70]

There are numerous passages that specifically address the "believing men" and ask them to do this or that for the "believing women." To be specific, the verses dealing with polygamy address men and instruct them on marriage. There is no similar verse that addresses women and instructs them about the way to ask men for marriage. Subsequently, it is generally culturally unacceptable and

"Islamically" unorthodox for a woman to ask a man to marry her, although there are reports that a number of women "offered" themselves to the Prophet in marriage and he accepted some offers and turned down others.[71] Similarly, verse [Q4:V4] specifically instructs men not to transgress against women and did not ask women to demand their rights from men and require them to fight back when men transgress.[72] The Qur'ānic verses on inheritance are explicitly patriarchic; while verse [Q4:V12] begins by addressing men and telling them directly that they are entitled to one-half of what their wives leave behind (to you; *lakum*), the next sentence of the same verse keeps addressing men, telling them that "for their wives one-forth of what they leave behind" (to them; *lahunna*). If the Qur'ānic language is not patriarchic, why does not it address women the same way it addressed men and say: "and to you women (*lakunna*) . . ."? Why the awkward shift from addressing men directly to addressing women as if they are absent or in seclusion and not to be addressed directly the way the believing men are addressed? Clearly, the Qur'ānic discourse is consciously realistically counting on men's goodwill to bring about fast change in terms of accommodating women and improving their status given the cultural milieu from which emerged the Qur'ān. I am not sure how Barazangi would understand those passages in a way that makes them less patriarchal.[73] Yet Barazangi is correct in identifying society as the culprit in creating a "language" and value system that are inherently discriminatory against women. I am not so sure however that her reformist project of changing Islamic law is a practical one, nor is it in the interest of women and other individuals to do so for a number of reasons.[74]

The Qur'ān consists of nearly 6665 verses. From that total, less than 200 verses could be broadly considered legal verses that proscribe or sanction acts and behavior. As it was shown in chapter 2, the crimes for which there is an explicit legal proof in the Qur'ān are few and even fewer crimes for which a punishment is also explicitly prescribed. So to argue, as did Wadud and `Abd al-Rahman, that the Qur'ān maintained a neutral stance on gender and class equality (*musāwāt*) is not unusual for a discourse that does not seem to be overly concerned with imposing legal controls. In fact, the Semitic scripture in general does not lend itself to elaborate and extensive prohibitions and sanctions. The Hebrew Bible, a document of many chapters and lengthy narratives, limited itself to very few purely mundane-legal enunciations: Ten Commandments to be exact. Even after the Jewish religion accumulated, in an accretive fashion, more elaborate legal ordinances in the form of the Midrashic and Mishnaic traditions, Jesus, who saw himself as one who was reaffirming the Jewish law, scrapped most of those extra legal restrictions. If we were to consider Muhammad as a continuation of the Semitic line of prophets, he too reduced the corpus of laws to a smaller body; hence, the limited legal prohibitions and sanctions that are readily available in the Qur'ān.

If we were to consider Islamic law as the record of Muslims' understanding of the Qur'ān, then such a law must be reflective of the mentality and values of the people who participated in the process of understanding. The discipline that emerged as Islamic law is in fact called "*fiqh,*" which means understanding. Therefore, Islamic law is hardly God's law, at least not in the eyes of its early framers. They were much too humble (and their language reflected that) to claim authorship of a document that is representative of the divine will.[75] Only later generations have come to see their work as part and parcel of "God's Path" or *sharī`ah*. The role of society in "manufacturing" law is further underscored by Mālikī jurisprudence, which considered local customs (*`urf*) to be a source of Islamic law. In other words, Mālik himself recognized that stable and functional communities can be a source of acceptable laws as long as ensuing laws do not violate explicit divine commands (which are few in number). Understanding the Qur'ān as a fluid and dynamic process is much more effective in ending abusive laws and social practices and creating new ones. With this in mind, it should be clear where I disagree with Barazangi and others who contend that a new reformed Islamic legal system will solve the problem of discrimination against women. As the debate between her and other Muslim women scholars shows, even a reformed Islamic law to which she would contribute will run the risk of discriminating against her other two colleagues at least. Therefore, the solution lies in working to establish Islamic civil society and civil institutions, not in creating laws that will be enforced by states' apparatus that may or may not be sympathetic to individual, minority, and women's rights. Civil institutions are more important than laws, because laws tend to be applied mechanically and do not "customize" justice on a case-by-case basis. Civil institutions such as private arbitration agencies, community councils, professional organizations, and other nongovernment organizations will be better positioned to provide individualized services to those in need without establishing precedents that could be used to limit the rights of others. With this kind of understanding in mind, it becomes clear why a *no-legal-action* stance is more effective in establishing justice than rigid legal rulings—reformed or otherwise.

I must emphasize that the no-legal-action position is different from a court's determination of a case as being moot. A no-legal-action position leaves the door open for legal intervention in the future whenever the act or behavior is deemed harmful or injurious to the person (or persons) involved. In contrast, for the court to consider a case moot necessarily implies that whatever legal ruling is implemented or upheld is satisfactory and requires no further legislative intervention. In this instance, a person has less legal recourse. When a no-legal-action position is in place, individuals affected by a particular practice will always have recourse to the law. No-legal-action promotes a discussion and an understanding of concepts such as justice and fairness, but it does not lock them legally to the detriment of some, even if that "some" is one or two individuals in the entire society.

Admittedly, it should be recalled that cases of human rights are claims against states (or individuals representing the state). Creating new laws or reforming existing ones to shift the effects of the laws from one direction to another is ultimately an exercise that empowers the state and limits the sphere of influence of civil and civic institutions. Furthermore, those who wish to "reform" the laws by abrogating the old ones and replacing them with new ones that reflect the interest of the majority of the people are necessarily arguing from a hedonistic utilitarian position that is far from being accommodating to individual, minority, and women's rights. If we were to recognize women's rights and their claim to justice and fairness as a claim to the protection of human dignity, it should become clear why sacrificing the dignity of one person cannot be justified by the preservation of the "happiness" of the greatest number of people.[76] To be sure, and for clarification purposes, if women were to successfully force the government of country X to ban polygamy, the practice will be considered a felony or a crime depending on the language of the new law. Once that happens, a woman who is actually benefiting from a polygamous marriage will be found guilty of something that others (not her) see as wrong, immoral, or illegal. Similarly, if men were to campaign and force a government of country Y to make it the right of men to enter into polygamous marriages, such a law will be a destructive and destabilizing threat to the well-being of women who do not wish to be involved in polygamous marriages. That is the nature of the law: While it may protect the rights of some, it also has the potential of harming others at the same time. Therefore, if enacting laws can be avoided by relying on alternative civil institutions, or in the case where a society is controlled by a tyrannical or dictatorial regime, it will be in the interest of the public to have a no-legal-action stance on certain social issues rather than to have a mechanical law enacted in the name and in the interest of the powerful and dominant elite.[77] In most claims of rights and entitlements, it may be the case that no-legal-action is more advantageous then clear proscription or sanction that strengthens the already powerful state's arm and weakens the civil institutions that tend to provide support in the form of "individualized" justice, if you will.

In all cases, and with respect to the issues of polygamy and inheritance laws, the system as it exists today is clearly skewed toward the preservation of the interest of men. It is so because the historical understanding that produced classical Islamic law did not keep up with the pace of change in society and social roles. There are many voices within the Muslim community that are demanding a change in the status quo. These voices, as we have seen in the previous chapters, come from different backgrounds, but in Muslim countries, the discussion is muted for the most part under the pretext of preserving religious values.[78]

With all this said, one might wonder about the motive and driving force behind Muslim's resistance to change if such a change is in fact supported by the basic legal proofs. Perhaps part of the answer could be found in the heritage of suspicion and mistrust that is the result of years of colonialism, interference, and manipulation by the West. If the prediction that the U.S. Supreme Court overturns the ban on polygamy materializes, should the rest of the world community pressure the U.S. government to undo such a ruling in order to protect women's rights? Many would argue that doing so will be foreign interference in the affairs of a sovereign nation. But is that not exactly what is happening when the West issues condemning reports to other nations for violating basic human rights? If this trend—where the Muslim world is asked to live up to liberal standards while the West is sliding down the opposite direction and falling under the control of conservative regimes—continues, not only the purpose and function of the law will be brought to the realm of doubt, but also the ethical and moral capital that was spent on improving the status of women and minorities will be wasted because of perceived double standards and sheer hypocrisy.

One more pattern may be another reason behind the slow progress in the area of creating civil institutions in the Muslim world and that is the distrust toward religious Muslim voices who are speaking for issues of human rights. Western governments have always and consistently sided with secular Arab and Muslim leaders and "conspired" to marginalize religious groups or religious individuals.

Undoubtedly, the Muslim world remains suspicious of Western interference and meddling in the internal affairs of indigenous peoples.[79] Frankly, the West needs to work harder to atone for its colonial past and its arrogance before asking the Muslim world to follow its example on the path to better treatment of human beings, and not just women. It may be the case that women's rights are just as much threatened in the Muslim world as they are in the West. The basis for discrimination and abuse might be under the guise of religion or liberalism but it is abuse, discrimination, and injustice nonetheless. When taken in its global context and without accusatory attitudes or arrogance, we will be able to see other issues and other problems that need to be addressed and resolved.

For example, another outcome of this study is the evident need to better understand the origins and function of legal rulings: Is it actually the case that laws protect and preserve individual rights or is it possible that some rights are better protected when the law is completely silent about certain issues? In other words, in a society of many competing interests and in a legal system built on contested notions of justice, is it more protective to minority's rights for the judicial and legislative bodies to take a no-legal-action stance instead of taking a definitive position in favor of one side? In the context of Islamic law, is the debate on polygamy and inheritance rights a direct consequence of the Qur'ānic ambiguity that intentionally avoided a clear stance on those matters?[80]

The fact that I am ending this section with a series of questions is testament to how much work needs to be done on these subjects. With emerging interdisciplinary approaches and the cooperative research embraced by true comparativists, I am confident that very soon we will see fresh perspectives and new ideas emerging to shed more light on this and other subjects of paramount importance to societies and to scholarship.

Inclusion and Exclusion of Women

During the pre-Islamic era, the Arabs had seen society divided along the wealth, health, color, and gender fault lines. Wealthy individuals controlled the economic and political sphere. They decided the prices and declared wars and relied on paid servants and imported slaves to enforce their decisions. If one was not wealthy or was stricken by an illness or a disability, he would be better off under the earth then on it. According to many historical reports, a son born to a wealthy and healthy man from a dark-skinned woman is as good as a slave. The poetry of `Antarah Ibn Shaddād speaks to these facts. The status of a woman was dependent on the status of the man to whom she is attached by blood or by marriage, but in all cases her status could never overcome that of men who are leaders of the tribe or clan. The pre-Islamic laws of inheritance and the polygamous marriage practices ensured that her status remained subordinate to men.

Islamic laws of inheritance and Qur'ānic restriction imposed on polygamous families changed some of the practices but did not fully uproot the ideas and mentality of men and women. Even when radical changes were being instituted by the Qur'ān, the language of these new teachings addressed men and asked them to make the accommodations. It did not address women and ask them to reject the established order and replace it with the one it proposes.[81] In doing so, the Islamic discourse that emerged with time was allowed to keep its cultural distinctions, which meant the preservation of a language that is exclusive of preferences. Arguably, the language is the vehicle of meaning and values, and it could be argued that values and meanings were preserved by a discourse that did not challenge the legitimacy of the language itself. The signature of social expectations and social roles is embedded in the dominant culture, and without the reformation of language, the "genes" of social order and social relations are passed from one generation to another.

By its nature, the religious discourse is about preserving traditions and practices; in the case of Islam, it is more than just preserving tradition and practices. Since the founder of the faith established himself as the political authority as well the spiritual guide, Islam, more than any other religion, became more than a private discourse on metaphysical matters. It provided a comprehensive view of the world and asked its adherents to live by a system that sees politics and religion as two sides of the same coin. In such an arrangement, the social control mechanism of Islam transcends that of a typical state in that it hardly requires police power to enforce the laws and practices. The power of the scripture in the form of what I dubbed *communicative justice* guaranteed that compliance is achieved by the largest number of individuals. Believers are reminded of the place and function of the scripture in their daily life and it was argued that the scripture, the explicit parts of it at least, cannot be ignored or altered for short-term gain. It remains unaffected by social protest and reasoned contestations.

Furthermore, the doctrine of *al-amr bi-'l-ma`rūf wa-'l-nahyi `an al-munkar* (enjoining good and speaking against evil) adds another layer of societal pressures that shape and inform public morality. In short, Islamic communal life supersedes the interests of the individual, and the laws are created with that goal in mind. Nonetheless, I have established in this study that the explicit text of the Qur'ān was indeed overruled by the rulings of the jurists. From numerous cases examined for this study, and from many more cases that did not fall within its scope, it is evident that Qur'ānic heirs, in many cases, were excluded in favor of heirs not mentioned therein. Since the majority of heirs explicitly mentioned in the Qur'ān for whom a specific portion was predetermined were women, the jurists' exclusion is therefore an exclusion of women in the interest of men. In the words of Coulson, who reached a similar conclusion, "there is no exception at all to the rule that a Qur'ānic heir does not exclude any male agnate."[82] With that in mind, the exclusion of women clearly contravenes the explicit determination of the Qur'ān. During the early days of the Islamic civilization, the exclusion might have been dictated and justified under the pre-Islamic customary tribal laws as well as the social order that dominated then. There is no evidence that shows that, with the changing circumstances and social conditions, such laws and juridical rulings were revised to be more inclusive of the rights and interests of women.

Even today, there are no efforts by Muslim and Arab women to reconstruct the language of their respective communities to include idioms and paradigms that represent their understanding of concepts and their standards of assigning meaning. One would think that in a segregated society women would be able to develop their own unique grasp of the meanings and their conceptualizations totally independent from men's influence. What happened however is that women have become "bilingual": They have their language and their reference points when they are in their private women-only space; but they remained fluent and proficient in understanding the point of view and the standards of men. In mixed environments, they use the male standards and use their own when they are alone.

In Muslim communities where the boundaries between men and women are diminished, women are generally adopting the language of men as the standard. Not only are their achievements measured against those of men, but even their sense of beauty is decided according to men's standards.

Conclusion

It is said that there is some "truth" in every joke, at least in the mind of the author/transmitter of the joke and possibly in the mind of the audience that decodes it. Jokes are usually anecdotal comments about someone's intelligence, look, ethnicity, or aptitudes. Historically, in Arabic cultures, and in order to avoid embarrassing oneself or others, jokes were attributed to a fictitious person named Juḥā. Persian and Turkish speaking Muslims have a similar personality, Mullah Nasruddine. In current times, other peoples (from neighboring countries or neighboring cities) are the subject of ridicule and funny jokes. Moroccans joke about Algerians, Algerians joke about Tunisians, Tunisians joke about Libyans, and so on. Often we hear men joking about women and sometimes women joking about men (mostly in private). Satirizing "others" is a way of attributing incompleteness and inaptitude (and rarely intelligence or other complementary traits) to a person other than the active agent (speaker/speakers) or the community. The funniest jokes are the crude stereotypes and wild generalizations that represent "others" as inferior or "irrationally" different from the active agents.[1] Before women "publicly" reciprocated, they were the main subject of jokes expressing inaptitude, strangeness, incompleteness, and everything negative. Now imagine, if every joke represents 1% of the true attitude of the author and the audience, after telling one hundred jokes about the same group of people, a completely (100%) constructed identity emerges into the real world whereby the represented entity is anything but an equal. Subsequently, new attitudes, new perceptions, and perhaps new identity of the subject of the jokes are manufactured.

To some extent, the Muslim woman is thus produced. From countless stereotypical generalizations, fossilized archaic representations, discriminating religious teachings, and oppressive political and social powers, emerges the "woman" as a different other, different from the elite who shape and decide identity and characteristics of the collective community. Unlike other entities that are represented by the elite as "others" such as ethnic, religious, and linguistic groups, woman's identity is more complex since women are members of all these groups including the elite. A woman rarely becomes part of the elite unless she is (or was) associated to a man who is one of the elite. Consequently, the projects of emancipation of women are unable to rely exclusively on the politics of sameness or difference. If one were to argue deservedness of equality and dignity on the ground that not only women worldwide are the same but also that women are members of the same human race as men, in this case one will find oneself as part of a hegemonic and imperialistic project that stands charged of dominating and controlling men and women of the Third World. If one were to argue that women are different and therefore require special care and different standards, one would automatically justify the inequity. This complex situation is even more so for Muslim women due to internal and external circumstances.

In a time when the West was speaking in favor of human rights and writing nice-sounding declarations of intent to respect human life and human dignity since, in the Western view, all peoples are "members of the human family,"[2] most of their governments were engaged in murderous wars, exploitive practices, and colonial endeavors that killed and maimed millions of indigenous peoples in Africa, Asia, and the Americas.[3] Even within the boundaries of the Western world, historical documents recorded acts of killing, torture, genocide, war crimes, and ethnic cleansing. The enduring question that still finds resonance in the twenty-first century is whether or not morality and abstract ethical thinking have any impact on the practices of honoring the ideals to which the majority of peoples subscribe.

The colonial legacy and Western powers' refusal to acknowledge responsibility for their exploitive activities provide credible context for those who reject any attempt to improve the status of women and underrepresented minorities in the name of resisting colonial influence. Calls for modernity are automatically translated into "westernization," a word that triggers memories of peoples under occupation. The way the West has failed to improve the lives of the peoples they victimized is similar to the way the Muslim society has failed to remedy the status of half of its population—women. The gap between rhetoric and reality is wide but it may be the need to address the status of women that will force the Muslim community to revise many long-held customs and norms. In that regard, the exploration of the concepts of justice and fairness in the context of Islamic law and ethics is a good starting point. The unity of the human race did not prevent some from colonizing others, nor did the unity of humankind as expressed in the Qur'ān impel Muslim thinkers to accept women's right to dignity and entitlements: "Humankind, be mindful of your Lord Who created you from one single soul, from that single soul He created its mate, and from the two souls He spread many men and women."[4]

If every culture, every religion, and every ideology contains condemnation of abuse of others and a golden rule that establishes the common link between members of the larger society, then why do some people transgress against the dignity and well-being of others? Is it the helplessness of the victims or hubris of the victimizer? Or is it the nature of society and the power of language that decide on the degree of justice and fairness each human being is awarded?

Aside from the power of the law, especially if such a law is rooted in a belief system, society depends on the religious discourse to create and preserve public morality, ethics, appropriateness, customs, respect, and the various value systems that contribute to creating an orderly community. The religious system in turn relies on human emotions and linguistic paradigms to communicate the cultural and social norms and customs. These processes operate in a matrix of sounds and images, dicta that transcend the elitism of written and reasoned instructions. The role of imagination, orality, and models in communicating certain "truths" to the masses are paramount. However, modern scholarship knows very little about the formation and application of images and paradigms and even less about the way orality mediates between written enunciations and the "consumers" of the information that emanates from the processes that create public images and attitudes (stories, proverbs, jokes, maxims). In particular, the Islamic discourse is rich with tools that guide and inform the framers of the laws, the subjects of such laws, and interpretations. In the first chapter of this study, I highlighted the place and functions of stories, idioms, models, metaphors, and paradigms as signifiers of beliefs and judgments. The story of the encounter between the "man of the Commandments" and the "knower" underscores the function played by paradigms and models in expanding the perception of order and purpose beyond reason. In that chapter, I suggest that acts of injustice could be contextualized in the religious discourse to relativize harm. In a sense, women and other social groups who are not enjoying equal economic and political status are made to accept such arrangements by appealing to stories and idioms such as the ones that justified the "illegal" and "unethical" behavior of the "knower."

In the second chapter, I delineated the nature of the Islamic jurisprudential philosophy vis-à-vis matters of social justice and redress of grievances. I emphasized the role of communicating consequences to the adherents in a powerful hedonistic discourse that assured full compliance with the prohibitions and obligations imposed on individuals and on the community. I showed the Qur'ānic communicative approach to justice to rely on threats of torture and enticements of fulsome rewards to instill in the individual a settled disposition of revulsion of acts, thoughts, and feelings deemed bad (*fāsid* or *qabīḥ*), and attraction to acts, thoughts, and feelings deemed good (*ḥasan* or *ṣāliḥ*). These teachings, which are transformed into a comprehensive belief system, assured men's loyal compliance and especially women's obedience (who are shown in chapter 4 to be more willing to follow established rules).

In the third chapter, I accounted for the full range of interpretations of the verses dealing with polygyny and explored the possibility of interpretations that are consistent with the letter and spirit of those verses. I argued that one possible interpretation of verse [Q4:V3] is to understand it to proscribe polygyny involving orphan women and discourage polygyny with other (nonorphan) women. I exhaustively examined the *Tafsīr* literature only to conclude that that particular interpretation was not listed despite the fact that it could be derived from the language and context of verse [Q4:V3]. I suggested that one possible explanation of the missing interpretation is the fact that, despite Muslim scholars' claim to the contrary, interpretations are rarely based on linguistic and syntactical analysis of the legal proofs and usually rely on authorizing oral traditions. To be sure, interpretations become authoritative once authorized and implemented by the Companions and that process elevates them to the category of consensus-based precedents that cannot be overturned by later consensus even if such consensus is near unanimous. This discovery might explain the reason behind traditional Muslim scholars' resistance to restrictions on polygyny.

The fourth chapter focused on the laws of inheritance and the Qur'ānic verses that formed the basis of such laws. I summarized the existing laws dealing with inheritance as codified by Sunni and Shi`ite scholars and I examined the exegetical and Ḥadīthic materials that contributed to determining the shares for each legal heir. Here too, I have shown that there are other possible interpretations that conform to the grammatical and syntactical rules yet are not accepted as legal rulings. This confirms my earlier conclusion arguing that interpretation in Islam does not rely exclusively on reason and logical analysis of the language; rather it is empowered and supplanted by tradition. Reason is applicable only in the absence of authorizing traditions. Since the meaning of the verses dealing with inheritance was fixed during the lifetime of the Prophet and the Companions who authored and implemented them, the meaning of social justice that was pegged to those verses was also locked. For example, many cases of inheritance were decided by applying the principle of *`awl*, which was authored by the second Caliph. Despite the existence of traditional views (Ibn Abbās's for instance) that challenge the basis of *`awl*, Sunni scholars still adhere to it and consider it part of the nonreversible principles of determining inheritance laws. The power of oral reports and precedent disengaged the final legal rulings from the explicit enunciations of the Qur'ān, which is counter to Muslim scholars' claim that explicit Qur'ānic verses cannot be overruled by human opinion.

In order to examine the extent of explicitness of the Qur'ānic verses dealing with inheritance, I have collected and analyzed their interpretations by more than nine hundred participants. On the one hand, the data establish that, contrary to Muslim scholars' view, it is the shares of females that are explicitly stated in the Qur'ān and not that of males. On the other hand, the data also show that men and women are bound by the cultural and societal determinations of the meaning and scope of justice and fairness. In other words, the participation of women in the interpretive process would not necessarily add a sympathetic voice to the cause of women. In fact, it was shown that women, more than men, closely follow the rules and boundaries established by society.

The final chapter provides an account of the findings and solutions advanced by Islamist and Islamicist thinkers and scholars whose research also focused on the status of Muslim women. Their recommendations ranged from total rejection of any and all religious systems in favor of a secular discourse to radical reformation of religious and cultural traditions. The majority of these views were premised on the assumption that women's participation in the interpretive processes and in governance will necessarily balance the outcome and increase advocacy for women. Based on my analysis of the historical documents and the quantitative analysis of the sources of Islamic law, I remain unconvinced that women's participation alone is the most effective way of promoting basic human rights and advocating for minorities and disadvantaged persons. I have shown that not all women were abused and not all men were abusers: "Women from noble families, especially when they had property of their own, not only had the same *de facto* rights as their husbands, but were sometimes able to demonstrate their superiority as well."[5] In other words, the oppression of women was due to their gender as it was due to their economic and social status at the same time. To be sure, even if a woman were to be selected to the Caliphate, it is very unlikely that the conditions of all women thereafter would have improved. For all that we know, Muslim women were just as committed to the preservation and transmission of the Islamic worldview as men. "For the most part, these women were people of their time, just as ruthless, scheming, and extravagant as their male counterparts."[6] In the light of these findings, I disagree with scholars such as Mernissi (and many others) who contend, as the title of Mernissi's work (*The Veil and the Male Elite*) indicates, that women's status is due to the *males'* dominance of the economic, religious, educational, and political life to the exclusion of women.[7] I have introduced examples showing many successful and prominent women involved in the defense and preservation of the status quo. Therefore, I identify the cause of the problem to be the societal and cultural elitism that relies on wealth-manufactured majoritism to create and preserve an environment that is less accommodating to historically disadvantaged social groups. This of course would imply that legal reform would not end discrimination, especially when such reforms are imposed from the top down.[8] Governmental actions merely shift power from one group of elites to another and strengthen the state, which does not necessarily represent the underprivileged and underrepresented groups especially in majority-based democracies.

Alternatively, I argue for the creation and protection of civil society institutions that would resist the power of the state and challenge the oppressive nature of society in order to improve the conditions of women and minorities and the poorest in the community.[9] It is through educational and advocacy civil institutions that guide and encourage critical thinking and unhindered access to learning (for both men and women) that the status of women is improved. After all, highly educated women among ignorant men could be as detrimental to social justice as noneducated women among elitist men. Educated women among ignorant men may stir up resentment and violence in *the* group of people (males) that has historically relied on violence to monopolize power. Educational institutions on the other hand, not only empower women to speak against injustice but also prepare men to accept new ideas and novel interpretations of society's traditional heritage. More importantly, the presence of civil society institutions ensures that contestation of discriminatory social norms and practices are not conducted in the name of sexism and ethnicism, but in the name of justice and fairness. In order to create a paradigm of political and social power that is responsive to the universal demands for respecting human dignity, the reign of the privileged few and the tyranny of majoritism (based on wealth, ethnicity, religion, ideology, or otherwise) must end. Human rights and human dignity of a single person ought *not* be determined and preserved by popular vote, nor should it be sacrificed for the dignity and rights of the many. The culture of majoritism must be curbed in favor of a culture of absolute respect for human dignity.

Appendix A

Timeline of Scholars and Major Figures

The dates are in accordance with the Islamic calendar (which starts on July 16, 622 CE, the date of the Messenger's arrival in Madīnah). The year corresponds to the date of death of each authority (unless otherwise indicated). I either included a short description of each scholar's specialization or cited one of his major publications in order to remove any discrepancies, given that sometimes more than one person shared the same name and/or the same *kunyah*.

Year	Scholar or renowned person (major publication or title/description)
11	Muḥammad (Messenger and Prophet)
13	Abū Bakr al-Ṣiddīq (first Caliph)
17	Mu`āth Ibn Jabal (Companion, *Qāḍī*)
18	Abū `Ubaydah Ibn al-Jarrāḥ (Companion)
23	`Umar Ibn al-Khaṭṭāb (the second Caliph, Companion)
32	`Abd Allāh Ibn Mas`ūd (Companion)
32	Abū al-Dardā' (*Ḥadīth* transmitter)
35	Uthmān Ibn `Affān (Caliph/Companion)
37	`Ammār Ibn Yāsir (Companion)
40	`Alī Ibn Abū Ṭālib (fourth and last of the *Rāshid* Caliphs)
45	Zayd Ibn Thābit (Companion/Qur'ān *Ḥāfiẓ*)
54	Usāmah Ibn Zayd (Companion and military *Amīr*)
58	`Ā'ishah Bint Abū Bakr al-Ṣiddīq (Prophet's wife)
58	Abū Hurayrah (*Ḥadīth* transmitter)
60	Mu`āwiyah Ibn Abī Sufyān (First Umayyad Caliph)
68	Ibn `Abbās (*Ḥadīth* transmitter)
68	Abū al-Aswad al-Du'alī (Reformed Arabic script)
73	`Abd Allāh Ibn `Umar (Companion, son of the second Caliph)

74 Mālik Ibn Abū `Āmir (*Ḥadīth* transmitter, Mālik's grandfather)
78 Jābir Ibn `Abd Allāh (Companion)
95 al-Ḥajjāj Ibn Yūsuf (Umayyad governor)
96 Ibrāhīm al-Nakh`ī (*Faqīh* from Kūfah)
97 `Urwah Ibn al-Zubayr (One of the seven *fuqahā'* from Madīnah)
101 `Umar Ibn `Abd al-Azīz (Umayyad Caliph)
104 Mujāhid (author: *Tafsīr Mujāhid*)
110 Ibn Sīrīn (*Faqīh* and *ḥadīth* transmitter from Baṣrah)
110 Ṭāwūs (*Tafsīr* and *fiqh* scholar)
122 Zayd Ibn `Alī (Shi`ite Imām, Zaydī Shi`ites)
131 Wāṣil Ibn `Aṭā' (Mu`tazilite thinker from Baṣrah)
136 Zayd Ibn Aslam (*Faqīh* from Madīnah)
143 Yaḥyā Ibn Sa`d al-Anṣārī (*Qāḍī* and *faqīh* from Madīnah)
148 Ja`far al-Ṣādiq (Seventh Imam, Ismā`īlī Shi`ites)
150 Abū Ḥanīfah ("Founder" of the Ḥanīfah School of law)
158 Ismā`īl Ibn Ja'far (*Qāḍī* and *faqīh* from Madīnah)
160 Shu`bah Ibn al-Ḥajjāj (collector of *ḥadīth*)
161 Sufyān al-Thawrī (*Ḥadīth* collector)
169 Nāfi` Ibn `Abd al-Raḥmān Ibn Abū Nu`aym (*qāri'* from Madīnah)
169 al-Khalīl Ibn Aḥmad al-Farāhīdī (Reformed the writing system)
179 Mālik Ibn Anas (Author of *al-Muwaṭṭa'*)
181 Ibn al-Mubārak (*Kitāb al-zuhd wa-'l-raqā'iq*)
182 Abū Yūsuf (*Kitāb al-āthār*)
189 al-Shaybānī, Muḥammad Ibn al-Ḥasan (*faqīh* from Kūfah)
193 Ziyād Ibn `Abd al-Raḥmān (Transmitter of *Muwaṭṭa'*)
197 `Abd Allāh Ibn Wahb (*al-Muwaṭṭa', kitāb al-muḥārabah*)
197 Warsh (*Qāri'* of the Qur'ān from Egypt)
198 Sufyān Ibn `Uyaynah (*Ḥadīth* scholar)
198 Yaḥyā Ibn Sa`d al-Qaṭṭān (*Ḥadīth* scholar)
204 al-Shāfi`ī (*Kitāb al-umm*)
204 Ibn al-Kalbī (*Jamharat al-nasab*)
211 `Abd al-Razzāq al-Ṣan`ānī (*al-Muṣannaf*)
218 Ibn Hishām (*Sīrat Ibn Hishām*)
220 Qālūn (Qur'ān reciter from Madīnah)
224 Abū Ubayd (*Kitāb al-nāsikh wa'l-mansūkh*)

230 Ibn Sa`d (*al-Ṭabaqāt al-kubrā*)
231 al-Naẓẓām (Mu`tazilite thinker)
234 Ibn al-Madīnī (*`Ilal al-ḥadīth, Ma`rifat al-rijāl*)
234 Yaḥyā Ibn Yaḥyā al-Laythī (Transmitter of *Muwaṭṭa'*)
235 Ibn Abī Shaybah (*Muṣannaf*)
238 Ibn Ḥabīb `Abd al-Malik (*al-Wāḍiḥah*)
240 Suḥnūn (Compiler of *Muwaṭṭa'* Mālik)
240 Suwayd al-Ḥadathānī [aka Abū Sa`īd] (Transmitter of *Muwaṭṭa'*)
240 al-Iskāfī (Mu`tazilite from Baghdād)
241 Aḥmad Ibn Ḥanbal (*Musnad*)
254 Muḥammad al-Mahdī ([Birth date] 12th Imam, Twelvers Shi`ites)
255 al-Dāramā (*Sunan*)
256 al-Jāḥiẓ (Renowned Mu`tazilite literary figure)
256 al-Bukhārī (*Ṣaḥīḥ al-Bukhārī*)
256 Muḥammad Ibn Suḥnūn (Transmitter of *Muwaṭṭa'*)
261 Muslim (*al-Jāmi` al-ṣaḥīḥ*)
273 Ibn Mājah (*Sunan*)
275 Abū Dāwūd (*Sunan*)
276 Ibn Qutaybah (*Kitāb ta'wīl mukhtalaf al-ḥadīth*)
277 al-Fasawī, Abū Yūsuf Ya`qūb Ibn Sufyān (*Kitāb al-ma`rifah*)
279 al-Tirmidhī (*Ḥadīth* collector)
298 Yaḥyā Ibn `Awn (*Ḥadīth* transmitter)
303 Abū `Alī al-Jubā'ī (Mu`tazilite scholar debated Ibn Ḥanbal)
303 al-Nasā'ī (*al-Sunan*)
309 al-Ḥusayn Ibn Manṣūr (authority on *naskh*)
310 al-Ṭabarī (*Tafsīr* and *Tārīkh*)
312 `Abd Allāh Ibn Sulaymān al-Ash`ath (authority on *naskh*)
317 al-Zubayr Ibn Aḥmad al-Zubayrī (Authority on *naskh*)
324 Ibn Mujāhid (*Kitāb al-sab`ah fī al-qirā'āt*)
327 Ibn Abī Ḥātim (*Taqdimatu al-ma`rifah , al-Jarḥ wa-'l-ta`dīl*)
330 Abū al-Ḥasan al-Ash`arī (Ash`arite theological school)
333 Abū al-`Arab M. Ibn Tamīm (*Ṭabaqāt `ulamā' ifrīqiyyah*)
338 Aḥmad Ibn M. al-Murādī [al-Naḥḥās] (authority on *naskh*)
354 Ibn Ḥibbān (*Kitāb al-thiqāt*)
363 Ibn Muḥammad al-Nu`mān (*Da`ā'im al-islām*)

370 al-Jaṣṣāṣ (*Aḥkām al-qur'ān*)
377 al-Ḥasan Ibn `Abd al-Ghaffār al-Fārisī (*al-Ḥujjah*)
381 Ibn Mihrān al-Isbahānī (*al-Mabsūṭ fī al-qirā'āt al-`ashrah*)
386 Ibn Abī Zayd al-Qayrawānī (*Kitāb al-jāmi`*)
403 Abū Bakr al-Bāqillānī (*Nukat al-intiṣār linaql al-qur'ān*)
429 Abū Manṣūr Baghdādī (*Uṣūl al-dīn*)
430 Abū Nu`aym (*Ḥilyat al-awliyā'*)
437 Makkī Ibn Abī Ṭālib (*al-Nāsikh wa'l-mansūkh*)
444 al-Dānī (*al-Muḥkam fī naqt al-maṣāḥif*)
456 Ibn Ḥazm (*Jamharat ansāb al-`arab*)
463 al-Khaṭīb al-Baghdādī (*Taqyīd al-'ilm*)
463 Ibn `Abd al-Bārr (*al-Intiqā' fī faḍā'il al-a'immah*)
464 Abū Bakr Abd Allāh Ibn Muḥammad al-Mālikī (*Riyāḍ al-nufūs*)
468 al-Wāḥidī (Qur'ān commentator)
474 al-Bājī (*Iḥkām al-fuṣūl fī aḥkām al-uṣūl*)
475 Ibn Khālawayh (*Mukhtaṣar fī shawādhdh al-qur'ān*)
475 Ibn Mākūlā (*al-Ikmāl*)
478 al-Juwaynī (*al-Shāmil fī uṣūl al-dīn*)
483 al-Sarakhsī (*al-Mabṣūṭ*)
520 Ibn Rushd al-Qurṭubī—al-Jadd (*al-Bayān wa'l-taḥṣīl*)
543 Ibn al-`Arabī (*Aḥkām al-qur'ān*)
562 al-Sam`ānī (*al-Ansāb*)
571 Ibn `Asākir (*Tārīkh dimashq*)
593 al-Marghīnānī (*al-Hidāyah* and *Sharḥ bidāyat al-mubtadī*)
595 Ibn Rushd al-Qurṭubī—al-Ḥafīd (*Bidāyat al-mujtahid*)
597 Ibn al-Jawzī (*Manāqib `Umar Ibn `Abd al-`Azīz*)
630 Ibn al-Athīr (*al-Kāmil fī al-tārīkh*)
631 Āmidī (jurisprudence scholar)
676 al-Nawawī (*Tahdhīb al-asmā'*)
681 Ibn Khallikān (*Wafayāt al-a`yān*)
684 al-Qarafī (*al-Dhakhīrah*)
685 al-Bayḍāwī (*Anwār al-tanzīl wa-asrār al-ta'wīl*)
700 Niẓām al-Dīn Ibn Muḥammad al-Nīsābūrī (*Gharā'b al-qur'ān*)
711 Ibn Manẓūr (*Lisān al-`arab*)
728 Ibn Taymiyyah (*Ṣiḥḥat uṣūl madhhab*)

738 Yaḥyā Ibn `Abd Allāh al-Wāsiṭī (*al-Nāsikh wa al-mansūkh*)
741 Ibn Juzayy (*al-Qawānīn al-fiqhiyyah*)
751 Ibn Qayyim al-Jawziyyah (*A`lām al-muwaqqi`īn*)
774 Ibn Kathīr (*al-Bidāyah wa'l-nihāyah*)
776 Khalīl Ibn Isḥāq (*al-Mukhtaṣar*)
790 al-Shāṭibī (*al-Muwāfaqāt fī uṣūl al-sharī`ah*)
799 Ibn Farhūd (*al-Dībāj al-mudhahhab*)
833 Ibn al-Jazarī (*Ghāyat al-nihāyah fī ṭabaqāt al-qurrā'*)
836 Aḥmad Ibn al-Mutawwaj al-Baḥrānī (*al-Nāsikh wa'l-mansūkh*)
840 Aḥmad Ibn Yaḥyā Ibn al-Murtaḍā (*al-Baḥr al-zakhkhār*)
845 Ibn Sa`d (*al-Ṭabaqāt*)
852 Ibn Ḥajar (*Fatḥ al-bārī fī sharḥ ṣaḥīḥ al-bukhārī*)
853 Muḥammad al-Rā`ī al-Andalusī (*Intiṣār al-faqīr*)
864 Jalāl al-Dīn al-Maḥallī (*Tafsīr al-jalālayn*)
883 Aḥmad Ibn Ismā`īl al-Absḥītī (*al-Nāsikh wa-'l-mansūkh*)
911 al-Ṣamhūdī (*Wafā' al-wafā' bi-akhbār dār al-muṣṭaafā*)
911 Jalāl al-Dīn al-Suyūṭī (*Tafsīr*)
925 Muḥammad Ibn Zakkariyā' al-Rāzī (Ethics and medicine)
950 al-Fārābī (philosophy and ethics)
1004 al-Ramlī (*Nihāyat al-muḥtāj ilā sharḥ al-minhāj*)
1025 Ibn al-Qāḍī (*Jadhwat al-iqtibās*)
1032 Aḥmad Bābā al-Tinbuktī (*Nayl al-ibtihāj bi taṭrīz al-dībāj*)
1033 al-Karmī (author on *naskh*)
1037 Ibn Sīnā (Philosophy, medicine, and ethics)
1089 Ibn al-`Imād (*Shadharāt al-dhahab*)
1101 al-Khirshī (*Sharḥ al-khirshī `alā mukhtaṣar al-khalīl*)
1104 Muḥammad Ibn al-Ḥasan al-Ḥurr al-`Āmilī (*Wasā'il al-shī`ah*)
1122 al-Zurqānī (Egyptian scholar who commented on the *Muwaṭṭa'*)
1190 `A iyyat Allāh Ibn `Aṭiyyah al-Ajhūrī (*Irshād al-raḥmān*)

Appendix B

Glossary of Key Arabic Terms and Their Derivatives

This glossary is meant to aid readers in understanding some of the key Arabic words that are used in this work; as such, each of the key words and their derivatives is followed by a very brief definition or translation. The pronunciation (audio clips) of these terms as well as a more comprehensive list of similar words is available online at www.souaiaia.com. To locate a word within the text, see the Index section of this book.

` (`ayn)

`adālah*, *`Adl: Justice, fairness; someone who is *`adl* could also mean a person of probity.

`adhāb: Punishment, torture.

`āla: To divide something equitably.

`ālim (al-): The one who knows; it is one of the ninety-nine attributes of God.

`amal: Action, practice, deed.

`aqīdah: Articles of faith, dogma, creed.

1. Belief in God (*Allāh).*
2. Belief that *Muḥammad* is the Messenger of God.
3. Belief in the Books (Torah, *Zabūr* [Psalms], *Injīl* [Gospels], *Qur'ān*).
4. Belief in the existence of angels and *jinn.*
5. Belief in the Last Day, Paradise, Hell . . .
6. Belief in *qaḍā'* and *qadar.*

`aql*: Reason, mind, intellect. In his treatise *On the Meanings of the Intellect (fī ma`āni al-`aql), al-Fārābī gives a list of the meanings of the intellect or reason as used by the general public, the *mutakallimūn,* and Aristotle:

1. Prudence or sound judgment in determining what is right and what is wrong.

2. The *mutakallimūn* use it when referring to certain actions enjoined or repudiated by reason (generally received by the public as a whole or for the most part).
3. For Aristotle, it is a "faculty of the soul whereby man is able to attain certainty by recourse to universal, true and necessary premises, known neither by deduction nor reflection, but rather naturally and instinctively."
4. A part of the soul that is able to gain, through habituation and prolonged experience, a certain apprehension of premises pertaining to volitional matters, which are susceptible to being sought or shunned. This reason grows with age.
5. Potential, actual, acquired and active reason.

`ārif: Knower.

`aṣabah: Category of heirs as classified in Islamic law of inheritance.

`awl: A legal doctrine adopted by the second Caliph and applies when the number of heirs is greater than the predetermined shares.

`ibādī: My servants.

`iffah: Temperance, purity, abstinence.

`illah: Legal purpose, justification.

`ilm: Science; genuine knowledge.

`iqāb: Punishment.

`ishq: Erotic passion. According to *al-Fārābī,* it is a disposition of the human soul to seek the satisfaction of "beastly" passion and renounce divine things.

`ulamā': Scholars, learned persons.

`ulūm al-`amaliyyah (al-): Practical sciences; generally, refers to legal sciences.

`aql, `āqil wa-ma`qūl: Plato believed that it is the active intellect or the unmoved mover.

A

A`ḍā' wa-'l-jurūḥ (al-): Body parts and wound s.

Adillah al-shar`iyyah (al-) or *al-aḥkām al-uṣūliyyah*: Legal rules (5).

Af`āl: Actions.

Āḥād: Singular.

Aḥkām al-khamsah (al-): Legal rulings (∞).

Aḥkām al-khamsah (al): The five judgments or normative categories; the way in which Islamic law and ethics have traditionally categorized human behavior. The five categories classifies behavior as obligatory (*wājib, farḍ*), recommended (*mandūb, mustaḥabb*), indifferent, morally neutral or permissible (*mubāḥ*), reprehensible (*makrūh*), and forbidden (*ḥarām*).

Aḥkām: Legal rulings.

Ahl al-`ilm: People of knowledge.

Ahl al-ḥaqq: Literally, "the people of the truth." It could also mean "the people of the true one," i.e., "the people of God."

Ahl al-kalām (also *mutakallimūn*): Muslim theologians (see *kalām*). According to *al-Fārābī,* the methods used by theologians essentially recourse to persuasive (*iqnā`ī*) or dialectical (*jadalī*) arguments, in which imaginative representations tend to replace demonstrative proofs. *Al-Fārābī* believed that these arguments are inferior to dialectical ones.

Ajsām al-basīṭah (*al-*): Simple bodies, primary elements. According to *Ibn Rushd* they are four:

1. *al-Nār*: the fire
2. *al-Hawā'*: the air
3. *al-Mā'*: the water
4. *al-Arḍ*: the soil.

Akhbār: Neutral statements, informative narratives.

Akhlāq (sing. *khuluq*): Character, manners; relating to individual mannerism, nature, see [Q68:V4]. According to *Ikhwān al-Ṣafā,* it is a natural disposition that prepares each and every member part of the body to enable the soul to act.

Akhlāṭ (sing. *khalīṭ*): Mixtures.

Alfāẓ (sing. *lafẓ*): (pronounced) Terms.

Allā ta`dilū: That you do not act justly.

Allā ta`ūlū: That you do not act fairly.

Allā tuqsiṭū: That you do not act equitably.

Allāh: The God.

Amr: Positive command.

Arkān: Pillars. They are the ritual practices (*`ibādāt*).

1. Declaration of faith. (see *Shahādah*).
2. Performance of obligatory prayers (see *Ṣalāh*).
3. Mandatory alms tax (see *Zakāh*).
4. Fasting all days of *Ramaḍān* (see *Ṣawm*).
5. Undertaking the journey of pilgrimage (see *Ḥajj*).

Āthār (sing. *Athar*): Traditions.

Awlād (sing. *walad*): Children.

B

Badan: Body.

Bāri' (*al-*): The Creator.

Bāṭin: Hidden.

Bay`ah*: It is an oath of allegiance to the caliph, once he has been established as such. Traditionally this endorsement of the caliph had to be open/public. A later development of the *bay`ah distinguished between the *bay`ah khāṣah* (done only by Muslims) and *bay`ah `āmmah* (secondary to *bay`ah khāṣah,* and done by non-Muslims too).

Bayt al-māl: Treasury.

Bayyinah: Evidence, proof.

Bilā kayfa: Without having to explain how.

Bilā limādhah: Without having to explain why.

Burhāniyyah: From the Arabic noun *Burhān* = proof; demonstrative philosophy.

D

Dalīl (pl. *dalā'il* or *adillah*): Proof.

Ḍarūrāt tubīḥ al-maḥḍūrāt (*al-*): Necessities override prohibitions.

Dhā maṣlaḥah: A thing that is praiseworthy.

Dhāt: Self.

Diyah: Monetary fine (redress) paid to homicide or wounds victims.

F

Fa'in khiftum allā tuqsiṭū: If you fear that you are unable to act fairly.

*Faḍīlah (*pl. *Faḍā'il*): Excellence, merit, virtue.

Faḥṣ: Inquiry, examination.

Falā tankiḥūhunna: Then do not marry them.

Falsafah: Philosophy; the word was derived from the Greek *philosophia.*

Faqīh (pl. *fuqahā'*): Legal scholar, he who is versed in Islamic law.

Farā'iḍ (sing. *farīḍah* or *farḍ*): Legal obligations.

Fawāḥish (sing. *fāḥishah*): Obscenities

Fi`l fāsid: An act that is blameworthy.

Fi`l ṣāliḥ: An act that is praiseworthy.

Fiqh: Islamic law. Literally, it means "understanding" or "knowledge."

Fitnah: Social upheaval, civil war. *Fitnah* is often used to refer to the civil war between *`Alī Ibn Abī Ṭālib* and *Mu`āwiyah Ibn Abī Sufyān.*

G

Ghaffār (al-): The Forgiver; it is one of the ninety-nine attributes of God.

Ghalabah: Literally, it means "victory," "overcoming something." *Ghalabah* is a gender, ethnic, tribal, and linguistic-based dominance that forces the acceptance of one's rule.

Ghāyah: Purpose.

Ghīrah: Jealousy.

H

Ḥadd: Definition; punishment for capital crimes as categorized in Islamic law.

Ḥadīth (pl. *al-aḥādīth*): The Arabic word has many meanings: "saying," "uttering," "conversation," "speech," "report." In Islam, it means "tradition." It is a record of the sayings or doings of the Prophet and his Companions. The *Ḥadīth* is considered as a source of Islamic law, dogma, and ritual second only to the *Qur'ān*.

Ḥajb: Exclusion.

Ḥajj: Pilgrimage to *Mecca*. It is the fifth of the five pillars (*Arkān*) of *Islām*.

Ḥaqq (al-): The Truth. One of the ninety-nine attributes of God.

Ḥarām: Forbidden.

Ḥayā': Bashfulness, shyneṣṣ

Ḥayy (al-): The Living. One of the ninety-nine attributes of God.

Ḥikmah: Wisdom.

Ḥilm: Forbearance, indulgence, gentleness.

Ḥudūd: Boundaries; refers to some capital offenses in Islamic law.

Ḥukkām: Rulers.

Ḥukm: Legal ruling.

Hum: They (masculine pronoun).

Hunna: They (feminine pronoun).

Ḥusn al-dhātī (al): Inherent goodness.

Huwa: He.

I

Ījāb: Offer.

I`tidāl: Moderation.

Ibāḥah: Permissibility.

Iblīs: Satan.

Iḥtikār: To establish a monopoly.

Ijmā`: In jurisprudence this term can be translated as "consensus" along with the *Qur'ān*, the *Sunnah*, it is one of the main sources of law and ethics in Islam.

Ijtihād: Informed independent reasoning.

Ikhlāṣ: Sincerity, faithfulness, fidelity.

Ikhtilāṭ: Admixture, combination.

Ikhtiyār (al-): Men's free will to choose.

Ikhwān al-Ṣafā: A secret group of Muslim philosophers, theologians and intellectuals who flourished most probably in Basra in the fourth to tenth or fifth to eleventh centuries. They were believed to be *ismā`īlī*. They are the authors of fifty-two epistles (*Rasā'il*) that were encyclopedic in range, covering subjects as diverse as music, astronomy, embryology, and philosophy. According to *Ikhwān al-Ṣafā*, all souls (living beings) are moved by the desire to live (*shahwat at-baqā'*) and contempt of death (*karāhiyyat al-fanā'*). *Ikhwān al-Ṣafā* also believe that humans act only when faced with:

a. Positive and negative commands: *amr wa-nahy*
b. Promise of positive reward and promise of painful reward: *wa`d wa-wa`īd*
c. Praise and bashing: *madḥ wa-dhamm*
d. Enticement and threat: *targhīb wa-tarhīb*

Imām:
a. Leader of the prayers.
b. For *Shī`ah*, he is the successor of the Prophet and is believed to be infallible.

Imām al-ma`ṣūm (al-): Infallible Imam.

Imān wa-`amal: Faith and deeds.

Imān: Faith, belief.

Ins: Humankind.

Iqnā` (adj. iqnā`ī / iqnā`yyah): Persuasion. According to *al-Fārābī,* persuasion is a form of conjecture (*ẓann*), in which one believes a thing to be such and such, although it is possible for it to be otherwise.

Irādah: Volition, want, will.

Irtidād: To revert to a previously held belief.

Islām: Literally, it means "submission." *Islām* is one of the three Semitic religionṣ It was founded by *Muḥammad* in the seventh century.

Isti`dād: Preparedness.

Istiḥbāb: One of the five legal rules, reference, desirability.

Istiḥsān: To prefer.

Istiqrā': To rely on some kind of deductive reasoning.

Istiṣḥāb: To assume that an established state of being still exists.

Ittiṣāl: Conjunction.

J

Jabbār (al-): The Restorer. It is one of the ninety-nine attributes of God.

Jabr (al-): Opposite of *ikhtiyār*; to compel.

Jabriyyah: Early Muslims who believed in predetermination.

Jadal (adj. *Jadalī / jadaliyyah*): Dialectic.

Jāhiliyyah: Derives from the Arabic noun *jahl* (state of ignorance). It is used to refer to the pre-Islamic period.

Jawhar: Core.

Jazā': Reward (positive reward).

Jism: Body.

K

Kabīrah: Grave moral or religious wrong.

Kahf (al-): The cave.

Kalām: Literally it means "speech." In Islam however, *`ilm al- kalām* is theology. Therefore, *kalām* includes the debates that took place in early Islam and that dealt with the theological subjects on which some scholars disagreed.

Kāna: He was.

Kānat: She was.

Kānū: They (masc. pl.) were.

Karāhah: Dislike.

Karam: Generosity, nobility.

Karāmah: Dignity.

Karīm (al-): The Generous. It is one of the ninety-nine attributes of God.

Khalīfah (pl. *khulafā')*: Caliph. Originally the word meant "successor" (i.e., of the Prophet). In Islam, the caliph is the head of the community of believers. His functions are secular as well as religious The first four caliphs are called *al-khulafā' al-rāshidūn* (the wise caliphs). In the *Qur'ān,* the title of *khalīfah* is given to both *Ādam* and *Dāwūd* (David).

Khalq: Creation. According to *al-Māturīdī,* God created everythings.

Kharajites (in Arabic *khawārij)*: Derived from the Arabic root *"kharajah"* (means "to go out," "to secede"); a revolutionary and egalitarian group that revolted against the Caliph *`Uthmān Ibn `Affān* and later against *`Alī Ibn Alī Ṭālib.* In the battle of *Ṣiffīn,* opposing *`Alī Ibn Abī Ṭālib* and *Mu`āwiyah Ibn Abī Sufyān* they refused any form of arbitration saying that the judgment should be left only to God.

Khāṣṣah: The elite. For *al-Fārābī*, the philosopher should be regarded as a member of the elite in an absolute sense.

Khawf: Fear; it is a principal virtue (a first-order virtue) in Sufi teaching.

Khayr: As adjective, means "charitable," "good." As nouns, means "goodness," "welfare."

Khilāfah al-rāshidah (al-): Righteously guided Caliphate.

Khilāfah: Caliphate.

Khuluq ḥasan: Good character, virtuous manner.

Kitāb (al-): The Book.

Kunna: They (fem. pl.) were.

L

Lā yuḥibb: He does not like.

Lā yuḥibbu al-mu`tadīn: He does not like aggressors.

Lā: Do not.

Ladhdhah (pl. *ladhdhāt*): Pleasure, bliss, enjoyment. According to *al-Ghazālī,* the ultimate pleasure (*a`ẓam ladhdhah*) is knowing God.

Lutf: Divine grace; it is a *Shi`ite* doctrine arguing that there should be always an infallible *imām* that exists to interpret the Qur'an and determine the Laws.

M

Mā ṭāba lakum: What you find desirable.

Mā: What.

Madhāhib (sing. *madhhab*): Schools of thought.

Madhhab al- ladhdhāt: Hedonism.

Mafsadah: A bad thing.

Maḥabbah: Platonic love; it is a principal virtue (a first-order virtue) in Sufi teaching.

Maḥrūrī al-ṭibā`: Hot-tempered persons.

Makrūh: Reprehensible, discouraged; one of the five normative categories (see *al-aḥkām al-khamsah).*

Maktūb: Written, fateful.

Mālik (al-): The ruler or the owner; one of the ninety-nine attributes of God.

Mālik al-Mulk: The owner or the ruler of the universe; one of the ninety-nine attributes of God.

Mandūb: Recommended (also *mustaḥabb)*; one of the five normative categories (see *al-aḥkām al-khamsah).*

Mansūkh: Abrogated.

Manṭiq: Logic. According to *al-Fārābī,* logic is a tool which, when used properly, will yield to certainty *(yaqīn)* in all theoretical and practical sciences and is absolutely indispensable for attaining that goal.

Mashkūk: Doubtful.

Masjid al-ḍirār: The name of a mosque from the time of the Prophet.

Maṣlaḥah: Good.

Mathnā: In threes.

Mizāj: Mixture; also, temperament, mood, humor, state of mind, physical constitution.

Mu`ālajat al-ḍarar: Managing the harm.

Mu`tazilah* (or *Mu`tazilites): The word derives from the Arabic verb *i`tazala*; to seclude oneself. In effect, the term refers to some scholars who disagreed with theologians on a number of points among which the doctrine of a created *Qur'ān,* and man's free will.

Mubāḥ: Permissible, morally neutral; one of the five normative categories (see *al-aḥkām al-khamsah).*

Mudda`ī (*al-*): Plaintiff; the claimant.

Mufti: A person who is qualified to issue religious edicts.

Mughālaṭah: Sophistry.

Muḥāsabah: Self-examination or accounting for one's actions; a supporting mystical virtue or a second-order virtue in Sufi teaching.

Muḥdath: That which is created in time. Plato believed that the world is created in time, while Aristotle is alleged to hold that it is eternal.

Muḥtasib: Market controller.

Mujtahid: Jurist.

Mujtama` (al-): Society, association, community.

Mukhāṭabah: Modes of address; talking to someone.

Munāfiq: Hypocrite, liar.

Munkir (al-): The defendant.

Murāqabah: Vigilance; a supporting mystical virtue or a second-order virtue in Sufi teaching.

Mustaḥabb: Recommended (see *mandūb)*; one of the five normative categories (see *al-aḥkām al-khamsah*).

N

Nafs (pl. *nufūs, anfus*): Soul; self.

Nahy: Negative command.

Nāmūs: Law, natural law, moral law, possibly religious law. *Ikhwān al-Ṣafā,* organize all living beings in categories. According to them, plants rank under animals, animals rank under humans, humans rank under wise people, wise people rank under the people of law (*nāmūs*), who in turn, rank under angels.

Nār: Literally, fire; it is a common name by which "hell" is referred to in the *Qur'ān.*

Nāsikh: Abrogator.

Naskh: Abrogation.

Naẓar: Literally, sight, discernment; deliberation; opinion.

Nikāḥ: Marriage.

Niyyah: Intention.

Nubuwwah: Prophetic office.

Nūr (al-): The Light; it is one of the ninety-nine attributes of God. Angels are believed to be created from *nūr,* as opposed to humans (*ins*) from clay, and *jinn* from fire.

Nuṭq: Speech. Philosophers divided *nuṭq* in two parts:

1. The power to conceive of; intelligible in the practical and theoretical fields.
2. The power of expression in spoken language.

Q

Qadariyyah: Early Muslims who believed in free will.

Qadhf: To falsely accuse a woman of adultery.

Qāḍī: Judge.

Qalb: Heart. According to *al-Ghazālī*, it is the same as *al-rūḥ* (the soul, the spirit). The virtues of the heart are:

a. Virtues of devils: *akhlāq al-shayāṭīn.*
b. Virtues of domestic animals: *akhlāq al-bahā'im.*
c. Virtues of predatory animals: *akhlāq al-sibā`.*
d. Virtues of angels: *akhlāq al-malā'ika*h.

Qarābah: Blood relation.

Qaṭ` al-ṭarīq: Road banditry.

Qatl: Murder.

Qiṣāṣ: Reciprocal punishment.

Qisṭ: Fairness.

Qiyās: Analogy or "analogical reasoning"; a method of extracting (deriving) legal rulings when none exists in the *Qur'ān, Sunnah,* and *ijmā`*. In his writings, *al-Fārābī* is critical of this method of analogy on the ground that it is reducible to similarity (*shabah*) rather than deduction in the strict sense. According to him, there are five types of *qiyās*: the demonstrative, the dialectical, the sophistical, the rhetorical, and the poetical.

Qubḥ al-dhātī (al-): Inherent badness; a doctrine of the *mu`tazilah*.

Qabūl: Acceptance.

Qudrah: Power to perform an act.

Qurb (also *muqārabah*): Proximity. According to *al-Fārābī,* when humans attain the highest stage of theoretical knowledge, they attain the stage of union with the Active Intellect. *Al-Fārābī* sometimes calls this stage conjunction (*ittiṣāl*).

Quwwah: Power, force.

R

Ra'y: Opinion. According to *al-Fārābī,* both conjecture and certainty are species of opinion (*ra'y*), which is liable to truth or falsity.

Radd: To return something.

Raḥīm (al-): The Compassionate. It is one of the ninety-nine attributes of God.

Raḥmān (al-): The Merciful. It is one of the ninety-nine attributes of God.

Rajā': Hope; it is a principal virtue (a first-order virtue) in Sufi teaching.

Ramaḍān: it is the ninth month of the Muslim lunar calendar; it is believed that the *Qur'ān* was descended during that month. It is also the month of fasting. During the fast the believer must abstain from food, drink, and sexual intercourse during daylight hours.

Ribā: Usury.

Riḍā': Satisfaction; it is a virtue produced by love, by pleasant acts, feelings.

Ru'yah: Vision.

Rubā`: In fours.

Rūḥ: Soul.

Rushd: Maturity, guidance, conscious awareness.

S

Sa`ādah: Happiness. According to *al-Ghazālī,* happiness is achieved through:

a. The power of anger: *quwwat al-ghaḍab*
b. The power of lust: *quwwat al-shahwah*
c. The power of knowledge: *quwwat al-`ilm*

Ṣabr: Patience. It is a principal virtue (a first-order virtue) in Sufi teaching.

Ṣafḥ: Forgiveness.

Ṣaḥābah: Companions of the Prophet.

Salaf: Early generation of Islamic authorities.

Ṣalāh: Ritual prayer. A Muslim does his/her prayer five times a day. *Ṣalāh* is the second of the five *Arkān* (pillars) of *Islām.*

Sariqah: Theft.

Ṣawm: Fasting during the month of *Ramaḍān.* It is the third of the five pillars (*Arkān*) of *Islām.*

Shahādah: Profession of faith that a person must recite in order to become a Muslim. It is the first of the five pillars (*Arkān*) of *Islām* and is declared once in one's lifetime.

Shahwah (pl. *shahawāt):* Craving, desire, passion, lust, appetite (see *Ikhwān al-Ṣafā,* and *al-Ghazālī*).

Shajā`ah: Courage.

Shakk: Doubt. According to *al-Fārābī, shakk* is the suspension of judgment with respect to two opinions equally credible.

Shar`: "The road leading to water" (or to the source of life); it is also coined to refer to law.

Shawq: Yearning.

Shī`ah*: Originally meant "group," "party," "followers of someone;" it is derived from *Shī`at `Alī* (followers of *`Alī Ibn Abī Ṭālib). The *Shi`ites* believe that it is *`Alī Ibn Abī Ṭālib* (cousin and son-in-law of the Prophet) rather than *Abū Bakr* who should have succeeded *Muḥammad.* In the civil war (*fitnah)* between *`Alī Ibn Abī Ṭālib* and *Mu`āwiyah Ibn Abī Sufyān* they supported *`Alī Ibn Abī Ṭālib.* They also argue for the need for infallible *imām* to guide the community.

Shukr: Gratitude, thankfulness.

Shurb al-khamr: Drinking wine.

Ṣidq: Truthfulness; a supporting mystical virtue or a second-order virtue in Sufi teaching.

Sīrah (pl. *siyar*): History of one's way of life.

Sunnah: Literally, it can mean "trodden path," "way," "rule," "manner of acting" or "mode of life." Originally it meant "customary practice." Since the behavior of the Prophet is believed to be virtuous and exemplary, the acts of *Muḥammad* provide the norms and set the model of human life and behavior. These virtuous acts are then converted into obligations of which total constitutes the *sharī`ah.* Customarily, *Sunnah* and *Ḥadīth* are used interchangeably (see *Ḥadīth*).

Ṣūrah: According to *Ibn Rushd*, the *ṣūrah* is the entity that does enjoy neither power (*quwwah*) nor preparedness (*isti`dād*).

T

Ta`līm: Instruction, teaching.

Ta`ṣīb: A method of distrubuting inheritance.

Ta`zīr (al-): Discretionary punishment.

Ṭā`ah: Obedience.

Ta'wīl: The interpretation of the words of the Lawgiver or His ordinances

Ta'yīd: Support.

Ṭabī`ah* (pl. *ṭabā'i`): Nature.

Tafakkur: Meditation, deliberation, pondering.

Tafsīr al-ishārī (al-): Interpretation based on hints; deductive interpretation.

Tafsīr al-riwā'ī (al-): Interpretation based on tradition.

Tafsīr: Commentaries on the Qur'an.

Taḥrīm: Proscription.

Ṭalāq rij`ī: Revocable divorce.

Ṭalāq: Divorce. A saying attributed to the Prophet states that among all things permitted by God, divorce is the most blameworthy. Thus divorce is clearly permitted in Islam but not encouraged. If the divorce is done by repudiating a marriage three times then this repudiation cancels any opportunity for reconciliation. Otherwise, it should be followed by a waiting period of three menstrual cycles that is supposed to give the spouses a chance for reconciliation and/or to determine if the wife is pregnant.

Taqiyyah: Dissimulation of one's religion, especially in time of persecution or danger. The practice is permitted by the *Shī`ah.*

Taqṣīr: Poor judgment.

Taqwā: Piety.

Taṣawwur: Conception.

Tasdīd: Leading, guiding, directing; conducting.

Tawakkul: Trust in God, rely on God.

Tawbah: Repentance, atonement.

Tawbīkh: To scold or reprimand an offender; to shame an offender.

Tawḥīd: Declaration of divine unity.

Tazwīr: To falsify testimony or evidence.

Thābit yaqīnan (al-): That which is positively evident.

Thawāb (al-): Positive reward.

Thulāth: In threes.

U

Ummah (pl. *umam*): Nation or community. This was a highly emotive word in early Islamic history in the time of the Prophet and remains so among the Arabs today.

Uns: Intimacy; it is a virtue produced by love.

Uṣūl al-dīn: Reformed Islamic theology.

Uṣūl al-fiqh: Means "the roots" or "sources" of law; foundation of law; Islamic jurisprudence.

Uṣūl: Roots, origins; foundations.

W

Wa`d: Promise of good reward for the faithful who upholds a virtuous Islamic life.

Wā`iz: Deterrent.

Wa`īd: Threat. "Promise" of painful reward for those who led a nonvirtuous life that contradicted the code of morality established in the *Qur'ān* and *Sunnah.*

Wa'd: Infanticide.

Wadūd (al-): The Loving. It is one of the ninety-nine attributes of God.

Wājib: (farḍ); Required; obligatory; one of the five categories in which Islamic law and ethics have traditionally divided human behavior.

Walā': Patronage.

Y

Yā: Vocative O!

Yakrah: He dislikes, he hates.

Yamīn: Oath.

Yaqīn: Certain knowledge, certainty (see *manṭiq*).

Yatāmā (al-): Orphans.

Yathrib: The pre-Islamic name of Madīnah.

Z

Ẓāhir: Appearance, superficial.

Zakāh: Alms tax, Almsgiving; it is the fourth of the five pillars (*Arkān*) of *Islām.*

Ẓann: Conjecture.

Zindīq (pl. *zanādiqah*): Nonbeliever, heretic, "free thinker."

Zuhd: Asceticism, soberness, by the mere necessities (shunning of luxury). It is a principal virtue (a first-order virtue) in Sufi teaching.

Ẓulm: Aggression.

Notes

Introduction

1. The Qur'ān makes the claim that God's justice will not let any act (good or bad) go unaccounted for, be it as small as an atom:

    > That day mankind will issue forth in scattered groups to be shown their deeds. Whoever had done good, be it as small as an atom's weight, he or she will see it; and whoever had done wrong, be it as small as an atom's weight, he or she will see it. [Q9:V6–8]

2. The idea that justice (or other similar concepts) is a social construct is well established in Western thought. But it is understood to mean that the concept of justice can be manipulated/changed by altering the social milieu and cultural environment. Hence, in any given era, a new understanding may emerge. While I conceive of justice as a social construct, I argue that, in the case of the Islamic discourse, the understanding of the concept of justice was developed and fixed during the formative period of Islamic law. As such, it is less susceptible to change despite the fact that it is a social construct.
3. Social and health sciences scholars have studied human behavior and compared social patterns in men and women. The literature on this subject is comprehensive and points to fundamental differences between men and women. See S. Berthoz, J. L. Armony, R. J. R. Blair, and R. J. Dolan (2002). "An fMRI Study of Intentional and Unintentional (Embarrassing) Violations of Social Norms." *Brain* 125: 1696–1708; R. J. R. Blair & L. Cipolotti (2000). "Impaired Social Response Reversal: A Case of 'Acquired Sociopathy.'"*Brain* 123: 1122–1141; L. Cahill (2003). "Sex-Related Influences on the Neurobiology of Emotionally Influenced Memory." *Annals of the New York Academy of Sciences*, 985: 163–73; L. Cahill, R. J. Haier, N. S. White, J. Fallon, L. Kilpatrick, C. Lawrence, S. G. Potkin, and M. T. Alkire (2001). "Sex-related Difference in Amygdala Activity During Emotionally Influenced Memory Stage." *Neurobiology of Learning and Memory*, 75: 1–9; L. Cahill, M. Uncapher, L. Kilpatrick, M. Alkire, and J. Turner (2004). "Sex-Related Hemispheric Lateralization of Amygdala Function in Emotionally Influenced Memory: An fMRI Investigation." *Learning and Memory*, 11: 261–66; J. Harasty, K. L. Double, G. M. Halliday, J. J. Kril, & D. A. McRitchie (1997). "Language-Associated Cortical Regions are Proportionately Larger in the Female Brain." *Archives of Neurology*, 54: 171–76; T. Rabinowicz, D. E. Dean, J. M. C. Petetot, and G. M. de Courten-Myers (1999). "Gender Differences in the Human Cerebral Cortex: More Neurons in Males; More Processes in Females." *Journal of Child Neurology* 14: 98–107; R. Reavis and W. H. Overman (2001). "Adult Sex

Differences on a Decision-Making Task Previously Shown to Depend on the Orbital Frontal Cortex." *Behavioral Neuroscience*, 115: 196–206; and E. S. Spelke (2005). "Sex Differences in Intrinsic Aptitude for Mathematics and Science? A Critical Review." *American Psychologist* 60: 950–58.

4. Although there are limited classical compilations dealing specifically with women's issues, Muslims' exegeses address such topics when they are dealing with stories where women are mentioned. For example, commentaries on the verses on polygamy and inheritance are rich with references to women and full of explanations. See al-Ṭabarsī, *Majma` al-bayān fī tafsīr al-Qur'ān* (Jordan: Aal al-Bayt Institute for Islamic Thought [Soft Collections], 2002); al-Rāzī, *al-Tafsīr al-kabīr* (Jordan: Aal al-Bayt Institute for Islamic Thought, 2002); al-Qurṭubī, *al-Jāmi` li-'aḥkām al-qur'ān* (Jordan: Aal al-Bayt Institute for Islamic Thought, 2002); al-Bayḍāwī, *Anwār al-Tanzīl wa-asrār al-ta'wīl* (Jordan: Aal al-Bayt Institute for Islamic Thought, 2002); Ibn Kathīr, *Tafsīr al-qur'ān al-karīm* (Jordan: Aal al-Bayt Institute for Islamic Thought, 2002); al-Shawkānī, *Fatḥ al-qadīr* (Jordan: Aal al-Bayt Institute for Islamic Thought, 2002); al-Māwardī, *al-Nukat wa-'l-`uyūn* (Jordan: Aal al-Bayt Institute for Islamic Thought, 2002); Abū Ḥayyān, *al-Baḥr al-muḥīṭ* (Jordan: Aal al-Bayt Institute for Islamic Thought, 2002); al-Tha`ālibī, *al-Jawāhir al-ḥisān fī tafsīr al-qur'ān* (Jordan: Aal al-Bayt Institute for Islamic Thought, 2002); al-Qummī, *Tafsīr al-qur'ān* (Jordan: Aal al-Bayt Institute for Islamic Thought, 2002); al-Ṭūsī, *al-Tibyān al-jāmi` li-`ulūm al-qur'ān* (Jordan: Aal al-Bayt Institute for Islamic Thought, 2002); and al-Fayḍ al-Kāshānī, *al-Ṣāfī fī tafsīr kalām allāh al-wāfī* (Jordan: Aal al-Bayt Institute for Islamic Thought, 2002).
5. The economic and social status of women in pre-Islamic times and in the early Islamic era determined the way women behaved in public and the way they were treated by society at large. See Wiebke Walther, *Women in Islam* (Princeton: Wiener, 1993), 90.
6. Nobility and wealth in pre-Islamic era and during the first century of the Islamic civilization played a major role. According to some reports, it was possible for a rich woman to reach a position of superiority over men because of her wealth. See Wiebke Walther, *Women in Islam* (Princeton: Wiener, 1993), 115.
7. It is a reasonable assumption that if a practice required a legal intervention (Qur'ānic prohibition), then it must be widespread because laws dealing with social matters are rarely created in a vacuum. See chapter 3.
8. For a historical account of the status of women before and after the rise of Islam, readers are advised to consult Leila Ahmed, *Women and Gender in Islam: Historical Roots of a Modern Debate* (New Haven: Yale University Press, 1992).
9. Zaynab Ridwan, *al-Mar'ah bayna al-mawrūth wa-'l-taḥdīth* (Cairo: al-Hay'ah al-Misriyyah al-`Ammah li-'l-Kitab, 2004), 34.
10. The Prophet Muhammad's view of women is expressed in the way he felt about Khadījah. Even as a successful person who was at that time married to numerous wives, he held the view that Khadījah was his favorite wife. It is reported that his loyalty to the memories of Khadījah made the younger wife `Ā'ishah jealous to the point that she demeaned her in his presence to which he responded: "He [God] has never given me a better one [than Khadījah]." See Walther, *Women in Islam*, 104. In another tradition, he is reported to have said (according to Musnad Ahmad and Musnad Hāshim): The favorite women from among the people of paradise are

Khadījah Bint Khuwaylid, Fāṭimah Bint Muhammad, Mariam Bint Imrān [Jesus' mother], and Āsiyā Bint Muzāḥim [Pharaoh's wife]. See *Insāniyyat al-mar'ah*, 298.

11. See Ibn Ḥazm, *al-Muḥallā* (Beirut: Dar al-Fikr, 1997), 9:429; *Jamharat ansāb al-arab*, 150; and *al-Iṣābah*, 7:727; Ibn Sa'd, *al-Ṭabaqāt* (Beirut: Dar Sadir), 8:268; Ibn Sa'd, *Asad al-ghābah* (Beirut: Dar Ihya' al-Turath al-Arabi), 6:162; and Taqī al-Dīn al-Fāsī's *al-`Iqd al-thamīn fī tārīkh al-balad al-amīn*, 8:252.
12. `Alī Ibn Abī Bakr al-Haythamī, *Majma` al-zawā'id wa-manba` al-fawā'id* (Beirut: Dār al-Kitāb al-Ilmiyyah, 1988), 9:264; and Yūsuf Ibn Abd Allah Ibn Abd al-Barr, *al-Istī`āb fī asmā' al-aṣḥāb* (Egypt: Nahdat Misr li-'l-Tiba'ah wa-'l-Nashr wa-'l-Tawzi'), 4:1823.
13. See Muslim's *Ṣaḥīḥ*, chapter on sowing and planting, 2:155; chapter on divorce, 57; and chapter on breastfeeding, 122; and Abu Dāwūd's *Sunan*, chapter on divorce, 44.
14. Women in early and late Islam held high political positions. As late as the thirteenth century, a woman and a former slave (Shajarat al-Durr) held the office of the Ayyubid Sultan. See Walther, *Women in Islam*, 4 and 120.
15. See *Fatḥ al-bārī*, 6:93; and Ibn al-Jawzī, *Ṣafwat al-ṣafwah* (Beirut: Dar al-Ma`rifah, 1985), 2:23.
16. See volume *al-jihād wa-'l-siyar* in al-'Asqalānī, *Fatḥ al-bārī*, (Beirut: Dar al-Ma`rifah, 1989), 6:89; al-`Asqalānī, *al-Iṣābah* (Beirut: Dar al-Kutub al-'Ilmiyyah) 8:223; *al-Ṭabaqāt*, 3:546, 8:435; Ibn Kathīr, *al-Bidāyah wa-'l-nihāyah* (Beirut: Maktabat al-Ma`ārif, 1985), 6:227–28, 7:84, and 7:158; and *Tahdhīb al-tahdhīb*, 5:111.
17. See A. E. Souaiaia, *The Function of Orality in Islamic Law and Practices: Verbalizing Meaning* (UK: Mellen, 2006), 310–20.
18. See *al-Ṭabaqāt*, 8:34; *al-Iṣābah*, 8:4; *al-Durr al-manthūr*, 25; *Asad al-ghābah*, 6:131–35; Ṭabarī's *Tārīkh*, 5:460–61; *al-`Iqd al-farīd*, 1:340–60; and *Balāghāt al-nisā'*, 30–38 and 70–75.
19. See Ibn al-Athīr's *Asad al-ghābah*, 5:469; and Ibn Ḥajar al-`Asqalānī's *al-Iṣābah*, 8:98–105.
20. See Walther, *Women in Islam*, 110.
21. See Walther, *Women in Islam*, 143.
22. Muhammad Ibn Ahmad Ibn `Uthmān al-Dhahbī, *Mīzān al-i`tidāl fī naqd al-rijāl* (Beirut: Dar al-Ma'rifah, 1963), 4:600–606.
23. See *Asad al-ghābah*, 5:551.
24. See Ibn Qāḍī, *Ṭabaqāt al-shāfi`iyyah* (Beirut: `Alam al-Kitāb, 1407 AH), 2:13.
25. See Ibn Kathīr, *al-Bidāyah wa-'l-nihāyah* (Beirut: Maktabat al-Ma`ārif, 1985), 14:72.
26. Historical records show that, during the lifetime of the Prophet, learned women were appointed as prayer leaders for mixed (men and women) congregations. See Walther, *Women in Islam*, 111. In March 2005, a Muslim woman made the news by leading mixed prayer; while such event might be groundbreaking for modern Muslim women, it seems that a precedent was established during the time of the Prophet Muhammad and that the practice was common in early Islam. See Ahmad Ibn `Alī al-Maqrīzī, *al-Khuṭaṭ al-maqrīziyyah* (Beirut: Dar Sadir), 2:440; and Jamal al-Banna, *Jawāz imāmat al-mar'ah al-rijāl* (Cairo: Dar al-Fikr al-Islami, 2005).

27. See al-Dhahbi, *al-`Ibar fī khabari man `abar* (Beirut: Dar al-Kutub al-`Ilmiyyah, 1985), 3:62; and Ibn Khallikān, *Wifāyāt al-a`y ān wa-anbā' abnā' al-zamān* (Beirut: Dar al-Fikr, 1969), 2:470–79.
28. See Ibn Ḥamīd, *al-Suḥub al-wābilah `alā ḍārā'iḥ al-ḥanābilah* (Beirut: Mu'assasat al-Risālah, 1996), 3:1227–29.
29. See Walther, *Women in Islam*, 108 and 143.
30. Since Western countries do not allow religious communities to adjudicate family law cases according to their own religious traditions, it is not really possible to determine whether or not Muslims living in the West would choose to live by Islamic law codes if given the option, but the attire remains a remarkable indicator since it is a visible form of expressing one's preference. For this reason, I will interject the topic of headscarf from time to time to make the point that the adherents may in fact "choose" a religious law even if they live in the Free World.
31. In 2006, some Canadian politicians considered initiating religious courts where Muslims could voluntarily adjudicate their disputes. The plan was halted due to public protests.
32. See, generally, Abdullahi An-Na`im, *Toward an Islamic Reformation* (New York: Syracuse University Press, 1990).
33. See Walther, *Women in Islam*, 232–39; and Zayzafoon, *The Production of the Muslim Woman*, 98–103.
34. The relationship between the legal proofs (*adillah*) and the legal rulings (*aḥkām*) as well as the history and origins of Islamic jurisprudence is discussed in detail in other works. See, generally, A. E. Souaiaia, *Verbalizing Meaning* (UK: Mellen, 2006).
35. For simplicity, I will use polygamy and polygyny interchangeably although in Islam only limited polygyny is recognized.

Chapter 1. Legal Absolutism and Ethical Relativism

1. The word "*ẓulm*" could also mean acting unjustly and unfairly. See the *qudusī* tradition: "*yā `ibādī, innī ḥarramtu al-ẓulma alā nafsī waja`altuhu bainakum muharraman; falā taẓālamū.*" See Ahmed Zakki Yamani, *al-Islām wa-'l-mar'ah* (Cairo: Matba'at al-Madani, 2004), 124.
2. See the failure of the world community to reach a consensus regarding a definition to the point that it was left out of the International Criminal Court (ICC) Rome Document.
3. Izutsu defines *ẓulm* to mean "to act in such a way as to transgress the proper limit and encroach upon the right of some other person." See Toshihiko Izutsu, *The Structure of Ethical Terms in the Koran* (Tokyo: Keio Institute of Philological Studies, 1959), 152.
4. For a discussion of ethical concepts of the Qur'ān, see Toshihiko Izutsu, *Ethic-Religious Concepts in the Qur'ān* (Montreal: McGill University Press, 1966).
5. All translations of Arabic passages into English are the author's.
6. This story is the subject of many commentaries; for details see Sunni, Shi`ite, Zaydī, Ibādī, and Sufi exegetes such as: al-Ṭabarī, *Jāmi` al-bayān fī tafsīr al-qur'ān* (Jordan: Aal al-Bayt Institute for Islamic Thought [Soft Collections], 2002); al-Zamakhsharī, *al-Kashshāf* (Jordan: Aal al-Bayt Institute for Islamic Thought [Soft Collections], 2002); al-Janābidhī, *Tafsīr bayān al-sa`ādah fī*

*maqāmāt al-`ibādah* (Jordan: Aal al-Bayt Institute for Islamic Thought [Soft Collections], 2002); al-'A`qam, *Tafsīr al-'a`qam* (Jordan: Aal al-Bayt Institute for Islamic Thought [Soft Collections], 2002); al-Huwwārī, *Tafsīr kitāb allāh al-`azīz* (Jordan: Aal al-Bayt Institute for Islamic Thought [Soft Collections], 2002); Atfīsh, *Taysīr al-tafsīr* (Jordan: Aal al-Bayt Institute for Islamic Thought [Soft Collection]), 2002); Ibn `Arabī, *Tafsīr al-qur'ān* (Jordan: Aal al-Bayt Institute for Islamic Thought [Soft Collections], 2002); and Ibn `Ajībah, *al-Baḥr al-madīd fī tafsīr al-qur'ān al-majīd* (Jordan: Aal al-Bayt Institute for Islamic Thought [Soft Collections], 2002).

7. For historical analysis of the story of Moses and the knower, read the authoritative and comprehensive article by Brannon Wheeler, "The Jewish Origins of the Quran 18:65:82? Reexamining Arent Jan Wensink's Theory," *Journal of the American Oriental Society* 118, 2 (Apr.–Jun. 1998): 153–71.
8. Even the name of Moses' helper (Joshua) is the subject of serious debate. See Brannon M. Wheeler, "Moses or Alexander? Early Islamic Exegesis of Quran 18:60–65," *Journal of Near Eastern Studies* 57, 3 (Jul. 1998): 191–215; and Brannon M. Wheeler, "The Jewish Origins of Quran 18:65–82? Reexamining Arent Jan Wensinck's Theory," *Journal of the American Oriental Society* 118 2 (Apr.–Jun. 1998), 153–71.
9. See the commentaries on [Q18:V65–82] in Ismā`īl Ibn 'Umar Ibn Kathīr, *Tafsīr al-qur'ān al-`aẓīm* (Beirut: Dār al-Mufīd, 1981); Muḥammad Ibn Aḥmad Qurṭubī, *al-Jāmi` li-aḥkām al-Qur'ān* (Beirut: Dār Iḥyā' al-Turāth al-Arabī, 2002); and Ṭabarī, *Jāmi` al-bayān `an ta'wīl āy al-qur'ān* (Egypt: Muṣṭafā al-Bābī, 1968).
10. There is no consensus regarding the location or name of the seas referenced in this story. Some exegetes contend that "juncture of the two seas" is a reference to where the Mediterranean Sea intersects the Atlantic Ocean. Others argue that it is a reference to the area where the Persian Gulf Sea intersects the Indian Ocean.
11. The word "*`ārif*" is coined by Sufis to refer to the teacher (or master). It is taken from another cognate that also means "knower."
12. Shi'ite concept of divine grace (*luṭf*) is essentially built on the assumptions of fallibility of reason and intellect and infallibility of divinely selected leaders.
13. See "On the sources of Islamic Tradition and Practices" *Journal of Law and Religion* 20, 2005), 101–25; and the forthcoming work, *Verbalizing Meaning: Function of Orality in Islamic Law and Practices*.

Chapter 2. The Domain of Ethics and the Law

1. H. L. A. Hart, *The Concept of Law* (Oxford: Clarendon, 1961), 5–10, 38–50, 150–210.
2. See for example, H. L. A. Hart, *Causation in the Law* (Oxford: Clarendon, 1962); Jeremy Bentham, *A Fragment on Government* (Cambridge: Cambridge University Press, 1988); H. L. A. Hart, *Law, Liberty, and Morality* (California: Stanford University Press, 1963); James Rachels, *The Elements of Moral Philosophy* (Boston: McGraw-Hill, 2003); John Austin, *The Province of Jurisprudence* (London: Weidenfeld & Nicolson, 1954); James Mill, *Analysis of the Phenomena of the Human Mind* (New York: Olms, 1982); John Stuart Mill, *On Liberty* (New York: Bantam, 1993); Auguste Comte, *Cours de philosophie positive* (Bruxelles:

Culture et Civilisation, 1969); and David Hume, *An Inquiry Concerning Human Understanding* (Indianapolis: Bobbs-Merrill, 1955).

3. Cornelia Geer Le Boutillier, *American Democracy and Natural Law* (New York: Columbia University Press, 1950); Peter J. Stanlis, *Edmund Burke and the Natural Law* (Ann Arbor: University of Michigan Press, 1965); Russell Hittinger, *A Critique of the New Natural Law Theory* (Notre Dame: University of Notre Dame Press, 1987); and Robert George, *In Defense of Natural Law* (Oxford: Oxford University Press, 2001).
4. In modern societies, such as Tunisia, that adopted European legal systems, inheritance laws are still shaped by personal statutes derived from classical Islamic law. In communities such as those in Jordan and Palestine, Islamic and civil laws coexist to form parallel legal systems.
5. See, Plato, *Apology* (London: Magnes, 1675); Plato, *Crito and Phaedo* (London: printed for M. Cooper, 1755); Plato, *Dialogues* (Oxford: Clarendon, 1953); Aristotle, *Eudemian Ethics* (Oxford: Clarendon, 1982); and see some counterarguments in Epicurus, *Épicure et les Épicuriens* (Paris: Presses Universitaires de France, 1964).
6. See, David Hume, *An Abstract of a Treatise of Human Nature* (Cambridge: Cambridge University Press, 1938); David Hume, *An inquiry Concerning the Principles of Morals* (New York: Liberal Arts Press, 1957); and David Hume, *A Treatise of Human Nature* (London: Dent, 1911).
7. In the words of Bentham, "nature has placed mankind under the governance of two sovereign masters; pain and pleasure. It is for them alone to point out that we ought to do, as well as to determine what we shall do." See also, Jeremy Bentham, *Deontology* (Oxford: Clarendon, 1983).
8. H. L. A. Hart, *The Concept of Law* (Oxford: Clarendon, 1961), 80–88.
9. This claim is the basis for the Mālikī school of thought's doctrine that expanded the legal sources to include the practice of the people of Madīnah at large.
10. It is said that Prophet Muhammad's manners and life was the application of the ethics of the Qur'ān. See Ibn Kathīr's *Tafsīr* of [Q68:V4] and [Q33:V21].
11. Abū Isḥāq al-Shirazi, *Ṭabaqāt al-fuqahā'* (Beirut: Dar al-Ra'id al-Arabi, 1970), 30–39.
12. A detailed account of the controversies associated with appointing the Prophet's successor can be gleaned from primary sources. See, Abū Ja`far Muhammad Ibn Jarīr al-Ṭabarī, *Tārīkh al-rusul wa-'l-mulūk* (Egypt: Dar al-Ma`arif, 1969), 3:180–95; Abū `Abdallāh Muhammad Ibn Ismā`īl Ibn al-Mughīrah, *Ṣaḥīḥ al-bukhārī* (Cairo: Dar al-Sha`b), 6:10–15; and Abū Abdullah Muhammad Ibn Sa`d, *Ṭabaqāt al-ṣaḥābah wa-'l-tābi`īn wa-'l-`ulamā'* (Beirut: Sadir), 2:240–50.
13. In Islamic tradition, only God is sovereign as He is the only Legislator and Ruler. However, the Caliph will be seen as the human sovereign as he derives that sovereignty from God.
14. Ibn Khaldān, *kitāb al-`ibar* (Princeton: Princeton University Press, 1969).
15. The role of social norms, politics, and precedent are aptly highlighted in a study by David S. Powers who made the connection between the role played by influential Muslim leaders and the formulation of early Islamic law. See David S. Powers, *Studies in Qur'an and Ḥadīth* (Berkeley: University of California Press, 1986), 1–7, 17–18, 106–109, 113–222. See also, Norman Calder, *Studies in Early Muslim Jurisprudence* (Oxford: Clarendon, 1993), 162.

16. Ahmad Hijazi Ahmad Saqqa, *al-Khawārij al-harūriyūn wa-muqāranat mabādi'ihum bi-mabādi' al-firaq al-Islāmiyyah: Ahl al-Sunnah, al-Mu`tazilah, al-Shī`ah, al-Murji'ah* (Cairo: Maktabat al-Kulliyat al-Azhariyyah, 1980); and Elie Adib Salem, *Political Theory and Institutions of the Khawārij* (Baltimore: Johns Hopkins Press, 1956).
17. Abd al-Qāhir al-Baghdadi, *al-Milal wa-'l-niḥal* (Beirut: Dar al-Mashriq, 1970), 75. The Kharajites challenged all principles adopted during al-Saqīfah meeting and proposed alternative social and political systems. See Abu al-Ḥasan al-Ash`arī, *Maqālāt al-islāmiyyīn* (Cairo: Maktabat al-Nahḍah al-Misriyyah, 1950), 1:150–98; and Sa`d al-Dir al-Taftāzānī, *Sharh al-`aqā'id al-nafīsah* (Cairo: PU, 1939), 480–89.
18. For Shi`ite theological and philosophical doctrines, see Nāṣir al-Din Muhammad Ibn al-Ḥasan al-Ṭūsī, *Kashf al-Murād* (Qom: shukura, 1413 AH), 373–423. For perspectives on Shi'ite social and political history, see Abū Ja`far Muḥammad Ibn Jarīr al-Ṭabarī, *Tārīkh al-rusul wa-'l-mulūk* (Egypt: Dar al-Ma`ārif, 1969), 5:400–12, 5:550, 5:560, 5:585–620.
19. That is, to argue for following a legal path to salvation as opposed to a philosophical or mystical ones.
20. For the history of Islamic thought, the attitudes of various scholars toward certain disciplines, and the function and place of scholars, see Ibn Taymiyyah, *Dar' ta`āruḍ al-`aql wa-'l-naql* (Cairo: Dar al-Kutub, 1981); and Abū al-Ḥasan al-Ash`arī, *Maqālāt al-islāmiyyīn* (Cairo: Maktabat al-Nahḍah al-Misriyyah, 1950). From the secondary sources, see Wael B. Hallaq, *A History of Islamic Legal Theory* (UK: Cambridge University Press, 1997); and John Burton, *The Sources of Islamic Law* (Edinburgh: Edinburgh University Press, 1990).
21. The progression from the discipline of *kalām* to jurisprudence is evident from the opinions held by major jurists in regard to the methodology and the outcome of *kalām*. Al-Shāfi`ī, for instance, sees the discipline of *kalām* as an activity that focuses on nonpractical matters and he rejects it saying "*lā shay'a abghaḍu ilayya min al-kalāmi wa-ahlih.*" [There is nothing I dislike more than *kalam* and its people.] See Abd al-Hayy Ibn Ahmad Ibn al-Imad, *Shadharāt al-dhahab fī akhbār man dhahab* (Cairo: Maktabat al-Qudsi, 1931), 2:8–9; and Ahmad Ibn Mustafa Tashkubrizadah, *Miftāḥ al-sa`ādah* (Cairo: Dar al-Kutub al-Ḥadīthah 1951), 2:20–29.
22. Bernard G. Weiss, *Studies in Islamic Legal Theory* (Leiden: Brill, 2002).
23. See the discussion of speech moods in, Ma`rūf al-Dawālībī, *al-Madkhal ilā `ilm uṣūl al-fiqh* (Beirut: Dar al-Kitāb al-Jadīd, 1965), 160.
24. Ma`rūf al-Dawālībī, *al-Madkhal ilā `ilm uṣūl al-fiqh* (Beirut: Dar al-Kitāb al-Jadīd, 1965).
25. For theories on the systematization of Islamic law and jurisprudence in secondary and primary sources, see Norman Calder, *Studies in Early Muslim Jurisprudence* (Oxford: Clarendon, 1993), 197; Taqī al-Din `Alī al-Sabkī, *Takmilat al-majmū`* (Cairo: al-Tadamun, 1906), 10–98; and Yasin Dutton, *The Origins of Islamic Law* (Richmond: Curzon, 1999).
26. See Ghazālī, *al-Mustaṣfā min `ilm al-uṣūl* (Baghdad: Maktabat al-Muthannā, 1970).
27. Shafi'ite and the Malikite jurists do not distinguish between the two Arabic words used for this rule: *wājib* and *farḍ* (except in the context of the processions of *hajj*

where the two words mean different things). According to Shafi'ites, something that is deemed "obligation" must be carried out and in the case of failure to act, the subject will be punished by fire as in the case of not performing daily prayers for example. Hanbalite and Hanafite jurists distinguish between the two terms. See Wizārat al-Awqāf, *Kitāb al-fiqh `alā al-madhāhib al-arba`ah* (Cairo: Dar al-Kitāb, 1931), 737.

28. The case of morality as a force for self-policing can be strengthened by the idea that reward and punishment are not only manifested in the form of community or state intervention in this world or divine justice in the Hereafter, but also in the promise of *barakah* (divine grace and blessing) that will cause one's worldly possessions to grow and multiply for acting on desired or abstaining to act on undesired recommendations. In other words, although the subject knows that he will not be punished for not undertaking a recommended act, he will nonetheless perform it for the sake of that *barakah* that could enhance his personal well-being and bring immediate positive return.
29. See Jeanette Wakin, "The Divine Command in Ibn Qudāmah," in *Islamic Law and Jurisprudence*, ed. N. Heer (Seattle: University of Washington Press, 1990), 33–52; and Wael B. Hallaq, *A History of Islamic Legal Theory* (UK: Cambridge University Press, 1997), 40–58.
30. Keep in mind that this category of acts concerns only the acts that are purely good or bad; that is to say acts that do not consist of mixtures of goodness and badness. See al-Mishkīnī, *Iṣṭilāḥāt al-uṣūl* (Qom: al-Hadi, 1413 AH), 120.
31. This category of acts differs from the aforementioned one since all acts herein are a mixture containing badness and goodness at the same time. See al-Mishkīnī, *Iṣṭilāḥāt al-uṣūl* (Qom: al-Hadi, 1413 AH), 121.
32. For an illustration, see Figure 2.1. In order to better understand the Islamic system of judgments, it might be helpful to think of it as two spectrums spreading left and right and away from the zone of permissible acts. The further one moves away and toward the left of the permissible acts, the more contemptuous the judgment is about any given case. At the end of that section, one locates the limited number of proscribed acts. The same applies to desired acts which fall on the right side of the zone of permissible acts ending with those that are established obligations. Both proscribed and obligatory acts, are determined in the speech of the Qur'ān as explained earlier.
33. It is reported that the Prophet Muhammad said: "*abghaḍ al-ḥalāl ilā allāh al-ṭalāq*." (The most hated act before God is divorce). See Zaki Ali al-Sayyid Abu Ghaddah, *al-Zawāj wa-'l-ṭalāq wa-'l-ta`addud* (Cairo: NP, 2004), 171; and M. J. Maghniyyah, *Fiqh al-imām Ja`far al-Ṣādiq* (Qom: Ansariayn, 1999), 6:3.
34. According to some scholars, if a marriage is conflicting with one's commitment to honoring the parents which is a Qur'ānic obligation, divorce becomes necessary as well. See Abu Hamid al-Ghazālī, *Iḥyā' `ulūm al-dīn* (Abu Dhabi: al-Warrāq, 2004), 405.
35. See Figure 2.1.
36. There are numerous reports encouraging Muslims, especially the youths (*al-shabāb*) to marry. One report states that the Prophet said, "whoever amongst you, youths, is able, should marry (*man istaṭā`a minkum al-bā'ah falyatazawwaj*). See *Ṣaḥīḥ al-bukhārī*, chapter on marriage (*nikāḥ*), section *al-targhīb fī al- nikāḥ*. See similar reports in Aḥmad's *Musnad* and Muslim's *Ṣaḥīḥ*.

37. The way Muslim jurists define *`adālah* (required for judges and witnesses) shows the degree of influence morality exerts over the legal system. For example, some Muslim scholars argue that in order to accept one's testimony, the witness must be known to be: "believing, righteous, in control of his or her belly, private parts, hands, and tongue; and known to avoid all the *kabā'ir* such as drinking wine, committing adultery, engaging in usurious transactions, or undertaking any act punishable by fire in the Hereafter." See Abu Mansur Jamal and Din al-Hasan Ibn Ysuf al-Hilli, *Mukhtalaf al-shī`ah fī aḥkām al-sharī'ah* (Isfahan: Maktabat al-Imam Ali, 1404 AH), 142.
38. For Qur'ānic context for this doctrine, see, [Q2:V206], [Q2:V212], [Q2:V223–4], [Q2:V231], [Q2:V233], [Q2:V237], [Q2:V241], [Q2:V278], [Q2:V281–3], [Q3:V15], [Q3:V28], [Q3:V50], [Q3:V76], [Q3:V102], [Q3:V115], [Q3:V120], [Q3:V123], [Q3:V125], [Q3:V130], [Q3:V131–33], [Q3:V138], [Q3:V172], [Q3:V179], [Q3:V186], [Q3:V198], [Q3:V200], [Q4:V1], [Q4:V9], [Q13:V34], [Q19:V63], [Q39:V57] and nearly 260 other verses dealing with the same topic in similar manner.
39. The Qur'ān elaborates on this notion in [Q2:V51], [Q3:V9], [Q9:V114], [Q17:V7], [Q21:V9], [Q31:V9], [Q46:V17], [Q72:V25], [Q77:V7], and nearly 120 similar passages.
40. The term in this particular form is not used often in the Qur'ān, see [Q14:V14] and [Q50:V45]; but when combined with the similar concept in the form of punishment or torture, the frequency balloons to over 330 reference. See [Q2:V7], [Q3:V21], [Q4:V93], [Q6:V40], [Q8:V34], [Q10:V4], [Q11:V103], [Q16:V113], [Q22:V2], [Q25:V19], and [Q29:V29], among other passages.
41. Translation of Qur'ānic passages in this work is the author's.
42. The Qur'ān declares: "*wa-innaka la'alā khuluqin `aẓīm*" [Surely you are (a person) of superb character] [Q68:V4]. See also, [Q33:V21].
43. According to a report on the authority of Qatādah, `Ā'ishah said the mannerism and character of the Prophet was whatever was stated in the Qur'ān, "*kāna khuluquhu al-qur'ān*." See Ibn Kathīr's *tafsīr* of [Q68:V4].
44. Abū Hurayrah reported that the Prophet said, "*innamā bu`ithtu li'utammima ṣāliḥ al-akhlāq*." See tradition 8595 in Aḥmad Ibn Ḥanbal's *Musnad*.
45. I am not aware of any recent critical study of this legal doctrine known as "*al-yad*" in Islamic law. It is a very developed concept especially in Shi'ite jurisprudence. It can be defined as ownership by way of the extension of the status quo. That is to say that a person who has been treating a thing or a person as his property will be seen in the eyes of the law as the owner despite the lack of proof of ownership. This concept is especially prevalent in the Qur'ānic discourse when dealing with women slaves. Since the Qur'ān encouraged emancipating slave men, a slave woman was kept under the status quo unless she gets married. The Qur'ān referred to them as "*mā malakat aydīkum/aymānukum*." See Abu Mansur Jamal and Din al-Hasan Ibn Yusuf al-Hilli, *Mukhtalaf al-shī`ah fī aḥkām al-sharī`ah* (Isfahan: Makatabat al-Imam Ali, 1404 AH), 197; and M. J. Maghniyyah, *Fiqh al-imām Ja'far al-Ṣādiq* (Qom: Ansariayn, 1999), 6:111–15.
46. See, among other passages, the following: [Q2:V222], [Q2:V276], [Q3:V14], [Q3:V31–32], [Q3:V57], [Q3:V76], [Q3:V119], [Q3:V134], [Q2:V165], [Q2:V177], [Q2:V190], [Q2:V195], [Q2:V205], [Q3:V140], [Q3:V146], [Q3:V148], [Q3:V159], [Q4:V36], [Q4:V107], [Q4:V148], [Q5:V13], [Q5:V18],

[Q5:V54], [Q5:V87], [Q5:V93], [Q6:V141], [Q7:V31], [Q7:V55], [Q8:V58], [Q9:V4], [Q9:V7], [Q9:V23–24], [Q9:V108], [Q12:V30], [Q16:V23], [Q20:V39], [Q22:V38], [Q28:V56], [Q28:V76–77], [Q30:V45], [Q31:V18], [Q38:V32], [Q40:V40], [Q49:V7], [Q49:V9], [Q57:V23], [Q60:V8], [Q61:V4], [Q76:V8], [Q89:V20], [Q100:V8].

47. [Q2:V216].
48. From the Qur'ānic discourse, one could gather the impression that emotions are the result of manipulation. Things will be made to look good. (See [Q3:V14].) The practice and example of the Prophet Muhammad explicitly ties faith to love: "*lā tadkhulūna al-jannata ḥattā tu'minū wa-lā tu'minū ḥattā taḥābbū*" [You will not enter paradise unless you believe, and you will not believe until you love one another]. See Muslim's *Ṣāḥīḥ*, chapter *al-īmān*; tradition 81; and Ahmad's *Musnad*, tradition 10238.
49. Commenting on the laws of adultery discussed in John 8, Jesus for example is reported to have said: "If your right eye causes you to sin, gouge it out and throw it away. It is better for you to lose one part of your body than for your whole body to be thrown into hell." Matthew 5:29.
50. According to some scholars, only an innocent person or someone who was not found guilty of similar crime could carry out the punishment. See M. J. Maghniyyah, *Fiqh al-imām Ja`far al-Ṣādiq* (Qom: Ansariyan, 1999), 6:258.
51. See verse [Q11:V103], which states in clear terms that "there are lessons for those who fear (*khāfa*) the punishment or torture (*`adhāb*) of the Hereafter."
52. See M. J. Maghniyyah, *Fiqh al-imām Ja`far al-Ṣādiq* (Qom: Ansariayn, 1999), 4:301.
53. Modern Western courts (U.S. courts for example), too, rely on the power of oath, which must be one of the residual influences of religion. For instance, in civil and criminal cases, the defendant, the plaintiff, and the witnesses (but not the lawyers) are asked to swear to tell the truth and nothing but the truth. However, such courts do not consider oath to be a means of establishing innocence as is the case in Islamic law.
54. See [Q2:V224–25], [Q3:V77], [Q5:V89], [Q16:V91], and [Q66:V2].
55. Abu Mansur Jamal and Din al-Hasan Ibn Yusuf al-Hilli, *Mukhtalaf al-shī`ah fī aḥkām al-sharī`ah* (Isfahan: Makatabat al-Imam Ali, 1404 AH), 142.
56. M. J. Maghniyyah, *Fiqh al-imām Ja`far al-Ṣādiq* (Qom: Ansariayn, 1999), 6:60–69.
57. One could argue that the mere publication of legal sentences and the reliance of states on violence in order to enforce the laws are in themselves forms of threats. Similarly, the system of reward money in return for providing and assisting in the arrest and conviction of criminals is an acknowledgment of the power of incentives in motivating people to act. These incentives, it must be noted, are appealing to emotions in that they provide means (pecuniary) for achieving happiness and pleasure.
58. As the Arabic name indicates, this is a category and not a specific case. The punishment is mentioned in the Qur'ān but the practice is generally not in conformity with that. The rulers and judges take generous leeway in assigning harsher punishments beyond what is expressed in the Qur'ān [Q4:V15–17], [Q27:V54–56], and [Q29:28]. That difference can be seen as a window into the mind of early Arab jurists and their theory on crime and punishable and deter-

rence. For example, sodomy for them is punished by death, fire, and the destruction of house over the subject. When asked for the reason this excessive harshness, it was reported that death alone is not enough, because the Arabs did not see much of a threat in killing. See the decree of the Caliph Abu Bakr as advised by `Alī in, M. J. Maghniyyah, *Fiqh al-imām Ja`far al-Ṣādiq* (Qom: Ansariayn, 1999), 6:266–67.

59. Some Muslim scholars include wine drinking in this category although the Qur'ān does not mention a punishment for it; but since Muslim scholars see the Prophet's tradition as a form of revelation, they argue that the punishment is therefore determined by God too.
60. Some Muslim scholars include slander (*qadhf*) in this category although the Qur'ān explicitly determines the punishment for this offense: eighty lashes as per [Q24:V4–5].
61. See al-Māwardī, *al-Aḥkām al-sulṭāniyyah wa-'l-wilāyāt al-dīniyyah* (Abu Dhabi: al-Warrāq, 2004), 38.
62. See [Q24:V22], and, [Q64:V14].
63. The legal procedure in Islamic law establishes the judges as truth seekers and not mere referees. In the absence of solid proof, judges depend on the degree of piety in the litigants. It is reported that the Prophet said: "Indeed I issue my ruling based on the apparent evidence (*al-ẓāhir*). As you (two litigants) argue your case before me, one of you might be more able to express his evidence better than the other. If I rule (*ḥakamtu*) and award one of you something that he knows is not his, he should not take it because what I awarded him is indeed a piece of fire." See Ibn Ḥazm, *al-Iḥkām fī uṣūl al-qur'ān* (Abu Dhabi: al-Warrāq, 2004), 423.
64. H. L. A. Hart, *Punishment and Responsibility* (Oxford: Oxford University Press, 1968), 1–39.
65. For examples of consequentialist theories, see J. Wilson, *Thinking about Crime* (New York: Basic, 1983); and N. Walker, *Why Punish?* (Oxford: Oxford University Press, 1991).
66. H. L. A. Hart, *Punishment and Responsibility* (Oxford: Oxford University Press, 1968), 8–10.
67. J. G. Murphy, "Marxism and Retribution," *Philosophy and Public Affairs* 2 (1973): 217–43; J. L. Anderson, "Reciprocity as a Justification for Retributivism," *Criminal Justice Ethics* 16 (1997): 13–25; and M. S. Moore, *Placing Blame: A Theory of Criminal Law* (Oxford: Oxford University Press, 1997).
68. See R. Matthews, *Informal Justice* (London: Sage, 1988); and L. Walgrave, *Restorative Justice and the Law* (Devon: Willan, 2002).
69. "*wa-ammā al-`iqāb fahwa al-ḍarar al-mustaḥaqq al-wāqi' `alā jihat al-istikhfāf wa-'l-ihānah.*" See Abu al-Salah al-Ḥalabī, *al-Kāfī fī al-fiqh* (Isfahan: Maktabat al-Imam Amir al-Mu'minin, 1403 AH), 462.
70. The concept of pain (*al-alam*), be it inflicted upon the subject as a punishment or an illness, was discussed by Muslim scholars from all theological and legal schools of thought. See Nāṣir al-Din Muhammad Ibn al-Hasan al-Ṭūsī, *Kashf al-murād* (Qom: Shakura, 1413 AH), 356–60; and Abu al-Salah al-Ḥalabī, *al-Kāfī fī al-fiqh* (Isfahan: Maktabat al-Imam Amīr al-Mu`min īn, 1403 AH), 462.
71. Abu al-Salah al-Ḥalabī, *al-Kāfī fī al-fiqh* (Isfahan: Maktabat al-Imam Amīr al-Mu`minīn, 1403 AH), 466–73.
72. Al-Ghazālī for instance, argues that all people will be punished in hell, the only

difference is that some would suffer for a very short time (the duration of a blink of an eye); others would suffer forever. See Abu Hamid al-Ghazālī, *Iḥyā' `ulūm al-dīn* (Abu Dhabi: al-Warrāq, 2004), 1130.

73. *"kullamā naḍijat julūduhum baddalnāhum julūdan ghayrahā liyadhūqū al-`adhāb"* [Q4:V56]. See also, [Q44:V45–6], [Q88:V6], [Q56:V50–5], and [Q18:V29].
74. In states with parallel legal systems, the community is largely governed by two distinct nonserial legal systems. That is, to have two or more legal systems (for example civil and religious) and each acts independently from the other. In other words, such legal systems are not hierarchized as is the case in the United States, where the relationship between federal and states' laws are explicitly spelled out.
75. In the United States, there is a system whose function fits what is described above. It consists of the state giving financial incentives (in the form of tax credits) in order to encourage social practices such as marriage and adoption or economic ventures such as tax cuts for entrepreneurs. Similarly, when the state wants to discourage the public from certain behavior, it imposes higher taxes if such activity is facilitated through trade activities. For example, to discourage people from smoking, governments impose higher taxes on the sale of tobacco products.

Chapter 3. Basis for the Practice of Polygamy

1. One of the fundamental principles guiding jurisprudence in Western legal thought is equality before the law. Islamic laws of inheritance do not follow this principle: A brother and a sister from the same parents receive different shares according to Muslim jurists from all major legal schools of thought (Shi'ite and Sunni tendencies alike). See detail on this matter when I introduce specific cases in chapter 4.
2. I would like to thank Professor Diana Cates who read and generously commented on this chapter. I am grateful for her constructive and insightful suggestions.
3. I use the phrase "posited ideas" to refer to the notion that Islamic law is, as the Arabic word (*fiqh*) indicates, an understanding. To be sure, it is a human understanding even if it is based on what Muslims see as divine revelations. See Abdullahi An-Na`im, *Toward an Islamic Reformation* (New York: Syracuse University Press, 1990).
4. The word "*`adl*" is generally used as an adjective describing a person of probity, whereas the word "*`adālah*" refers to the concept of justice.
5. See the various explanations that Muslim scholars introduced to contextualize polygamy in the rest of the chapter.
6. See, generally, Muhammad Sabuni, *al-Itqān fī `ulūm al-qur'ān* (Beirut: Dar al-Irshad, 1970).
7. There is no consensus regarding the identification of the "Companions." Some would argue that they are any Muslim who lived and met the Prophet in person. Others would limit the pool of "Companions" to those who fought the battle of Badr (the first battle). There are some who would argue that they are those who were promised paradise. Whatever the case may be, one could simplify the definition of a Companion as a person who was a confidant of the Prophet.
8. Abu Zahrah, *Malik* (Egypt: Matba'at al-Itmad, 1955), 322.
9. I will use the phrase "legal ruling" to refer to the Arabic term *ḥukm* (sometimes specified as *al-ḥukm al-shar`ī*, which means the legal or ethical finding). This is

the actual law or ruling in regard to the specific case. The legal ruling is the keying of any of the five legal rules (*al-ḥukm al-uṣūlī*) to the specific case.

10. The concept of *al-maṣāliḥ al-mursalah* (a concept for which I coined the phrase "inherent well-being") is especially of great importance as it implies that there are certain rights that are natural or absolute and that cannot be restricted by written order or specific enunciation.
11. Ma`rūf al-Dawālībī, *al-Madkhal ilā `ilm al-uṣūl* (Beirut: Dar al-Kitāb al-Jadīd, 1965), 238, and 307–11.
12. Although most Muslim scholars state that polygamy is "*mubāḥ*," not mandatory or even recommended, few would go as far as supporting its prohibition when the circumstances have changed. See Zaki Ali al-Sayyid Abu Ghaddah, *al-Zawāj wa-'l-ṭalāq wa-'l-ta`addud* (Cairo: NP, 2004), 234.
13. Acts do not fall under one of the five rules as it is generally suggested; rather, I would argue that acts are judged to fall anywhere in a continuous spectrum of rules (judgments). This spectrum has clear regions marking the acts that are obligatory, recommended, permissible, contemptuous, and proscribed. But some of the acts are more contemptuous than others. For example, as per tradition of the Prophet, divorce is so contemptuous that it is almost proscribed.
14. Louis M. Epstein, *Marriage Laws in the Bible and the Talmud* (Cambridge: Harvard University Press, 1942), 17–18.
15. Louis M. Epstein, *Marriage Laws*, 15–16.
16. For more on the history and nature of the pre-Islamic Arab communities see Hitti 1967; Smith 1903; and Arberry 1957. See also the historical background presented prior to the interpretive treatment of verse [Q4:3] in al-Ṭabāṭabā'ī 1974, 4:151–66. Also, see A. J. Arberry, *The Seven Odes: The First Chapter in Arabic Literature* (London: Allen & Unwin, 1957); Philip K. Hitti, *History of the Arabs* (New York: St. Martin's, 1967); and W. Robertson Smith, *Kinship and Marriage in Early Arabia* (London: Black, 1903).
17. Zaki Ali al-Sayyid Abu Ghaddah, *al-Zawāj wa-'l-ṭalāq wa-'l-ta`addud* (Cairo: NP, 2004), 234.
18. See the passage regarding the practice of burying female babies alive upon birth: *wa-idhā al-maw'ūdatu su'ilat, b'ayyi thanbin qutilat* [Q81:8–9].
19. Giladi, Avner, "Some Observations on Infanticide in Medieval Muslim Society," *International Journal of Middle Eastern Studies* 22 (1990) 185–200.
20. In addition to the loss of life among men in wars and raids, the system of "revenge" also affects the population of men, since the retribution was in the form of "a free man for a free man and a slave for a slave."
21. It is incorrect to think of polygamy as an innovation by the pre-Islam Arabs. Jewish communities practiced polygamy all the way until the Roman times when Theodosius banned the custom in 393 CE. But even the legal monogamy that was enforced by the Greeks and the Romans was "often supplemented with institutionalized concubinage and widespread prostitution." See Eugene Hillman, *Polygamy Reconsidered* (New York: Orbis, 1975).
22. Since polygamy refers to "having more than one *spouse* at the time, and because Islamic law does not recognize the marriage of one woman to more than one man, using the word "polygamy" is technically inaccurate. However, for simplicity, I will be using it with the understanding that polygamy in the Islamic context refers

to the instance where one man is married to two, three, or four wives (limited polygyny).

23. The same problem of cultural dominance over reformist religions has also faced the Christian Church in recent years forcing Pope Pius XII to decree that "[n]ative custom has the privilege of '*melior condicio possidentis*.' Before in effect decreeing the eventual suppression of a custom, the missionary must prove that it is indissolubly linked with error or immorality or absurd superstition. Insofar as this proof is not conclusive, the custom holds. It has the force of law." See Eugene Hillman, *Polygamy Reconsidered* (New York: Orbis, 1975), 4.
24. According to Islamic traditions, the *imām* (or *mujtahid*) is empowered to temporarily suspend a law even if it is explicitly mentioned in the Qur'ān. This was done by the second Caliph `Umar on many occasions including the suspension of *ḥadd al-sariqah* during the drought years and the reversal of *mut`ah* marriage.
25. The second verse of chapter 4 (*al-nisā'*) explicitly addresses the treatment of orphans. The opening of verse 3 mentions orphans (*wa'in khiftum allā tuqsiṭū fū al-yatāmā …*). Clearly, this chapter has in mind orphans and women as the title and word choice indicate. Based on some traditions, scholars have argued that the mention of orphans in this context is merely for establishing an analogy to make men understand that it is hard to establish justice among many wives: "*fakamā takhāfūna allā tuqsiṭū fī al-yatāmā, fakhāfū allā tuqsi ū wa-ta`dilū fī al-nisā'*." The alternative understanding of the same verse is prohibition: "*fa'in khiftum yā ma`shara awliyā' al-yatāmā allā tuqsiṭū … falā tankiḥūhunna, walākin ankiḥū ghayrahunn …*" See the tradition reported on the authority of al-Muthannā and that on the authority of Abū Ja`far in al-Ṭabarī's *tafsīr* of verse [Q4:V3].
26. The role of human agency in determining the meaning of divine revelations in the Islamic discourse has been widely discussed. See Hadia Mubarak, "Breaking the Interpretive Monopoly," *Hawwa* 2, 3 (2004), 261–89.
27. See, generally, Norman Calder, *Studies In Early Muslim Jurisprudence* (Oxford: Clarendon, 1993); John Burton, *The Sources of Islamic Law* (Edinburgh: Edinburgh University Press, 1990); G. H. A. Juynboll, *Studies on The Origins and Uses of Islamic Ḥadīth* (Brookfield, VT: Variorum, 1996); Ignaz Goldziher, *Muslim Studies* (Albany: State University of New York Press, 1967); and J. Schacht, *The Origins of Muhammadan Jurisprudence* (Oxford: Clarendon, 1979).
28. This tradition, or variations of it, was reported on the authority of Ibn Ḥanbal. Similar reports were presented by al-Shāfi`ī, Abū Ḥanīfah, and al-Bukhārī. See Ibn Kathīr's *Tafsīr*, al-Ṭabarī's *Tafsīr*, and al-Qurṭubī's *Tafsīr* of [Q4:V3].
29. Clearly even early Muslim scholarship was not convinced that the language of verse [Q4:V3] prohibits marrying more than four wives, and for that reason, the cap was mainly established based on the traditions mentioned in Ibn Kathīr's *tafsīr* of [Q4:3], rather than by relying on the Qur'ānic text itself.
30. According to al-Shāfi`ī, the Sunnah established that God does not permit anyone, other than the Prophet, to marry more than four women (*lā yajūzu li-'aḥadin ghayra rasūli allāh … `an yajma`a bayna akthari min arba` niswah*). This view is shared by all Muslim scholars except some Shi'ites who allowed uncapped polygamous marriages. For more on this discussion, see Ibn Kathīr's *Tafsīr* of verse [Q4:V3]. The Shi`ite law on polygamy is articulated in Maghniyyah's work (Maghniyyah, 1999, 5:197).

31. Some of the traditions that were used to fix the interpretations of the verse [Q4:V3] were reported in the works of al-Shāfi`ī, al-Tirmidhī, al-Bukhārī, al-Bayhaqī, and al-Dāraqaṭnī, and the names of the Companions were mentioned therein. See the commentary on verse [Q4:V3] in Ibn Kathīr's *Tafsīr*.
32. See the commentary on verse [Q4:V3] in Ibn Kathīr's *Tafsīr* .
33. Al-Qurṭubī for instance argued that if a man does not fear *qisṭ* (fairness), then he shall be able to marry up to four orphans; al-Qurṭubī's *Tafsīr* of [Q4:V3]. Al-Ṭabarī on the other hand, argued that if one fears *qisṭ* even in regard to one, then he shall not marry an orphan at all. See al-Ṭabarī's *Tafsīr* of [Q4:V3].
34. See the tradition reported on the authority of al-Zubayr Ibn Bakkār (al-Qur ubī's *tafsīr* of verse [Q4:V3]) who contends that a woman approached the Caliph `Umar Ibn al-Khaṭṭāb to complain about her husband who abandoned her in bed in pursuit of acts of piety and worship. When Ka`b al-Asdī was asked by the Caliph to render a judgment in this case, he ruled that she had the right to satisfy her sexual needs, arguing that God allowed a man up to four wives, which would require him to spend at least one night and one day with each of them and have three nights and three days to himself to worship (*inna allāha `azza wa-jalla qad aḥalla laka mina al-nisā' mathnā wa-thulāth, wa-rubā`, falaka thalāthat ayyām wa-layālīhinna ta`bud fīhinna rabbak*).
35. According to Ibn Kathīr, the dominant view prohibits marrying more than four wives at the same time but the Prophet was excluded from this restriction, based on the opinion of al-Shāfi`ī. There are some among the Shi`ites who allow up to nine wives and other Shi`ites who do not restrict the number of wives at all. For more on the various views regarding the limitation of polygamy, see Ibn Kathīr's *Tafsīr* of verse [Q4:V3].
36. That is to say the right of an orphan woman (just like any other woman) to marry has been contravened.
37. Women's participation in the interpretive process was lacking. This should not be confused with women who narrated Prophetic traditions such as `Ā`ishah, whose authority as a transmitter of Ḥadīth is limited to Sunni Islam and is not recognized in Shi`ite Islam.
38. See the list of influential Muslim scholars and community leaders in Appendix A.
39. A good account of the style of life of the Arabs before Islam and during the early years of the Islamic community can be gathered from a number of historical accounts such as al-Dhahbī's *Tārīkh al-islām* and Jawwad Ali's *al-Mufaṣṣal fī tārīkh al-`arab qabla al-islām.*
40. Al-Qurṭubī explicitly states that if a man fears that he cannot establish justice among orphans, he should marry some other women (*ghayrihinn*). See Al-Qurṭubī's *Tafsīr* of verse [Q4:3].
41. Limitation in the sense of prohibiting men from marrying orphans in polygamous marriages.
42. This view is widely reported in the Ḥadīth compilations as well as in the exegetical works. For more on this understanding, see the commentaries on verse [Q4:3] in al-Ṭabarī's *Tafsīr*, al-Qurṭubī's *Tafsīr*, and Ibn Kathīr's *Tafsīr*.
43. According to Arab grammarians, *mā* is used with nonhuman subjects (*ghayr al-`āqil*); hence, in this context, it refers to the number of women and not to the category/class of women per se.

44. Muhsin al-Kashani, *Kitāb al-kāfi fī tafsīr al-qur'ān* (Tehran: Dār al-Kutub al-Islāmiyyah, 1998).
45. The Qur'ānic verse states: "You are never able to be fair and just (*ta`dilū*) as between wives, even if it is your ardent desire. Do not turn away (from a woman) altogether, so as to leave her (as it were) hanging (in the air). If you come to a friendly understanding, and practice self-restraint, then God is Oft-Forgiving, Most Merciful" [Q4:129].
46. `Abdullāh Ibn `Umar al-Bayḍāwī, *Anwār al-tanzīl* (Iran: Ufest, 1977), 1:202–203.
47. Muhammad Hussein al-Tabataba'i, *al-Mīzān fī tafsīr al-qur'ān* (Beirut: Muassasat al-A`lami li-'l-Maṭbū`āt, 1974), 4:167.
48. According to Sunni and Shi`ite scholars, temporary marriage (*zawāj al-mut`ah*) is sanctioned in the Qur'ān [Q4:V24]. Sunni scholars argue that the verse was abrogated. Shi`ite scholars dispute that assertion and claim that it was rescinded by the Caliph `Umar instead. See Fakhr al-Dīn al-Rāzī, *al-Tafsīr al-kabīr* (Istanbul: PU, 1307 AH), 3:286; and Ahmad Ibn Ḥanbal's *Musnad* where he talks about the sermon in which the Caliph `Umar banned *mut`ah:* "Two *mut`ah* were practiced during the time of the Prophet (i.e. temporary marriage and *mut`at al-ḥajj*) but I am proscribing both and I will punish anyone who practices either." Commenting on this same event, al-Rāzī summarized the Sunni interpretation of `Umar's decree by saying that they were pronounced in a gathering of Companions and no one protested. Therefore, the situation must have been as follows: either (1) everyone knew that *mut`ah* was forbidden, so they remained silent, (2) they all knew that it was permitted, yet they remained silent out of negligence and in order to placate `Umar, or (3) they did not know whether it was forbidden or permitted, so they remained silent since the matter had been clarified for them, so they had no reason to protest.
49. The words *mathnā*, *thulāth*, and *rubā`* are understood to imply polygyny. It follows then that *āḥād* would then refer to monogamy, which is not mentioned as an option in verse [Q4:V3], suggesting that monogamy is the norm when marrying from the class of orphan women.
50. Muhammad Abduh (d. 1905) argued that verse [Q4:V129] makes it virtually impossible to establish justice among all four wives and thus concluded that monogamy ought to be the norm. See Abduh and Rida, 1934.
51. See [Q4:V3] and [Q4:V129].
52. A study in Saudi Arabia has concluded that the practice of allowing men to marry up to four wives is the principal cause of divorce in the Kingdom. The report from the sociology department of King Saud University in Riyadh said that the Saudi courts grant between twenty-five and thirty-five divorces a day, with most occurring in the first three years of marriage. Report was released on April 29, 2001.

Chapter 4. Women in Islamic Law of Inheritance

1. Reconstructing pre-Islamic social order remains a challenging task due mostly to the lack of written and archeological records that would enable scholars to establish a definitive understanding of that era. Very few literary legacies from the pre-Islamic era survived, and they survived, because they were preserved as oral poetry and stories. The so-called *jāhiliyyah* poetry hints to a social order where

women are treated as objects of pleasure for men. Imru' al-Qays for instance, glorifies his adventures and his sexual relations with his father's wife. The Qur'ānic, unusually detailed prohibitions of sexual relations with immediate relatives suggest that such practices were prevalent. The accounts of pre-Islamic poetry and the Qur'ānic criticism of *jāhiliyyah* together point to a radically different social order from the one that emerged with Islam.

2. Zaynab Ridwan, *al-Mar'ah bayna al-mawrūth wa-'l-taḥdīth* (Cairo: al-Hay'ah al-Misriyyah al-`Ammah li-'l-Kitab, 2004), 34.
3. Ala Abu Bakr, *Insāniyyat al-mar'ah* (Cairo: Markaz al-Tanwir al-Islami, 2005), 21–22.
4. Zaynab Ridwan, *al-Mar'ah*, 33–36.
5. In Qur'ānic law prohibitions of marrying relatives is detailed: "It is herein decreed that you shall not marry your mothers, daughters, sisters, father's sisters, mother's sisters, brother's daughters, sister's daughters, foster-mothers (women who breastfed you), foster-sisters (women born to women who breastfed you), your wives' mothers, your step-daughters who are in your household with whose mother you had consummated a marriage—if you have not consummated the marriage then no restriction therein—and your true children's wives [not adopted children], and married women . . . " [Q4: V23–24].
6. See the poetry of Imru' al-Qays and other pre-Islamic poets; their poetry provides a telling account of the social order that existed then.
7. Nabil Luqa Babawa, *Zawjāt al-rasūl* (Egypt: PU, 2004), 39.
8. For specific examples of laws not reflecting the explicit Qur'ānic legal proofs, see, generally, A. E. Souaiaia, *Verbalizing Meaning* (UK: Mellen, 2006).
9. This claim is challenged in this study when the verses are analyzed from different perspectives and outside the traditional context.
10. This passage is problematic. The first part says "a brother *or* a sister" but the continuation of that says "for each of them . . . " [*falikulli wāḥidin minhumā* . . .] as if the verse presupposes that there are two, which would suggest that the "or" is mistakenly used instead of "and." However, when this verse is considered together with [Q4:V176], it becomes clear that "or" is used liberally to cover any combination of "a brother and a sister." That is to say: two brothers, one brother and one sister, or two sisters. In all cases there will be two individuals sharing the estate. It must be noted that most Muslim exegetes either consider [Q4:V12] and [Q4:V176] to be a case of abrogation, or one verse covers full siblings while the other covers half siblings. However, when taken without considering the commentaries, the explanation I provided would make sense in the Qur'ānic context alone.
11. The word "*kalālah*" has been a subject of a lively debate among early and modern scholars. The emerging consensus suggests that the term is used to refer to a deceased who is survived neither by children nor by parents. It has been suggested that children and parents bar the siblings from inheriting from their brother or sister, and that siblings inherit one another by way of *kalālah* only.
12. See, generally, Souaiaia, *Verbalizing Meaning*.
13. See, generally, Ibn Rushd, *Talkhīṣ al-siyāsah* (Beirut: Dar al-Tali'ah, 2002).
14. See al-Qurṭubī's *Tafsīr*, 2:1230.
15. Khaled Jamal Ahmed Hasan, *Ḥaqq al-mar'ah* (Egypt: Maktabat `Alam al-Ma`rifah li-'l-Nashr wa-'l-Tawzi`, 2004), 40.

16. Khaled Jamal Ahmed Hasan, *Ḥaqq al-mar'ah*, 44.
17. Khaled Jamal Ahmed Hasan, *Ḥaqq al-mar'ah*, 50.
18. This tradition is reported in all compilations of Ḥadīth with the exception of the one by al-Nasā'ī. See major exegetical works as well as Shawkānī's *Nayl al-awtār*, 6:56. Also, see Coulson, *Succession in the Muslim Family*, 29.
19. Khaled Jamal Ahmed Hasan, *Ḥaqq al-mar'ah*, 53–54.
20. See *Tafsīr mafātīḥ al-ghayb* commenting on al-Rāzī's *al-Tafsār al-kabīr* and his detailed commentary on [Q4:V11].
21. See al-Rāzī's comments in *al-Tafsīr al-kabīr* regarding [Q4:V11].
22. Ibn Abbās is reported to award one-half to two daughters as well. In other words, even the same authority is said to hold two radically different positions, which underscores the complexity of determining the shares for two daughters as opposed to the shares of more than two daughters. Ibn `Abbās's view where he awards one-half to two daughters is recorded in al-Tha'ālibī's *Tafsīr*; see his commentary on [Q4:V11] in *al-Jawāhir al-ḥisān fī tafsīr al-qur'ān*.
23. See al-Nasfī's commentary on [Q4:V11] in *Madārik al-tanzīl wa-ḥaqā'iq al-ta'wīl*.
24. See *Tafsīr mafātīḥ al-ghayb* expanding on al-Rāzī's *al-Tafsīr al-kabīr* and the detailed commentary on [Q4:V11].
25. This story has no basis in the Qur'ān and the Sunnah and its origins cannot be authoritatively established. See *Tafsīr mafātīḥ al-ghayb* expanding on al-Rāzī's *al-Tafsīr al-kabīr* and the commentary on [Q4:V11].
26. See Bawḍāwī's commentary on verse [Q4:V11] in *Anwār al-tanzīl wa-asrār al-ta'wīl*.
27. See Shawkānī's commentary on verse [Q4:V11] in *Fatḥ al-qadīr*.
28. See *al-Itqān wa-'l-iḥkām fī sharḥ tuḥfat al-ḥukkām* also known as *Sharḥ Mayyārah*, chapter *al-tawāruth wa-'l-farā'iḍ*, section *ahl al-farā'iḍ wa-uṣūlihā*.
29. See Souaiaia, *Verbalizing Meaning*.
30. Khaled Jamal Ahmed Hasan, *Ḥaqq al-Mar'ah*, 65.
31. Rules of inheritance in *aḥkām* materials are directly derived from tradition even if they do not explicitly state the legal proof. This practice is common among scholars from the Sunni as well as Shi'ite denominations. For examples on the statements of these rules, see Abū al-Ṣalāḥ al-Ḥalabī, *al-Kāfī fī al-fiqh* (Iṣfahān: Maktabat al-Imām, 1403 H), 363–381.
32. N. J. Coulson, *Succession in the Muslim Family* (UK: Cambridge University Press, 1971), 7.
33. It must be noted that the participants did not assign shares in hypothetical cases; they merely interpreted the test for the mandated share of each of the listed heirs.
34. By second- or third-generation translations, I mean the reconstruction of a written document from another work that is itself a translation of the original. For example, while in Morocco, I found a book by Ibn Rushd about political philosophy. The book was in Arabic and I did not know that such a book existed. Upon studying it further, I learned that it was an Arabic translation of the English translation of a Latin translation of the original work by Ibn Rushd (most of his Arabic works were burned). Since translation is, in my opinion, in effect a "passive" interpretation of an original work, one can only imagine the details that are either added or omitted by translators (or interpreters).

Chapter 5. Women in Modern Times

1. Zaki Ali al-Sayyid Abu Ghaddah, *al-Zawāj wa-'l-ṭalāq wa-'l-ta'addud* (Cairo: NP, 2004), 247.
2. The distribution of inheritance according to the Qur'ān can be found in [Q4:V11–12]; See Chapter 4.
3. Muslim scholars admit that the justice implied in the Qur'ān refers to fairness and justice in matters of financial support and not emotional "justice" because such demand for equity could never be attained: "*al-`adl al-maṭlūb hunā ... fī al-infāq wa-'l-mu`āmalah, ammā al-`adl wa-'l-musāwāt fī al-maḥabbah faghayr maṭlūb.*" See Maghniyyah 1999, 5:197.
4. Aware of the abuse of the conditional stipulation in the Qur'ān, even the conservative Ayatollah Muttaheri called for revision of the existing understanding (see Souaiaia, *Human Rights and Islam*, 142–3).
5. The idea that Muslim women earned many basic rights faster and earlier than their Western counterparts is not without merit. Only recently have Western women achieved the status of independent and full persons without being tied to male protectors and "as late as the seventeenth century, there were arguments in central Germany as to whether women were human beings." See Walther, *Women in Islam*, 60.
6. Jeff Spinner-Halev, "Feminism, Multiculturalism, Oppression, and the State." *Ethics* 112 (2001): 84–113
7. Admittedly, this charge is recognized by Muslim women who are writing on the subject from the West; see Valentine M. Moghadam, "Islamic Feminism and Its Discontents: Towards a Resolution of the Debate." *Signs: Journal of Women in Culture and Society* (2002): 27.
8. See Zaki Ali al-Sayyid Abu Ghaddah, *al-Zawāj wa-'l-ṭalāq wa-'l-ta`addud* (Cairo: NP, 2004), 241–45.
9. The case against "Islamic feminism" has been articulated by a number of Muslim women, most of whom are living outside the Muslim world. For a summary of their points of view, see Valentine M. Moghadam, "Islamic Feminism and Its Discontents: Towards a Resolution of the Debate." *Signs: Journal of Women in Culture and Society* (2002): 27.
10. Not only Muslims feel that Muslim women "had rights in the early period of Islam that were later taken away from them," but some Western scholars who examined documents from medieval to modern times reached similar conclusions. See Walther, *Women in Islam*, 7, 54, and 240.
11. From author's collection of audio tapes.
12. See Walther, *Women in Islam*, 238–39.
13. Yusuf al-Qardawi, *Markaz al-mar'ah fī al-ḥayāt al-islāmiyyah* (Cairo: Maktabat Wahba, 1996), 118.
14. The tradition was reported in the compilation of Abū Dāwūd, al-Nasā'ī, Ibn Mājah, al-Tirmidhī, and Ibn Ḥanbal on the authority of Abū Hurayrah.
15. In one of the most recent studies, which is representative of most works by Muslim scholars on this subject, one author suggests that "practically speaking, polygamy is very rare ... may be one or two men in every number of hundreds of men. See Muthanna Amin al-Kurdistani, *Ḥarakāt taḥrīr al-mar'ah min al-musāwāt ilā al-jandar* (Cairo: Dar al-Qalam li-'l-nashr wa-'l-tawzi`, 2004), 296.

16. Muthanna Amin al-Kurdistani, *Ḥarakāt taḥrīr al-mar'ah*, 292, and Ahmed Zakki Yamani, *al-Islām wa-'l-mar'ah* (Cairo: Matba'at al-Madani, 2004), 125.
17. Muthanna Amin al-Kurdistani, *Ḥarakāt taḥrīr al-mar'ah*, 293–96.
18. A Western academician who spent time in a number of Muslim countries identified "a woman's failure to bear children" as "one of the main reasons for a man to take a second wife." See Walther, *Women in Islam*, 87.
19. Amina Wadud, *Qur'an and Woman* (New York: Oxford University Press, 1999), 84.
20. Amina Wadud, *Qur'an and Woman*, 83.
21. Amina Wadud, *Qur'an and Woman*, 87–88.
22. See, generally, Eugene Hillman, *Polygamy Reconsidered* (New York: Orbis, 1975).
23. Generally, in Islamic law, divorce is to be initiated by the husband. It does not mean that divorce in Islamic law can never be sought by the wife. There are legal mechanisms that allow for the wife to compel the husband to divorce her. There are numerous examples supporting this claim from early Islam as well as from modern times. Sukaynah, the daughter of the grandson of the Prophet, Ḥusayn, is said to have been married and divorced four times. One of her husbands was Zayd Ibn `Amr (Grandson of the third Caliph `Uthmān). "She married him on the condition that he would never repudiate her on his initiative, nor touch another woman." See Walther, *Women in Islam*, 113. In modern times, Zaynab al-Ghazali was married twice and she stipulated in her marriage contract that she could seek divorce and her husband must grant it. See Lamia Shehadeh, *The Idea of Women in Fundamentalist Islam*, 121.
24. Muthanna Amin al-Kurdistani, *Ḥarakāt taḥrīr al-mar'ah*, 297.
25. Taqiuddin an-Nabhani, *The Social System in Islam* (Delhi: Milli, 2001), 141.
26. an-Nabhani, *The Social System in Islam*, 142.
27. an-Nabhani, *The Social System in Islam*, 143.
28. In Tunisia, even scholars and activists who attended religious educational institutions (al-Zaytounah) rooted their opposition to polygyny in reasoned and rational justifications. Al-Haddad, who is seen in modern Tunisia as one of the inspirational founding fathers of the country, argued that "because the essence of the Islamic faith is 'justice' and 'equality between people,' polygamy and gender inequality, like slavery, are to be abolished gradually." See Lamia Zayzafoon, *The Production of the Muslim Woman* (New York: Lexington, 2005), 103.
29. Nawal al-Sa'dawi, *Taw'am al-sulṭah wa-'l-jins* (Egypt: Dar al-Mustaqbal al-Arabi, 1999), 117.
30. Faridah al-Naqqash, *Ḥaqā'iq al-nisā' fī naqd al-uṣūliyyah* (Cairo: Markaz al-Qahirah li-Dirasat Huquq al-Insan), 45.
31. Zaki Ali al-Sayyid Abu Ghaddah, *al-Zawāj wa-'l-ṭalāq wa-'l-ta'addud* (Cairo: NP, 2004), 242.
32. Muhammad Mitwalli al-Sha'rawi, *al-Mar'ah fī al-qur'ān al-karīm* (Egypt: Akhbar al-Yawm, 1990), 30.
33. al-Sha'rawi, *al-Mar'ah fī al-qur'ān al-karīm*, 32.
34. Abu Ghaddah, *al-Zawāj*, 245.
35. Also see al-Kurdistani, *Ḥarakāt taḥrīr al-mar'ah*, 438.
36. Abu Ghaddah, *al-Zawāj*, 246–47.
37. Abu Ghaddah, *al-Zawāj*, 248–49.

38. Abu Ghaddah, *al-Zawāj*, 270.
39. Abu Ghaddah, *al-Zawāj*, 255–62.
40. Islamic thinkers made the link between the immorality of slavery and the treatment of women and predicted that both will end. See Zayzafoon, 103.
41. John Hartung, "Polygyny and Inheritance of Wealth." *Current Anthropology* (1982), 23.
42. Some of the arguments proposed by the proponents of the theory of natural law and utilitarianism have, explicitly and implicitly, supported the idea of "natural roles" that justified slavery.
43. Some Islamic thinkers justify discrimination against women on the basis of difference and function. Tunisian thinker Bin Abi Diaf argued that women are treated differently because of the privileges associated with or linked to "rationality, prophecy, and *jihād*." That is to say that, since men are more rational than women, and since God's prophets were all men, and since men are the ones who undertake *jihād*, then women's rights are not expected to be equal to men's. See Zayzafoon, 98.
44. The socioeconomic functions concluded by some scholars and observers after the study of African communities (see Eugene Hillman, *Polygamy Reconsidered* [New York: Orbis, 1975], 114–27) who practice polygamy does not extend to modern societies in which most needs highlighted therein are provided by a network of charities, volunteers, or government agencies. Additionally, even if those functions were to be found significant for modern communities, there is no set criteria that would prevent abuse of this institution that has been thus far, in Islam at least, up to the will and desire of men.
45. See the traditions attributed to Imām al-Ṣādiq (see al-Kāshānī, 186).
46. See Lévi-Strauss, 1992, 300–15; and Dumont, 1970, 114.
47. See Clignet's determination of function of polygamy in Africa (Joshi, 1995, 37).
48. Qur'ān [Q4:3].
49. See, generally, Souaiaia, *Verbalizing Meaning*.
50. Amina Wadud, *Qur'an and Woman*, 82–86.
51. Interpretations of other cultures through local lenses are sometimes biased and are guided by local concerns. The West has always reacted to Muslims' practices from their own perspectives, which are necessarily informed by their own experiences, history, hopes, and fears that may be different from the experiences, history, hopes, and fears of Muslims. For example, Western critics "condemned every practice that differed from what was common in their traditions. Their attitude toward divorce was typical: it was found to be barbaric and to foster the abandonment of women." (See Walther, *Women in Islam*, 8.) It took the West centuries to challenge and criticize the Catholic Church ban on divorce that, in most instances, disadvantaged women and forced them to stay in abusive relationships.
52. Jonathan Turley is the Shapiro Professor of Public Interest Law at George Washington Law School.
53. Morality, culture, and the law collide in every society and it is not absolutely clear whether the law determines morality and ethics, or morality and ethics inform legal reasoning. The reasoning of the court and the justices' personal points of view offer a glimpse of the nature of the discourse. I have selected representative passages from the thirty-six-page court's opinion to illustrate this point.

The case:

> Responding to a reported weapons disturbance in a private residence, Houston police entered petitioner Lawrence's apartment and saw him and another adult man, petitioner Garner, engaging in a private, consensual sexual act. Petitioners were arrested and convicted of deviate sexual intercourse in violation of a Texas statute forbidding two persons of the same sex to engage in certain intimate sexual conduct. In affirming, the State Court of Appeals held, *inter alia*, that the statute was not unconstitutional under the Due Process Clause of the Fourteenth Amendment. The court considered *Bowers v. Hardwick*, 478 U. S. 186, controlling on that point.

Justice Kennedy delivered the opinion of the court:

> Liberty protects the person from unwarranted government intrusions into a dwelling or other private places. In our tradition the State is not omnipresent in the home. And there are other spheres of our lives and existence, outside the home, where the State should not be a dominant presence. Freedom extends beyond spatial bounds. Liberty presumes an autonomy of self that includes freedom of thought, belief, expression, and certain intimate conduct. The instant case involves liberty of the person both in its spatial and more transcendent dimensions.

Justice O'Connor, concurring in the judgment:

> The Court today overrules *Bowers v. Hardwick*, 478 U.S. 186 (1986). I joined Bowers, and do not join the Court in overruling it. Nevertheless, I agree with the Court that Texas' statute banning same-sex sodomy is unconstitutional.

Justice Scalia, with whom the Chief Justice and Justice Thomas join, dissenting:

> "Liberty finds no refuge in a jurisprudence of doubt." *Planned Parenthood of Southeastern Pa. v. Casey*, 505 U.S. 833, 844 (1992). That was the Court's sententious response, barely more than a decade ago, to those seeking to overrule *Roe v. Wade*, 410 U.S. 113 (1973). The Court's response today, to those who have engaged in a 17-year crusade to overrule *Bowers v. Hardwick*, 478 U.S. 186 (1986), is very different. The need for stability and certainty presents no barrier . . .
>
> Countless judicial decisions and legislative enactments have relied on the ancient proposition that a governing majority's belief that certain sexual behavior is "immoral and unacceptable" constitutes a rational basis for regulation. See, e.g., *Williams v. Pryor*, 240 F. 3d 944, 949 (CA11 2001) (citing *Bowers* in upholding Alabama's prohibition on the sale of sex toys on the ground that "[t]he crafting and safeguarding of public morality . . . indisputably is a legitimate government interest under rational basis scrutiny"); *Milner v. Apfel*, 148 F. 3d 812, 814 (CA7 1998) (citing *Bowers* for the proposition that "[l]egislatures are permitted to legislate with regard to morality . . . rather than confined to preventing demonstrable harms"); *Holmes v. California Army National Guard* 124 F. 3d 1126, 1136 (CA9 1997) (relying on *Bowers* in upholding the federal statute and regulations banning from military service those who engage in homosexual conduct); *Owens v. State*, 352 Md. 663, 683, 724 A. 2d 43, 53 (1999) (relying on *Bowers* in holding that "a person has no constitutional right to engage in sexual intercourse, at least outside of marriage"); *Sherman v. Henry*, 928 S. W. 2d 464, 469–73 (Tex. 1996) (relying on *Bowers* in rejecting a claimed constitutional right to commit adultery). We ourselves relied extensively on *Bowers* when we concluded, in *Barnes v. Glen Theatre, Inc.*, 501 U. S. 560, 569 (1991), that Indiana's public indecency statute furthered "a substantial government interest in protecting order and morality," ibid., (plurality opinion); see

> also id., at 575 (Scalia, J., concurring in judgment). State laws against bigamy, same-sex marriage, adult incest, prostitution, masturbation, adultery, fornication, bestiality, and obscenity are likewise sustainable only in light of *Bowers*'s validation of laws based on moral choices.

Justice Thomas, dissenting:

> I join Justice Scalia's dissenting opinion. I write separately to note that the law before the Court today "is . . . uncommonly silly." *Griswold v. Connecticut*, 381 U.S. 479, 527 (1965) (Stewart, J., dissenting). If I were a member of the Texas Legislature, I would vote to repeal it. Punishing someone for expressing his sexual preference through noncommercial consensual conduct with another adult does not appear to be a worthy way to expend valuable law enforcement resources.
>
> Notwithstanding this, I recognize that as a member of this Court I am not empowered to help petitioners and others similarly situated. My duty, rather, is to "decide cases 'agreeably to the Constitution and laws of the United States.'"Id., at 530. And, just like Justice Stewart, I "can find [neither in the Bill of Rights nor any other part of the Constitution a] general right of privacy," ibid., or as the Court terms it today, the "liberty of the person both in its spatial and more transcendent dimensions," ante, at 1.

54. Polygamy was sanctioned by the teachings and early beliefs of the Mormon Church. However, for political reasons, it was abandoned in 1890. During that time period, the Utah territory sought statehood and since its chances of being admitted into the Union were directly dependent on its people's conformity to the standards of the larger community, the church leaders banned polygamy. The church now excommunicates members who practice it and has worked enthusiastically to distance itself from the estimated 50,000 polygamists in Utah, Arizona, and Idaho who say they are following fundamental Mormon doctrine.
55. Not only exegetical work was dominated by men but all other disciplines also were controlled by male scholars. I have compiled a list of the most influential scholars and religious authorities of the Islamic civilization and it does not show many women among them. It is true, as I have shown in the introduction, that there are many Muslim women who contributed to the rise of the Islamic civilization throughout times, but very few of them are taken as authority the way the individuals in the list are seen. See Appendix A.
56. Nimat Hafez Barazangi, *Woman's Identity and the Qur'an* (Gainesville: University Press of Florida, 2004), 113.
57. This reality becomes evident when one considers the outcome of the recent election in Kuwait in which women participated, for the first time, in large numbers. The highest female vote getter received only 1540 votes prompting commentators to suggest that "even women did not vote for women." See the Kuwait election results of June 29, 2006.
58. Slavery came to an end when the culture, including that of the slaveholders, no longer had the capacity to reconcile its moral purpose with the practices (holding persons in servitude) of the time. For example, the end of slavery in America was not contingent (or dependent) on the unanimous rejection of the practice by all the slaves. It was possible when the social environment made it possible for slaves *and* slave-holding communities to see it as degrading and cruel treatment of human beings. The same applies to women suffrage in America; it was necessary to change the mentality of women and men for that to happen.

59. Lynn Welchman (ed.), *Women's Rights and Islamic Family Law: Perspectives on Reform* (New York: Zed, 2004), 134–43.
60. For a survey of the opinions and ideas on the concept of justice in Islam, see Lawrence Rosen, *The Justice of Islam* (Oxford: Oxford University Press, 2000), 154–75.
61. See the discussion in Barazangi, *Woman's Identity and the Qur'an*, 70–85.
62. Barazangi, *Woman's Identity and the Qur'an*, 71.
63. Asma Barlas takes a similar position and argues that the Qur'ān is not and could not be patriarchic. See, Generally, Barlas, *"Believing Women" in Islam.*
64. Barazangi, *Woman's Identity and the Qur'an*, 77.
65. A closer reading of the writings of the so-called feminists of the Muslim world reveal that they are more critical of local and dominant cultures and less to the Qur'ānic discourse. Renowned feminist Mernissi for instance, argues that the subjugation of women in the Muslim world is due to "territorialized oppressive Islamic culture of the Maghreb" and not necessarily to the spirit of the Qur'ān. Others object even to the use of "Islamic culture" contending that oppressive restrictions imposed on women are rooted in "current ideological or political invention that masquerades as an authentic Islamic tradition." See Zayzafoon, *The Production of the Muslim Woman*, 2.
66. Leila Ahmed, *Women and Gender in Islam: Historical Roots of a Modern Debate* (New Haven: Yale University Press, 1992), 62.
67. Leila Ahmed, *Women and Gender in Islam*, 86–88.
68. For a detailed discussion of the accretive nature of Islamic law and practices, see Souaiaia, *Verbalizing Meaning*, 2006.
69. The evidence suggests that Muslim exegetes have relied on Jewish tradition to give meaning and context to ambiguous Qur'ānic passages. The articulation of Jewish laws governing marriage, property rights, and women are another thread that ties Semitic cultures together. For more on polygamy and family laws in Judaism and in the Bible, see, generally, Louis M. Epstein, *Marriage Laws.*
70. Barlas has made it her objective to show that the Qur'ānic discourse is not patriarchal, but her method and selection of passages for analysis did not help achieve her goal. See, generally, Barlas, *"Believing Women" in Islam.*
71. The word "Islamically" must be taken in the context of Islamic law. That is to judge a practice as valid or invalid in Islamic law. In that regard, mainstream Sunni and Shi'ite jurists concur that a marriage is valid only if the man utters the "offer" (*ījāb*) and the woman utters the "response" (*qabūl*).
72. See the language of verses [Q4:V2–4]. It will not be an exaggeration to assert that the language of the Qur'ān is overwhelmingly directed to men and only the passages or chapters that specifically deal with women's issues will be an exception.
73. See the full translation of verses [Q4:V11–12] in chapter 4.
74. Based on historical evidence, I argue that, to implement laws top-down amounts to the preservation of the elitists' project of furthering their political and economic programs on the expense of women and the poor. For example, women were used as pawns during the colonial Tunisia. Then, Bourguiba (the first president of Tunisia who is widely accredited for championing women's rights) encouraged the preservation of religious values (including the wearing of the headscarf) in order

to argue for a separate and distinct identity of Tunisians: hence, supporting his call for independence from France. Then, he responded to Durel's denial of the existence of a "Tunisian identity" by asserting that Islam, the veil, and territorial unity are quintessential elements of the Tunisian identity. See Zayzafoon, 101–102. After Tunisia's independence, in a speech that he delivered on December 5, 1957, he argued that the veil is an import that has nothing to do with religion. See Zayzafoon, 103. He went on to ban the veil and create a new national identity as he imagined it. In short, women were used as a tool for furthering a national agenda that was then monopolized by the westernized elite.

75. Legal opinions of all jurists of the classical era (including the so-called founders of the major schools of thought) usually conclude by the phrase "and God knows better;" suggesting that what they decree is just their opinion and their understanding. The plurality in Islamic schools of jurisprudence, each of which is equally authoritative, is another aspect of differentiating between positive Islamic law and Qur'ānic law.

76. For instance, Nawal Sa'dawi contended that, since polygamy is practiced by less than 2% of the society, it should be made illegal. But she does not seem to care whether the 2% of the population are involved in polygamous marriages due to necessity or other reasons.

77. I came to see the different ways laws can impact different social classes when I was in a discussion about the status of Muslim women. After a talk about this very same subject, the ensuing conversation included the topic of the limitation imposed by the Saudi government on women in the form of prohibiting them from driving. A Saudi woman, a very wealthy and highly placed one, interjected to justify the law by saying: "We don't need to drive. I for one have chauffeurs who drive me where I need to be and it is better that way." Assuming that every woman in Arabia is as wealthy as she is, that sounds reasonable. But when one learns that, even in Arabia, there are poor people who can't afford a car let alone a driver; it becomes clear how the laws impact different individuals in different ways. For instance, a rich woman is not affected by the prohibition on driving and therefore she is not bothered by it and probably would want the prohibition to remain to keep relying on the services of drivers. Another woman who is a widow or divorcee and who is the sole provider for her family and who needs to find a job driving rich people around or driving trucks for a living, for example, will be barred from driving, an activity that can earn her food. This is just an example from the real world that makes the case for undesirability of overlegislating if you will. Some laws legalizing "social activities or behavior" may benefit the elite or those who could escape it, but it may be an undue encroachment on a fundamental basic right (such as the right to work) of another person or group of people.

78. Even in Muslim countries that are seen as "friendly" or "accommodating" to women, there is no real free and open discussion of these and other issues. The problems and the solutions are the domain of the government and the people in charge. For this reason, any reform that is imposed top-down remains "alien" because it was not the product of a civil discourse facilitated by civil institutions. Bourguiba, for instance, appropriated the religious discourse and exerted a monopoly on its interpretation. In a speech on December 15, 1961, he attacked women wearing the veil charging them with "misunderstanding the Qur'ānic

verses." (See Zayzafoon, 117.) In the 1980s, he prosecuted, jailed, and executed Islamists who were engaged in the "reinterpretation of Islam." Either religion is a pubic discourse that anyone could "reinterpret" just as he did, or it is a private matter that should not be monopolized by anyone (including him and the government). But the reality is that in most Muslim countries, the absence of civil society institutions gives extraordinary powers to governments and these governments impose their will on people. The danger with this situation is that women, minorities, and the poor are at the mercy of the temperament of the political leaders.

79. See the characterization of the difference of opinion on this matter as a clash between Western intentions and Islamic resistance in Zaki Ali al-Sayyid Abu Ghaddah, *al-Zawāj wa-'l-ṭalāq wa-'l-ta`addud* (Cairo: NP, 2004), 239.
80. Admittedly, the Qur'ānic discourse is not unique in its "avoidance" of issuing a clear legal determination regarding polygamy. It would seem that all Semitic religious scripture took the same stance on this matter:

> The law-giver, finding polygamy at the root of Hebrew life did not or could not eradicate it by outright prohibition, but sought to eliminate it gradually by such laws as the required purification after contact with a woman, or the command to treat all wives alike, or the prohibition against castration. (See Louis M. Epstein, *Marriage Laws*, 5.)

81. Asma Barlas undertakes the ambitious project of proving that the Qur'ānic discourse is not patriarchic. She relies on what she calls "God's Self-Disclosure" that guides the Qur'ānic hermeneutics to support her claim. More specifically, she argues that the three principles (Divine Unity, Justness, and Incomparability) make the Qur'ānic discourse necessarily universal, just, and inclusive. As such, she argues that the Qur'ān is as much about and for women as it is for and about men. Even if we allow for the assumptions of the divine nature as described by Barlas, the same logic would support the view that distinguishes between the sexes (and classes and ethnicities). After all, according to this same view, humans do not share any of the attributes that describe the deity. Hence, since humans have no claim to a universal unity of being, justness, and incomparability, they are dependent on patriarchic and partial languages and expressions. To be sure, humans are of myriad colors, languages, ethnic backgrounds, aptitudes, and interests. They are, or could be, selfish, greedy, gluttonous, aggressive, and wicked. They are comparable to one another and exhibit no commitment to infallibility and goodness. And since the Qur'ānic discourse is directed at them and was meant to "educate" them, it must have taken into account all these characteristics for it to be effective and realist. In doing so, the Qur'ānic discourse spoke to the powerful, to the influential, to the people who can prevent or impose change. The result is a patriarchic discourse and the language of the Qur'ān is reflective of that.
82. Coulson, *Succession*, 38.

Conclusion

1. The power of jokes in dealing with serious issues, venting frustration, and galvanizing social attitudes was on display in Morocco in December 2006 when the weekly newspaper *Nichane* published a front-cover story, *Jokes: How Moroccans Laugh about Religion, Sex, and Politics*. The managing editor and the journalist who compiled the dossier were prosecuted and sentenced to three years in prison

(suspended; pending appeal), fined 80,000 dirhams, and their newspaper was banned (from publication and circulation) for two months (starting January 15, 2007; the day the court issued its ruling). The author was in Morocco for these events to observe and interview the parties involved in this and other cases for a forthcoming work.

2. See the preamble of the Universal Declaration of Human Rights.
3. It is not an exaggeration to estimate the number of people killed during the colonial wars in Africa, Asia, and the Americas to be in the millions. For example, during the Algerian liberation revolt alone, 1.5 million people lost their lives and scores more were wounded, displaced, or rendered refugees.
4. See [Q4:V1].
5. See Walther, *Women in Islam*, 115.
6. See Walther, *Women in Islam*, 119.
7. Mernissi is certain that it was men who denied women all the rights they did not have before Islam: "According to Mernissi, Islam's endorsement of a woman's right to inheritance created a 'bombshell' or a 'conflict' of interest between the *male* population of Medina and the Prophet of the new religion." See Zayzafoon, *The Production of the Muslim Woman*, 18; emphasis mine. It is very difficult to ascertain that claim because we know very little about Madīnah. But given that it was a diverse community with large Jewish and other religious communities, it is possible that some women there had enjoyed some rights just like the counterparts in Mecca (Khadījah and other rich women attached to the tribal leaders).
8. For example, countries that imposed prohibition on polygyny instituted new obligations on women. In Egypt and Tunisia (during Nasser and Bourguiba's reign, respectively), women were required to contribute equally to "the upkeep of the household." Turkey, which prohibited polygyny in 1926, was forced to pass at least eight "amnesty laws" between 1933 and 1970 because traditional marriages (performed by religious leaders) continued to exist. (See Walther, *Women in Islam*, 232–33). Furthermore, legal reform generally means the *re*construction of "woman" in the image of the ruling elite, which sometimes may be favorable to women and sometimes unfavorable. Bourguiba's Tunisia, for instance, while enacting the Personal Status Code (August 13, 1956) that supposedly liberated women, dissolved the confessional courts that offered alternatives to other ethnic and religious groups and imposed one man's vision on everyone. In doing so, Bourguiba essentially undermined the emergence of civil society institutions. (See Zayzafoon, *The Production of the Muslim Woman*, 121.) In short, legal reform is an unpredictable approach to dealing with questions of social justice and basic human rights because any regime can use it to continue to shift the balance of power. Without changing the culture that supports and nurture discrimination, all other solutions will remain temporary and short-lived.
9. Many scholars have concluded that financial support is a major factor in forcing some women to accept polygynous marriages especially if such widowed or divorced women have children. By creating and supporting charitable entities (that advocate for these women) that are part of the civil society institutions, these women will have options, and that would render polygyny less attractive.

Bibliography

`Abd al-Jalīl, Sa'īd. *al-Siyagh al-shar`iyyah li-qadāyā al-aḥwāl al-shakhṣiyyah*. Cairo: al-Maktabah al-Qānūniyyah, 1977.

`Abd al-Raḥīm, Muḥammad. *al-Qarābah wa-'l-mīrāth fī al-mujtama` bayna al-qawā`id al- shar`iyyah wa-'l-taṣarrufāt al-wāqi`iyyah*. Cairo: Maktabat al-Thaqāfah al-Dīniyyah, 1993.

`Adawī, `Abd al-Raḥmān. *al-Wasīṭ fī al-fiqh al-islāmī wa-'l-mawārīth*. Cairo: al-Maktabah al-Azhariyyah li-'l-Turāth, 1996.

`Alī, As`ad Aḥmad. *Tāj*. Dimashq: Dār al-Su'āl, 1987.

`Uthaymin, Muḥammad Ṣāliḥ. *Tashīl al-farā'iḍ*. Beirut: Mu'assasat al-Risālah, 1983.

Abū `Awanah, Ya`qūb Ibn Isḥāq. *Musnad al-qism al-mafqūd min musnad Abī `Awanah al-mustakhraj `alā ṣaḥīḥ Muslim*. Cairo: Maktabat al-Sunnah, 1995.

Abū `Ubayd, al-Qāsim Ibn Sallām. *Kitāb al-amwāl*. Cairo: Maktabat al-Kullīyāt al-Azhariyyah, 1968.

Abū al-`Abbās, Aḥmad Ibn-Jābir al-Balādhūrī. *Kitāb futūḥ al-buldān*. New York: [PA], 1924.

Abū al-Hudā al-Sayyadī, Muḥammad Ibn Ḥasan Wadī. *Ḍaw' al-shams fī qawlihi ṣallā allāhu `alayhi wa-sallam*. Dimashq: Maktabat al-Fārābī, 1974.

Abū Bakr, `Alā`. *Insānīyat al-mar`ah*. Cairo: Markaz al-Tanwīr al-Islāmī, 2005.

Abū Dāwūd Sulaymān Ibn al-Ash`ath al-Sijjistānī. *Sunan Abī Dāwūd*. Lahore: S. M. Ashraf, 1984.

Abū Ḥanīfah. *Sharḥ kitāb al-fiqh al-akbar*. Beirut: Dār al-Kutub al-`Ilmiyyah, 1995.

Abū Ḥayyān, Muḥammad Ibn Yūsuf. *al-Baḥr al-muḥīṭ fī tafsīr al-qur'ān*. al-Riyāḍ: Maktabat wa-Maṭābi` al-Naṣr al-Ḥadīthah, 1980.

Abū Ḥayyān. *al-Baḥr al-muḥīṭ*. Jordan: Aal al-Bayt Institute for Islamic Thought (Soft Collections), 2002.

Abū Isḥāq, Ibrāhīm al-Sāmirī. *Kitāb al-mīrāth das Buch der Erbschaft des Samaritaners Abū Isḥāq Ibrāhīm: kritische Edition mit Übersetzung und Kommentar*. Berlin: de Gruyter, 1974.

Abū Nu`aym al-Isbahānī Aḥmad Ibn `Abd Allāh. *al-Musnad al-mustakhraj `alā ṣaḥīḥ al-imām Muslim*. Beirut: Dār al-Kutub al-`Ilmiyyah, 1996.

Abū Zahrah, Muḥammad. *al-Mīrāth `inda al-ja`fariyyah ma`a tarjamat al-sayyid al-imām Abū `Abd Allāh Ja`far al-Ṣādiq*. Beirut, Dār al-Rā'id al-`Arabī, 1970.

Abu Zahrah. *Malik*. Egypt: Matba`at al-Itmad, 1955.

Afzal-ur-Rahman. *Role of Muslim Women in Society*. London: Seerah Foundation, 1986.

Ahmed, Leila. *Women and Gender in Islam: Historical Roots of a Modern Debate*. New Haven: Yale University Press, 1992.

al-A`qam. *Tafsīr al-a`qam*. Jordan: Aal al-Bayt Institute for Islamic Thought (Soft Collections), 2002.

al-Alūsī, Muḥammad Ibn `Abd Allāh. *Rūḥ al-ma`ānī fī tafsīr al-Qur'ān al-`aẓīm wa-'l-sab` al-mathānī*. Beirut: Dār Iḥyā' al-Turāth al-`Arabī, 1970.

al-Ash`arī, Abu al-Ḥasan. *Maqālāt al-islāmiyyīn*. Cairo: Maktabat al-Nahda al-Misriyyah, 1950.

———. *Maqālāt al-islāmiyyīn*. Cairo: Maktabat al-Nahda al-Misriyyah, 1950.

al-Baghdadi, `Abd al-Qahir. *al-Milal wa-`l-niḥal*. Beirut: Dar al-Mashriq, 1970.

al-Baghdādī, Aḥmad Ibn `Alī. *al-Wuṣūl ilā al-uṣūl*. Riyāḍ: Maktabat al-Ma`ārif, 1983.

al-Balādhūrī, Aḥmad Ibn Yaḥyā Ibn Jābir. *Ansāb al-ashrāf*. Beirut: Dār al-Nashr, 1975.

al-Banna, Jamal. *Jawāz imāmat al-mar`ah al-rijāl*. Cairo: Dar al-Fikr al-Islami, 2005.

al-Bayḍāwī. *Anwār al-Tanzīl wa-asrār al-ta`wīl*. Jordan: Aal al-Bayt Institute for Islamic Thought (Soft Collections), 2002.

al-Daqr, `Abd al-Ghani. *al-Imām al-Shāfi`ī*. Beirut: Dār al-Kitāb, 1972.

al-Dāwūdī, Aḥmad Ibn Naṣr. *Kitāb al-amwāl*. al-Ribāṭ: Markaz Iḥyā' al-Turāth al-Maghribī, 1988.

al-Dhahbī, Muhammad Ibn Aḥmad Ibn `Uthmān. *Mīzān al-i`tidāl fī naqd al-rijāl*. Beirut: Dar al-Ma`rifah, 1963.

———. *al-`Ibar fī khabari man `abar*. Beirut: Dar al-Kutub al-`Ilmiyyah, 1985.

al-Fawzān, Ṣāliḥ Ibn Fawzān Ibn `Abd Allāh. *al-Taḥqīqāt al-marḍiyyah fī al-mabāḥith al-farḍiyyah*. al-Riyāḍ: Maktabat al-Ma`ārif, 1986.

al-Fayḍ al-Kāshānī. *al-Ṣāfī fī tafsīr kalām allāh al-wāfī*. Jordan: Aal al-Bayt Institute for Islamic Thought (Soft Collections), 2002.

al-Ḥalabī, Abū al-Ṣalāh. *al-Kāfī fī al-fiqh*. Isfahan: Maktabat al-Imam Amīr al-Mu`minīn, 1403 AH.

al-Haythamī, `Alī Ibn Abī Bakr. *Majma` al-zawā`id wa-manba` al-fawā`id*. Beirut: Dār al-Kitāb al-Ilmiyyah, 1988.

al-Ḥillī, Abū Manṣūr Jamāl al-Dīn al-Ḥasan Ibn Yūsuf. *Mukhtalaf al-shī`ah*. Isfahān: [PA], 1403 H.

———. *Mukhtalaf al-shī`ah fī aḥkām al-sharī`ah*. Isfahan: Makatabat al-Imam Ali, 1404 AH.

al-Huwwārī. *Tafsīr kitāb allāh al-`azīz*. Jordan: Aal al-Bayt Institute for Islamic Thought (Soft Collections), 2002.

Ali, Syed Mohammed. *The Position of Women in Islam: A Progressive View*. Albany: State University of New York Press, 2004.

al-Janābidhī. *Tafsīr bayān al-sa`ādah fī maqāmāt al-`ibādah*. Jordan: Aal al-Bayt Institute for Islamic Thought (Soft Collections), 2002.

al-Kashani, Muhsin. *Kitāb al-kāfī fī tafsīr al-qur'ān*. Tehran: Dār al-Kutub al-Islāmiyyah, 1998.

al-Kurdistani, Muthanna Amin. *Ḥarakāt taḥrīr al-mar`ah min al-musāwāt ilā al-jandar*. Cairo: Dar al-Qalam li-'lnashr wa-'ltawzi`, 2004.

Allison, J. W. F. *A Continental Distinction in the Common Law*. Oxford: Clarendon, 1996.

al-Maqrīzī, Ahmad Ibn `Alī. *al-Khuṭaṭ al-maqrīziyyah*. Beirut: Dar Sadir, YA.

al-Maṭ`anī, `Abd al-`Aẓīm Ibn Ibrāhīm. *al-Fiqh Bayna `abqariyyat al-salaf wa-ma`ākhidh nāqidīh*. Cairo: Maktabat Wahbah, 1993.

al-Māwardī, `Alī Ibn Muḥammad Ḥabīb al-Baṣrī. *al-Aḥkām al-sulṭānīyyah wa-'l-wilāyāt al-dīnīyyah*. Egypt: Dār al-Fikr, 1983.

———. *al-Aḥkām al-sulṭāniyyah wa-'l-wilāyāt al-dīniyyah*. Abu Dhabi: al-Warrāq, 2004.

———. *al-Nukat wa-'l-`uyūn*. Jordan: Aal al-Bayt Institute for Islamic Thought (Soft Collections), 2002.

al-Nīsābūrī, Abū al-Ḥasan Muslim Ibn al-Ḥajjāj al-Qushayrī. *Ṣaḥīḥ Muslim*. Cairo: Dār al-Kitāb, 1334 AH.

al-Qardawi, Yusuf. *Markaz al-mar`ah fī al-ḥayāt al-islāmiyyah*. Cairo: Maktabat Wahba, 1996.

al-Qummī. *Tafsīr al-qur'ān*. Jordan: Aal al-Bayt Institute for Islamic Thought (Soft Collections), 2002.

al-Qurṭubī. *al-Jāmi` li-`aḥkām al-qur'ān*. Jordan: Aal al-Bayt Institute for Islamic Thought (Soft Collections), 2002.

al-Rāzī. *al-Tafsīr al-kabīr*. Jordan: Aal al-Bayt Institute for Islamic Thought (Soft Collections), 2002.

al-Sa`dawi, Nawal. *Taw`am al-sulṭah wa-'l-jins*. Egypt: Dar al-Mustaqbal al-Arabi, 1999.

al-Sa`dī, `Abd al-Hakim. *Mabāḥith al-`illah fī al-qiyās `inda al-uṣūliyyīn*. Beirut: Dār al-Bashā'ir al-Islāmiyyah, 1986.

al-Sabkī, `Alī Ibn `Abd al-Kāfī. *al-Ibhāj fī sharḥ al-minhāj*. Beirut: Dār al-Kutub al-`Ilmiyyah, 1984.

al-Sabkī, Taqī al-Dīn `Alī. *Takmilat al-majmū`*. Cairo: al-Tadamun, 1906.

al-Ṣābūnī, Muḥammad `Alī. *Tafsīr āyāt al-aḥkām*. Syria: Maktabat al-Ghazālī, 1977.

al-Sharbīnī, Shams al-Dīn. *al-Iqnā` fī ḥall alfāẓ Abī Shujā`*. Beirut: Dār al-Kutub al-`Ilmiyyah, 1994.

al-Shawkānī. *Fatḥ al-qadīr*. Jordan: Aal al-Bayt Institute for Islamic Thought (Soft Collections), 2002.

al-Shīrāzī, Abū Isḥāq. *Ṭabaqāt al-fuqahā`*. Beirut: Dār al-Rā`id al-`Arabī, 1970.

al-Ṭabarī, `Alī Ibn Ṣalāḥ Ibn `Alī Ibn Muḥammad. *Shifā` ghalīl al-sā`il `ammā taḥammalahu al-kāfil*. Yemen: Maktabat al-Yaman al-Kubrā, 1988.

———. *Tārīkh al-rusul wa-'l-mulūk*. Egypt: Dar al-Ma`ārif, 1969.

———. *Jāmi` al-bayān fī tafsīr al-qur'ān*. Jordan: Aal al-Bayt Institute for Islamic Thought (Soft Collections), 2002.

Al-Ṭabarsī. *Majma` al-bayān fī tafsīr al-qur'ān*. Jordan: Aal al-Bayt Institute for Islamic Thought (Soft Collections), 2002.

al-Tabataba'i, Muhammad Hussein. *al-Mīzān fī tafsīr al-qur'ān*. Beirut: Muassasat al-A`lami li-`l-Maṭbū`āt, 1974.

al-Taftāzānī, Sa`d al-Dīn. *Sharh al-`aqā`id al-nafīsah* Cairo: PU, 1939.

al-Tha`ālibī. *al-Jawāhir al-ḥisān fī tafsīr al-qur'ān*. Jordan: Aal al-Bayt Institute for Islamic Thought (Soft Collections), 2002.

al-Ṭūsī, Nāṣir al-Din Muhammad Ibn al-Ḥasan. *Kashf al-Murād*. Qom: shukura, 1413 AH.

———. *al-Tibyān al-jāmi` li-`ulūm al-qur'ān*. Jordan: Aal al-Bayt Institute for Islamic Thought (Soft Collections), 2002.

al-Zamakhsharī. *al-Kashshāf.* Jordan: Aal al-Bayt Institute for Islamic Thought (Soft Collections), 2002.

Amīn, Qāsim. *The Liberation of Women: A Document in the History of Egyptian Feminism*. Cairo: American University in Cairo Press, 1992.

An-Na`im, Abdullahi. *Toward an Islamic Reformation.* New York: Syracuse University Press, 1990.

Aristotle. *Eudemian Ethics*. Oxford: Clarendon, 1982.

Atfīsh. *Taysīr al-tafsīr.* Jordan: Aal al-Bayt Institute for Islamic Thought (Soft Collections), 2002.

Austin, John. *The Philosophy of Positive Law*. London: Murray, 1913.

———. *The Province of Jurisprudence.* London: Weidenfeld & Nicolson, 1954.

Badran, Badran Abū al-`Aynayn. *al-Fiqh al-muqāran li-'l-aḥwāl al-shakhṣiyyah bayna al-madhāhib al-arba`ah al-sunniyyah wa-'l-madhhab al-ja`farī wa-'l-qānūn.* Beirut: Dār al-Nahḍah al-`Arabiyyah li-'l-Ṭibā`ah wa-'l-Nashr, 1967.

Baḥrānī, Hāshim Ibn Sulaymān. *Kitāb al-burhān fī tafsīr al-qur'ān*. Tehran: Chapkhanah-i Afatab, 1956.

———. *Ghāyat al-marām*. Beirut: Mu`assat al-A`lamī li-'l-Maṭbū`āt, 1968.

Bannā, Jamāl. *Jawāz imāmat al-mar'ah al-rijāl*. Cairo: Dār al-Fikr al-Islāmī, 2005.

Bannon, Cynthia Jordan. *The Brothers of Romulus: Fraternal Pietas in Roman law, Literature, and Society*. Princeton: Princeton University Press, 1997.

Barazangi, Nimat Hafez. *Woman`s Identity and the Qur'ān: A New Reading.* Gainesville: University Press of Florida, 2004.

Barlas, Asma. *"Believing Women" in Islam*. Austin: University of Texas Press, 2002.

Barrāj, Jum`ah Muḥammad. *Aḥkām al-mīrāth fī al-sharī`ah al-islāmiyyah*. Amman: Dār al-Fikr li-'l-Nashr wa-'l-Tawzī`, 1981.

Barri, Zakariya. *al-Wasīṭ fī aḥkām al-tarikāt wa-'l-mawārīth*. Cairo: Dār al-Nahḍah al-`Arabiyyah, 1970.

Baveja, Malik Ram. *Woman in Islam*. New York: Advent, 1981.

Bentham, Jeremy. *A Fragment on Government.* Cambridge: Cambridge University Press, 1988.

———. *Deontology.* Oxford: Clarendon, 1983.

Berkey, Jonathan P. *Popular Preaching and Religious Authority in the Medieval Islamic Near East*. Seattle: University of Washington Press, 2001.

Binder, L. *The Study of the Middle East*. New York: Wiley, 1976.

Bloch, Maurice. *Ritual, History and Power: Selected Papers in Anthropology*. London: Athlone, 1989.

Bradley, Denis J. M. *Aquinas on the Twofold Human Good: Reason and Human Happiness in Aquinas's Moral Science*. Washington D.C.: Catholic University of America Press, 1997.

Brittain, John A. *Inheritance and the Inequality of Material Wealth.* Washington: Brookings, 1978.

Brockopp, Jonathan E. *Early Mālikī Law.* Leiden: Brill, 2000.

Buckland, W. W. *Roman Law and Common Law*. Cambridge: Cambridge University Press, 1952.

Bukhārī, Muḥammad Ibn Ismā`īl. *Al-Jāmi` al-ṣaḥīḥ*. Chicago: Kazi, 1979.

Burton, John. *The Sources of Islamic Law.* Edinburgh: Edinburgh University Press, 1990.

Calder, Norman. *Studies in Early Muslim Jurisprudence.* Oxford: Clarendon, 1993.

Chelhod, Joseph. *Le sacrifice chez les arabes.* Paris: Presses Universitaires de France, 1955.

Cilardo, Agostino. *Studies on the Islamic Law of Inheritance.* Napoli: Istituto Universitario Orientale, 1990.

Clanchy, M. T. *From Memory to Written Record.* Cambridge: Harvard University Press, 1979.

Cohen, Arnold J. *Jewish Civil Law.* Jerusalem: Feldheim, 1991.

Comte, Auguste. *Cours de philosophie positive.* Bruxelles: Culture et Civilisation, 1969.

Corbin, Henry. *terre celeste et corps de resurrection.* Correa: Buchet/Chastel, 1960.

Coster, W. *Kinship and Inheritance in Early Modern England: Three Yorkshire Parishes.* York [England]: Borthwick Institute of Historic Research, 1993.

Coulson, Noel J. (Noel James). *Succession in the Muslim Family.* UK: Cambridge University Press, 1971.

Council of Europe, Committee of Ministers. *Equality of Spouses in Civil Law: Resolution (78) 37, Adopted By The Committee Of Ministers Of The Council Of Europe On 27 September 1978, And Explanatory Memorandum.* Strasbourg: Council of Europe, 1979.

Crone, Patricia. *Roman, Provincial, and Islamic Law: The Origins of the Islamic Patronate.* New York: Cambridge University Press, 1987.

Dabab, `Alī Ibn Hilāl. *al-Shu`ā` al-fā'iḍ: sharḥ mukhtaṣar `ilm al-farā'id.* Cairo: Qusay Muḥibb al-Dīn al-Khaṭīb, 1977.

Dahir, Fu'ad. *Qānūn al-irth `inda ghayr al-muḥammadīyyīn.* Beirut: Y F. Dahir and Sultanah `Abd Allāh, 1996.

Dahl, Tove Stang. *The Muslim Family: A Study of Women`s Rights in Islam.* Boston: Scandinavian University Press, 1997.

Dhibani, `Abd al-Majid `Abd al-Hamid. *Aḥkām al-mawārīth wa-`l-tarikāt wa-'l-waṣiyyah fī al-sharī`ah al-islāmiyyah.* Tarābuls: al-Jāmi`ah al-Maftūḥah, 1995.

Dimashqi, Muhammad Munir. *Irshād al-rāghibīn fī al-kashf `an 'āy al-qur'ān al-mubīn.* Beirut: Dār al-Qalam, 1980.

Durkheim, Emile. *Les Formes Elementaires De La Vie Religieuse.* Paris: Librairie Felix Alcan, 1912.

Dutton, Yasin. *The Origins of Islamic Law.* Richmond, UK: CURZON, 1999.

Eliade, M. *Histoire Des Croyances et Des Idees Religieuses.* Paris: Payot, 1976.

———. *History of Religious Ideas.* Chicago: University of Chicago Press, 1965.

Engineer, Asgharali. *The Rights of Women in Islam.* New Delhi: Sterling, 1992.

Epicurus. *Épicure et les Épicuriens.* Paris: Presses Universitaires de France, 1964.

Epstein, Louis M. *Marriage Laws in the Bible and the Talmud.* Cambridge: Harvard University Press, 1942.

Evans-Pritchard, E. E. *Theories of Primitive Religion.* Oxford: Oxford University Press, 1965.

Fawzī, Ibrāhīm. *Aḥkām al-irth al-mukhtalaf `alayhā fī al-fiqh al-islāmī wa-'l-maṣādir allatī ishtaqqa minhā Qānūn al-aḥwāl al-shakhṣiyyah.* Beirut: Dār al-Ḥaqā'iq, 1987.

Fazlur, Rahman. *Approaches to Islam in Religious Studies: Review Essay, in Approaches to Islam in Religious Studies*. Tucson: University of Arizona Press, 1985.

Firdawsī. *Furūḍ*. Tehran: Mu'assasah-'i Mutala`at va Tahqiqat-i Farhangi, 1990.

Fontenrose, Joseph. *The Ritual Theory of Myth*. Berkeley: University of California Press, 1971.

Frazer, J. G. *The Golden Bough: A Study in Magic and Religion*. New York: Macmillan, 1927.

Freud, Sigmund. *Totem and Taboo: Some Points of Agreement between the Mental Lives of the Savages and Neurotics*. New York: Norton, 1950.

Geertz, Clifford. *Islam Observed*. London: Yale University Press, 1968.

———. *Religion as a Cultural System*. Missoula: Scholars Press, 1975.

George, Robert. *In Defense of Natural Law*. Oxford: Oxford University Press, 2001.

Gerami, Shahin. *Women and Fundamentalism: Islam and Christianity*. New York: Garland, 1996.

Ghazālī, A. *al-Mustaṣfā min 'ilm al-uṣūl*. Baghdad: Maktabat al-Muthannā, 1970.

Goldziher, Ignaz. *Muslim Studies*. Edited by S. M. Stern. Albany: State University of New York Press, 1967–1971.

Goodheart, Arthur L. *English Law and the Moral Law*. London: Stevens, 1953.

Griffiths, Paul J. *Religious Reading*. New York: Oxford University Press, 1999.

Grønvik, Ottar. *The Words for "Heir," "Inheritance," and "Funeral Feast," in Early Germanic*. Oslo: Universitetsforlaget, 1982.

Hallifax, Samuel. *An Analysis of the Roman Civil Law*. Cambridge: J. Archdeacon, 1779.

Hart, H. L. A. (Herbert Lionel Adolphus). *The Concept of Law*. Oxford: Clarendon, 1994.

———. *Causation in the Law*. Oxford: Clarendon, 1962.

———. *Law, Liberty, and Morality*. California: Stanford University Press, 1963.

———. *Punishment and Responsibility*. Oxford: Oxford University Press, 1968.

Hartung, John. "Polygyny and Inheritance of Wealth." *Current Anthropology* (1982).

Hasan, al-Amrani Zantar. *Aḥkām al-mīrāth fī fiqh al-sharī`ah al-islāmiyyah*. al-Dār al-Bayḍā': Dār al-Khattabī, 1992.

Hasani, Hashim Ma`rūf. *al-Wiṣāyah wa-'l-awqāf wa-irth al-zawjah wa-'l-`awl wa-'l-ta`ṣīb min al-aḥwāl al-shakhṣiyyah fī al-fiqh al-islāmī*. Beirut: Dār al-Qalam, 1980.

Heer, N. *Islamic Law and Jurisprudence*. Seattle: University of Washington Press, 1990.

Hekmat, Anwar. *Women and the Koran: the Status of Women in Islam*. Amherst, NY: Prometheus Books, 1997.

Ḥilmī, `Abd al-`Aẓīm Hasan Muḥammad Rashād `Abd al-Wahhāb. *al-Mīrāth wa-'l-waṣiyyah wa-'l-wilāyah `alā al-nafs wa-'l-māl*. Cairo: al-Hay'ah al-`Āmmah li-Shu'ūn al-Maṭābi` al-Amīriyyah, 1983.

Hittinger, Russell. *A Critique of the New Natural Law Theory*. Notre Dame: University of Notre Dame Press, 1987.

Hoeflich, Michael H. *Roman and Civil Law and the Development of Anglo-American Jurisprudence in the Nineteenth Century*. Athens: University of Georgia Press, 1997.

Holmgren, Jennifer. *Marriage, Kinship, and Power in Northern China*. UK: Variorum, 1995.

Hubert, Henri. *Sacrifice: Its Nature and Function*. London: University of Chicago Press, 1964.

Hujjātī, Muḥammad Bāqir. *Kashf ta'wīl al-qur'ān bi-'l-qur'ān*. Tehran: Daftar-i Nashr-i Farhang-i Islamī, 1987.

Hume, David. *A Treatise of Human Nature*. London: Dent, 1911.

———. *An Abstract of a Treatise of Human Nature*. Cambridge: Cambridge University Press, 1938.

———. *An Inquiry Concerning Human Understanding*. Indianapolis: Bobbs-Merrill, 1955.

———. *An inquiry Concerning the Principles of Morals*. New York: Liberal Arts Press, 1957.

———. *Philosophical Essays Concerning Human Understanding*. Indianapolis: Bobbs-Merrill, 1955.

Husari, Aḥmad. *al-Tarikāt wa-'al-waṣāyā fī al-fiqh al-islāmī*. `Ammān: Maktabat al-Aqṣā, 1972.

———. *al-Tarikāt wa-'l-waṣāyā fī al-fiqh al-islāmī*. `Ammān: Maktabat al-Aqṣā, 1980.

Ḥusayn, Aḥmad Farraj. *Niẓām al-irth fī al-tashrī` al-islāmī*. Beirut: al-Mu'assasah al-Jāmi`iyyah li-'l-Dirāsāt wa al-Nashr wa al-Tawzī`, 1996.

Ibn `Abd al-Barr, Yūsuf Ibn `Abd Allāh. *Jāmi` bayān al-`ilm*. Cairo: Maktabat Ibn Taymiyyah, 1996.

Ibn `Ajībah. *al-Baḥr al-madīd fī tafsīr al-qur'ān al-majīd*. Jordan: Aal al-Bayt Institute for Islamic Thought (Soft Collections), 2002.

Ibn `Arabī. *Tafsīr al-qur'ān*. Jordan: Aal al-Bayt Institute for Islamic Thought (Soft Collections), 2002.

Ibn Abd al-Barr, Yūsuf Ibn Abd Allah. *al-Istī`āb fī asmā` al-aṣḥāb*. Egypt: Nahdat Misr li-'l-Tiba`ah wa-'l-Nashr wa-'l-Tawzi`.

Ibn Abī Ḥātim. *Tafsīr al-qur'ān al-`Aẓīm: Musnad `an rasūl allāh wa-'l-ṣaḥābah wa-'l-tābi`īn*. Beirut: al-Maktabah al-`Aṣriyyah, 1999.

Ibn Abī Ṭalḥah `Alī. *Ṣaḥīfat `Alī Ibn Abī Ṭalḥah `an Ibn `Ayyās fī tafsīr al-qur'ān al-karīm*. Cairo: Maktabat al-Sunnah, 1991.

Ibn al-`Arabī, Muḥammad Ibn `Abd Allāh. *Kitāb al-qabas fī sharḥ Muwaṭṭa' Mālik Ibn Anas*. Beirut: Dār al-Gharb al-Islāmī, 1992.

Ibn al-Athīr, Izz al-Dīn. *al-Kāmil fī al-tārīkh*. Beirut: Dār Sader, 1967.

Ibn al-Hawwārī, Muḥammad. *al-Dirāyah wa-kanz al-ghināyah fī muntahā al-ghāyah wa-bulūgh al-kifāyah fī tafsīr khamsmi'at āyah min tafsīr al-qur'ān al-karīm*. Beirut, 1994.

Ibn al-Imad, Abd al-Hayy Ibn Ahmad. *Shadharāt al-dhahab fī akhbār man dhahab*. Cairo: Maktabat al-Qudsi, 1931.

Ibn al-Jawzī. *Ṣafwat al-ṣafwah*. Beirut: Dar al-Ma`rifah, 1985.

Ibn Ḥajar al-`Asqalānī, Aḥmad Ibn `Alī. *Fatḥ al-bārī bi-sharḥ ṣaḥīḥ al-bukhārī*. Cairo: Dār al-Kitāb al-Jadīd, Lajnat Iḥyā' al-Turāth al-Islāmī, 1970.

Ibn Ḥamīd. *al-Suḥub al-wābilah `alā ḍārā'iḥ al-ḥanābilah*. Beirut: Mu'assasat al-Risālah, 1996.

Ibn Ḥanbal, Aḥmad Ibn Muḥammad. *Marwiyyāt al-imām Aḥmad Ibn Ḥanbal fī al-tafsīr*. al-Riyāḍ: Maktabat al-Mu'ayyad, 1994.

Ibn Ḥazm. *al-Iḥkām fī uṣūl al-qur'ān*. Abu Dhabi: al-Warrāq, 2004.

———. *al-Muḥallā*. Beirut: Dar al-Fikr, 1997.

Ibn Ḥibbān, Muḥammad. *Ṣaḥīḥ Ibn Ḥibbān*. Beirut: Dār al-Kutub al-`Ilmiyyah, 1987.

Ibn Kathīr, Ismā`īl Ibn `Umar. *al-Bidāyah wa-'l-nihāyah*. Beirut: Maktabat al-Ma`ārif, 1985.

———. *Tafsīr al-qur'ān al-`aẓīm*. Beirut: Dar al-Ma`rifah, 1989.

———. *Tafsīr al-qur'ān al-`aẓīm*. Cairo: Maktabat al-Turāth al-Islāmī, 1993.

———. *Tafsīr al-qur'ān al-karīm*. Jordan: Aal al-Bayt Institute for Islamic Thought (Soft Collections), 2002.

Ibn Khaldūn, A. *Kitāb al-`ibar.* Princeton: Princeton University Press, 1969.

________, A. *Wifāyāt al-a`yān wa-`anbā' abnā' al-zamān*. Beirut: Dar al-Fikr, 1969.

Ibn Mufliḥ al-Maqdisī, Muḥammad. *Kitāb al-furū`*. Beirut: `Ālam al-Kutub, 1405 AH.

Ibn Qāḍī. *Ṭabaqāt al-shāfi`iyyah*. Beirut: `Alam al-Kitāb, 1407 AH.

Ibn Sa`d, Abū `Abd Allāh Muhammad. *Ṭabaqāt al-ṣaḥābah wa-'l-tābi`īn wa-'l-`ulamā`*. Beirut: Sadir, 1968.

———. *Asad al-ghābah*. Beirut: Dar Ihya` al-Turath al-Arabi, 1408 AH.

Ibn Taymiyyah. *Dar' ta`āruḍ al-`aql wa-'l-naql*. Cairo: Dar al-Kutub, 1981.

Izutsu, Toshihiko. *Ethic-Religious Concepts in the Qur'ān*. Montreal: McGill University Press, 1966.

———. *The Structure of Ethical Terms in the Koran*. Tokyo: Keio Institute of Philological Studies, 1959.

Jaffee, Martin S. *Torah in the Mouth*. Oxford: University Press, 2001.

Jawad, H. A. *The Rights of Women in Islam: An Authentic Approach*. Hampshire: Macmillan; New York: St. Martin's, 1998.

Jazīrī, `Abd al-Raḥmān. *al-Fiqh `alā al-madhāhib al-arba`ah*. Beirut: Dār Iḥyā' al-Turāth al-`Arabī, 1960.

Juynboll, G. H. A. *Studies on the Origins and Uses of Islamic Ḥadīth*. Brookfield, VT: Variorum, 1996.

Kafi, Muḥammad Ibn Yūsuf. *Iḥkām al-aḥkām `alā tuḥfat al-ḥukkām*. Beirut: Dār al-Kutub al-`Ilmiyyah, 1994.

Kahn-Freund, Otto. *Comparative Law as an Academic Subject*. Oxford: Clarendon, 1965.

Kelly, P. J. *Utilitarianism and Distributive Justice: Jeremy Bentham and the Civil Law*. Oxford: Clarendon, 1990.

Khan, Shamshad M. *Why Two Women Witnesses*. Birmingham, UK: IPCI, 1993.

Khū'ī, Abū al-Qāsim Ibn `Alī Akbar. *Bayān fī tafsīr al-qur'ān*. New York: Oxford University Press, 1998.

Kirk, G. S. et al. *Le Sacrifice dans L`antiquite*. Geneve: Vandeuvres, 1980.

Kishki, Muḥammad `Abd al-Rahim. *al-Mīrāth al-muqāran*. Baghdad: Dār al-Nadhir li-'l-Ṭibā`ah wa-'l-Nashr, 1969.

Knudten, Richard D. *The Sociology of Religion, an Anthology*. New York: Appleton-Century-Crofts, 1967.

Konvitz, Milton Ridvas. *Torah and Constitution: Essays in American Jewish Thought*. Syracuse: Syracuse University Press, 1998.

Kulaynī, Muḥammad Ibn Ya`qūb. *al-Uṣūl min al-kāfī*. Tehran: Dār al-Kutub al-Islāmiyyah, 1388–1391 H.

Lapin, Hayim. *Early Rabbinic Civil Law and the Social History of Roman Galilee: A Study of Mishnah.* Atlanta: Scholars Press, 1995.

Lassner, Jacob. *Demonizing the Queen of Sheba: Boundaries of Gender and Culture in Post-Biblical Judaism and Medieval Islam.* Chicago: University of Chicago Press, 1993.

Le Boutillier, Cornelia Geer. *American Democracy and Natural Law.* New York: Columbia University Press, 1950.

Lenski, Gerhard Emmanuel. *The Religious Factor: A Sociological Study of Religion's Impact on Politics, Economics, and Family Life.* Westport: Greenwood Press, 1977.

Lentz, Tony M. *Orality and Literacy in Hellenic Greece.* Carbondale: Southern Illinois University Press, c1989.

Lévi-Strauss, Claude. *The Savage Mind.* London: Weidenfeld & Nicolson, 1966.

Levy, Reuben. *An Introduction to the Sociology of Islam.* London: Williams & Norgate, 1931.

———. *Sociology of Islam*, vols. 1–2. London: Williams & Norgate, 1931.

Locke, John. *An Essay Concerning Human Understanding.* Oxford: Clarendon, 1924.

Ludwikowski, Rett. *The Beginning of the Constitutional Era: A Bicentennial Comparative Analysis of the First Modern Constitutions.* Washington, D.C.: Catholic University of America Press, 1993.

Lynn and Moberg (ed.). *Research in the Social Scientific Study of Religion.* Greenwich: JAI Press, 1989.

Mackenzie, D. A. *Myths of Babylonia and Assyria.* London: Gresham, YA.

Madkur, Muhammad Sallam. *al-Islām wa-'l-usrah wa-'l-mujtama`.* Cairo: Dār al-Nahḍah al-`Arabiyyah, 1968.

Maghniyyah, M. J. *Fiqh al-imām Ja`far al-Ṣādiq.* Qom: Ansariayn, 1999.

———. *al-Fiqh `alā al-madhāhib al-khamsah.* Beirut: Dār al-`Ilm li-'l-Malāyīn, 1962.

———. *al-Fuṣūl al-shar`iyyah `alā madhhab al-shī`ah al-imāmiyyah.* Beirut: Dār al-Thaqāfah, 1974.

———. *Fiqh al-imām Ja`far al-Ṣādiq.* Beirut, Dār al-'Ilm li al-Malāyīn, 1965.

Maḥallī, Jalāl al-Dīn Muḥammad Ibn Aḥmad. *Kitāb al-jalālayn fī tafsīr al-qur'ān al-`aẓīm.* Cairo: [1872 or 1873].

Mahmood, Saba. *Politics of Piety.* Princeton: Princeton University Press, 2005.

Maḥmūd, Sayyed Ṭāhir. *Hindu Law.* Allāhabad: Law Book Co., 1981.

Marcus, Julie. *A World of Difference: Islam and Gender Hierarchy in Turkey.* New Jersey: Zed, 1992.

Martin, R. *Approaches to Islam in Religious Studies.* Tucson: University of Arizona Press, 1985.

Matthews, R. *Informal Justice.* London: Sage, 1988.

Māturīdī, Muḥammad Ibn Muḥammad. *Tafsīr al-māturīdī al-musammā ta'wīlāt ahl al-sunnah.* Cairo: Lajnat al-Qur'ān wa-al-Sunnah, 1971.

Mbacké, Khadim. *Le Coran et la femme: mariage, divorce, viduité, allaitement et garde des enfants, succession.* Dakar: K. Mbacké, 1991.

McKenna, Marian C. *The Canadian and American Constitutions in Comparative Perspective.* Canada: University of Calgary Press, 1993.

Mernissi, Fatima. *The Veil and the Male Elite: A Feminist Interpretation of Women's Rights in Islam.* Massachusetts: Addison-Wesley, 1991.

———. *Women's Rebellion and Islamic Memory*. London; Atlantic Highlands: Zed, 1996.

Merryman, John Henry. *The Civil Law Tradition: An Introduction to the Legal Systems of Western Europe and Latin America*. California: Stanford University Press, 1985.

Michaud, Francine. *Un signe des temps: accroissement des crises familiales autour du patrimoine à Marseille à la fin du XIIIe siècle*. Toronto: Pontifical Institute of Mediaeval Studies, 1994.

Mihayl, Marion. *The Changing Status of Women in the Middle East*. Colorado State College, Museum of Anthropology, 1969.

Mihrpur, Ḥusayn. *Barrasi-i miras-i zawjah dar huquq-i Islam va Iran: tahlil-i fiqhi va huquqi-i irs-i zan az dara'i-i shawhar*. Tehran: Intisharat-i Ittila`at, 1368 H.

Mill, James. *Analysis of the Phenomena of the Human Mind*. New York: Olms, 1982.

Mill, John Stuart. *On Liberty*. New York: Bantam, 1993.

Miller, Robert K. Jr., and Stephen J. McNamee (editors). *Inheritance and Wealth in America*. New York: Plenum, 1998.

Minai, Naila. *Women in Islam: Tradition and Transition in the Middle East*. New York: Seaview, 1981.

Mol, Hans. *Identity and the Sacred: A Sketch for a New Social-Scientific Theory of Religion*. New York: Free Press, 1977.

Money-Kyrle, R. *The Meaning of Sacrifice*. London: Johnson, 1965.

Moore, M. S. *Placing Blame: A Theory of Criminal Law*. Oxford: Oxford University Press, 1997.

Moors, Annelies. *Women, Property, and Islam: Palestinian Experiences, 1920–1990*. New York: Cambridge University Press, 1995.

Mubārakfurī, Muḥammad `Abd al-Raḥmān Ibn `Abd al-Raḥīm. *Tuḥfat al-aḥwadhī bi-sharḥ jāmi` al-tirmidhī*. Cairo: Maṭba`at al-Madanī, 1963–1967.

Mukhopadhyay, Maitrayee. *Legally Dispossessed: Gender, Identity, and the Process of Law*. Calcutta: Bhatkal, c1998.

Muranyi, Miklos. *`Abd Allāh b. Wahb*. Wiesbaden: Harrassowitz, 1992.

Murata, Sachiko. *The Tao of Islam: A Sourcebook on Gender Relationships in Islamic Thought*. Albany: State University of New York Press, 1992.

Mūsā, `Abd al-Ḥalīm Maḥmūd. *al-Fiqh al-islāmī al-muyassar fī al-`aqā'id wa-'l-`ibādāt wa-'l-mu`āmalāt `alā al-madhāhib al-arba`ah*. Cairo: Dār al-Fikr al-`Arabī, 1964.

Mūsā, Muḥammad Yūsuf. *al-Tarikah wa-'l-mīrāth fī al-islām*. Egypt: Dār al-Kitāb al-`Arabī, 1960.

Muslim Ibn al-Ḥajjāj al-Qushayrī. *Jāmi` al-ṣaḥīḥ*. Cairo: Dār al-Ḥadīth, 1994.

Nadin, Mihai. *The Civilization of Illiteracy*. Dreshden: Dreshden University Press, 1997.

Nagendra, S. P. *The Concept of Ritual in Modern Sociological Theory*. India: Academic Journal of India, 1971.

Nasā'ī, Aḥmad Ibn Shu`ayb. *Sunan al-Nasā'ī*. Egypt: Muṣṭafā al-Bābī al-Ḥalabī, 1964.

Nāẓirī, Muḥammad Ibn Aḥmad. *Jawharat al-farā'iḍ: sharḥ miftāḥ al-farā'iḍ*. San`ā': Maktabat al-Yaman al-Kubrā, 1984.

Neusner, Jacob. *Ancient Judaism and Modern Category Formation*. Lanham, MD: University Press of America, 1986.

Newman, Edwin S. *The Law of Civil Rights and Civil Liberties*. New York, Oceana, 1957.

Newman, William M. *The Social Meanings of Religion: An Integrated Anthology*. Chicago: Rand McNally, 1974.

Ong, Walter J. *Orality and Literacy*. London: Methuen, 1982.

Otto, Rudolf. *The Idea of the Holly*. London: Oxford University Press, 1952.

Pals, Daniel L. *Seven Theories of Religion*. New York: Oxford University Press, 1996.

Peletz, Michael G. *A Share of the Harvest: Kinship, Property, and Social History among the Malays of Rembau*. Berkeley: University of California Press, 1988.

Peterson, Mark A. *Korean Adoption and Inheritance: Case Studies in the Creation of a Classic Confucian Society*. Ithaca: East Asia Program, Cornell University, 1996.

Pickering, W. S. F. *Durkheim's Sociology of Religion: Themes and Theories*. London: Routledge & Kegan Paul, 1984.

Plato. *Apology*. London: Magnes, 1675.

———. *Crito and Phaedo*. London: printed for M. Cooper, 1755.

———. *Dialogues*. Oxford: Clarendon, 1953.

Powers, David S. *Studies in Qur'ān and Ḥadīth: The Formation of the Islamic Law of Inheritance*. Berkeley: University of California Press, 1986.

Preus, J. Samuel. *Explaining Religion*. London: Yale University Press, 1987.

Quaegebeur, J. *Ritual and Sacrifice in the Ancient Near East*. Leuven: Uitgeverij Peeters en Department Orientalistiek, 1993.

Rachels, James. *The Elements of Moral Philosophy*. Boston: McGraw-Hill, 2003.

Radwan, `Abd al-Hasib. *Madhāhib ahl al-`ilm fī mīrāth al-khunthā al-mushkil*. Cairo: Dār al-Tawfīq al-Namūdhajiyyah, 1992.

Ratnaparkhi, M. S. *Uniform Civil Code: An Ignored Constitutional Imperative*. New Delhi: Atlantic, c1997.

Ridwan, Zaynab. *al-Mar`ah bayna al-mawrūth wa-'l-taḥdīth*. Cairo: al-Hay'ah al-Misriyyah al-`Ammah li-'l-Kitab, 2004.

Roby, Henry John. *Roman Private Law in the Times of Cicero and of the Antonines*. Cambridge: Cambridge University Press, 1902.

Rosen, Lawrence. *The Justice of Islam*. Oxford: Oxford University Press, 2000.

Rosenfeld, Jeffrey P. *The Legacy of Aging: Inheritance and Disinheritance in Social Perspective*. Norwood, NJ: Ablex, 1979.

Rouse, Carolyn Moxley. *Engaged Surrender: African American Women and Islam*. Berkeley: University of California Press, 2004.

Rumsey, Almaric. *Moohummudan Law of Inheritance and Rights and Relations Affecting It: Sunni Doctrine*. Lahore: Sang-e-Meel, 1981.

Sabuni, Muhammad. *al-Itqān fī `ulūm al-qur'ān*. Beirut: Dar al-Irshad, 1970.

Salem, Elie Adib. *Political Theory and Institutions of the Khawārij*. Baltimore: Johns Hopkins University Press, 1956.

Saller, Richard P. *Patriarchy, Property, and Death in the Roman Family*. Cambridge: Cambridge University Press, 1994.

Ṣamhūdī. *Kitāb wafā' al-wafā'*. Cairo: PU, 1908.

Saqqa, Ahmad Hijazi Ahmad. *al-Khawārij al-harūriyūn wa-muqāranat mabādi'uhum bi-mabādi' al-firaq al-islāmiyyah: ahl al-sunnah, al-mu`tazilah, al-shī`ah, al-murji`ah*. Cairo: Maktabat al-Kulliyat al-Azhariyyah, 1980.

Sarkar, Golapchandra. *Hindu Law: With an Appendix of Mahomedan Law of Inheritance*. Calcutta: Banerjee, 1903.
Schacht, J. *The Origins of Muhammadan Jurisprudence*. Oxford: Clarendon, 1979.
Schiffman, Lawrence H. *Reclaiming the Dead Sea Scrolls*. Philadelphia: Jewish Publication Society, 1994.
Schimmel, Annemarie. *My Soul Is a Woman: The Feminine in Islam*. New York: Continuum, 1997.
Schleifer, Aliah. *Motherhood in Islam*. Cambridge: Islamic Academy, 1986.
Schlesinger, Rudolf B. *Comparative Law: Cases, Text, Materials*. London: Stevens, 1960.
Sedgwick, John. *Rich Kids*. New York: Morrow, 1985.
Segal, R. A. *Ritual and Myth*. New York: Garland, 1996.
Shāfi`ī, Aḥmad Maḥmūd. *Aḥkām al-mawārīth*. Beirut: al-Dār al-Jāmi`iyyah, 1986.
Shalabī, Ḥamdī `Abd al-Mun`im. *al-Rā'id fī `ilm al-farā'iḍ*. Cairo: Maktabat Ibn Sīnā, 1989.
Shammas, Carole. *Inheritance in America*. New Brunswick: Rutgers University Press, 1987.
Sharpe, E. J. *Comparative Religion: A History*. Illinois: Open Court, 1986.
Shaw, Arthur. *Readings in the Philosophy of Law*. New Jersey: Prentice Hall, 1993.
Shaw, Malcolm N. *International Law*. Cambridge: Cambridge University Press, 1997.
Shehadeh, Lamia Rustum. *The Idea of Women in Fundamentalist Islam*. Gainesville: University Press of Florida, 2003.
Shifman, Pinhas. *Dine ha-mishpahah bi-Yisrael*. Jerusalem: Ha-Universitah ha-Ivrit bi-Yerushalayim, 1984.
Sibṭ al-Mardīnī, Badr al-Din Muḥammad Ibn Muḥammad. *Sharḥ al-rahbiyah fī al-farā'iḍ*. Beirut: Mu'assasat al-Kutub al-Thaqāfiyyah, 1989.
Smith, Margaret. *Muslim Women Mystics*. Oxford: Oneworld, 2001.
Smith, W. C. *The Meaning and End of Religion*. New York: Macmillan, 1962.
Smith, W. R. *Lectures of William Robertson Smith*. London: Black, YA.
Souaiaia, A. E. *The Function of Orality in Islamic Law and Practices: Verbalizing Meaning*. UK: Mellen, 2006.
———. Human Rights and Islam. New York: Universie, 2003.
Stanlis, Peter J. *Edmund Burke and the Natural Law*. Ann Arbor: University of Michigan Press, 1965.
Stowasser, Barbara Freyer. *Women in the Qur'ān, Traditions, and Interpretation*. New York: Oxford University Press, 1994.
Sulamī, `Izz al-Dīn `Abd al-`Azīz Ibn `Abd al-Salām. *Tafsīr al-qur'ān: Ikhtiṣār al-Nukat li-'l-Māwardī*. Beirut, Dār Ibn Ḥazm, 1996.
Sundberg, Jacob W. F. *Civil Law, Common Law and the Scandinavians*. Stockholm: Almqvist & Wiksell, 1969.
Suyūṭī, Jalāl al-Dīn. *Kitāb al-durr al-manthūr fī tafsīr bi-'l-ma'thūr*. Beirut: Muḥammad Amīn Damaj, 1972.
———. *Tartīb suwar al-qur'ān*. Beirut: Dār wa-Maktabat al-Hilāl, 1986.
Ṭabarī, Abī Ja`far Muḥammad Ibn Jarīr. *Jāmi` al-bayān `an ta'wīl al-qur`ān*. Dār al-Ma`ārif: PU, 1969.
Tabarsī, al-Faḍl Ibn al-Hasan. *Majma` al-bayān li-`ulūm al-qur'ān wa-majma` al-bayān fī tafsīr al-qur'ān*. Beirut: Dār al-Fikr, 1954–1957.

Ṭabāṭabā'ī, Muḥammad Ḥusayn. *al-Mīzān fī tafsīr al-qur'ān*. Beirut: Mu'assasat al-A`lamī li-'l-Maṭbū`āt, 1970.

Tariq, Bashir, *Legal Remedies in Islam*. Lahore: Irfan Law Book House: Khyber Law Publishers, 1994.

Taylor, John. *Elements of the Civil Law*. London: printed for T. Payne, 1772.

Tellegen, J. W. *The Roman Law of Succession in the Letters of Pliny the Younger, Zutphen*. Holland: Terra, 1982.

Thomas, Aquinas Saint. *Aquinas ethicus*. London: Burns & Oates, 1896.

Tirmidhī, Muḥammad Ibn `Isā. *Jāmi` al-ṣaḥīḥ*. Toshkent: Ghafur Ghulom Nomidagi Adabiët va Sanat Nashriëti, 1993.

Tirmidhī, Muḥammad Ibn `Isā. *Sunan al-Tirmidhī wa-ḥuwa al-jāmi` al-ṣaḥīḥ*. al-Madīnah al-Munawwarah: al-Maktabah al-Salafiyyah, 1965–1967.

Turner, V. *The Forest of Symbols*. New York: Cornell University Press, 1967.

Tushnet, Mark V. *Making Civil Rights Law: Thurgood Marshall and the Supreme Court*. New York: Oxford University Press, 1994.

Ṭūsī, Muḥammad Ibn al-Ḥasan. *al-Tibyān fī tafsīr al-qur'ān*. Najaf: al-Maṭba`ah al-`Ilmiyyah, 1957.

Tylor, Edward B. *Primitive Culture; Research into the Development of Mythology, Philosophy, Religion, Language, Art And Customs. 3d American from 2d English*. New York: Holt, 1883.

United Arab Republic. *al-Mīrāth wa-'l-waṣiyyah wa-'l-wilāyah `alā al-māl wa-'l-nafs*. Cairo: al-Hay'ah al-`Āmmah li Shu'ūn al-Maṭābi` al-Amīriyyah, 1971.

Vāhidī Nishābūrī, Abū al-Hasan `Alī. *al-Wasīṭ fī tafsīr al-qur'ān al-majīd*. Beirut: Dār al-Kutub al-`Ilmiyyah, 1994.

Venel, Nancy. *Musulmanes Francaise*. Paris: L`Harmattan, 1999.

Vreede-de Stuers, Cora. *Parda: A Study of Muslim Women's Life in Northern India*. New York, Humanities, 1968.

Wadud, Amina. *Inside the Gender Jihad*. Oxford: Oneworld, 2006.

———. *Qur'an and Woman*. New York: Oxford University Press, 1999.

Wagner, William G. *Marriage, Property, and Law in Late Imperial Russia*. Oxford: Clarendon, 1994.

Walgrave, L. *Restorative Justice and the Law*. Devon: Willan, 2002.

Walther, Wiebke. *Women in Islam*. Princeton: Wiener, 1993.

Wansbrough, John E. *Quranic Studies*. Oxford: Oxford University Press, 1977.

Wāqidī. *Kitāb al-maghāzī*. London: Maṭba` Jāmi`ah Uksfūrd, 1966.

Watson, Alan. *The Making of the Civil Law*. Cambridge: Harvard University Press, 1981.

Welchman, Lynn (ed.). *Women`s Rights and Islamic Family Law: Perspectives on Reform*. New York: Zed, 2004.

Wensinck, J. *Some Semitic Rites of Mourning and Religion*. Amsterdam: Koninklijke, 1917.

———. *The Ocean in the Literature of the Western Semites*. Amsterdam: j. Müller, 1918.

Westrup, Carl Wium. *Introduction to Early Roman Law*. London: Oxford University Press, 1934.

Widengren, Geo. *Mani and Manichaeism*. London: Weidenfeld & Nicolson, 1961.

———. *Mesopotamian Elements in Manichaeism*. Uppsala: Lundequistska, 1946.

Wilson, John. *Social Theory*. New Jersey: Prentice-Hall, 1983.
Wolff, Hans Julius. *Roman Law*. Norman: University of Oklahoma Press, 1951.
Yakan, Zuhdi. *al-Qānūn al-rūmānī wa-'l-sharī`ah al-islāmiyyah.* Beirut: Dār Yakan li-'l-Nashr, 1975.
Yamani, Ahmad Zaki. *al-Islām wa-'l-Mar'ah*. Cairo: Mu'ssasat al-Furqān li'l-Turāth al-Islāmī, 2004.
———. *al-Islām wa-'lmar'ah.* Cairo: Matba`at al-Madani, 2004.
Zamir, Muḥammad. *Human Rights Issues and International Law*. Dhaka: Dhaka University Press, 1990.
Zayd, `Abd al-`Azīz Muḥammad. *The Islamic Law of Bequest.* London: Scorpion, 1986.
Zayzafoon, Lamia Ben Youssef. *The Production of the Muslim Woman*. Lanham, MD: Lexington, 2005.
Ziadeh, Farhat Jacob. *Property Law in the Arab World*. London: Graham & Trotman, 1979.
———. *The Philosophy of Jurisprudence in Islam*. Leiden: Brill, 1961.
Zuhayli, Wahbah. *al-Waṣāyā wa-'l-waqf fī al-fiqh al-islāmī*. Dimashq: Dār al-Fikr, 1987.

Index